1913:
From General To Specific Welfare

How the 16th Amendment, 17th Amendment, and the Federal Reserve Act Transformed the Ultimate Goal of the United States Constitution from General to Specific Welfare

AARON KERKMAN

Copyright © 2018 by Aaron Kerkman.

All rights reserved. No part of this book may be reproduced in any written, electronic, recording, or photocopying without written permission of the publisher or author. The exception would be in the case of brief quotations embodied in articles or reviews and pages where permission is specifically granted by the publisher or author.

Aaron Kerkman/1913: From General To Specific Welfare
Printed in the United States of America

Although every precaution has been taken to verify the accuracy of the information contained herein, the author and publisher assume no responsibility for any errors or omissions. No liability is assumed for damages that may result from the use of information contained within.

1913: From General To Specific Welfare/ Aaron Kerkman -- 1st ed.

CONTENTS

Introduction 1

Part I: *Maximization of Satisfaction – The Why* 9

    Article I: The "Science" of Human Nature – Induction and Deduction 10

    Article II: Maximization of Satisfaction.................................... 12

    Section I: Minimizing Pain.. 14

    Section II: Seeking Pleasure 18

Part II: *Result of Our Premise – Government* 31

    Article I: Why We Institute Governments – The Theory 34

    Article II: Necessary Restraint 50

Part III: *United States Constitution Pre-1913*............................ 57

    Article I: Enumerated, Specific Powers................................... 73

    Article II: "Necessary and Proper" Applied............................ 82

    Article III: Taxes.. 84

    Article IV: Senators of the States (Statesmen, or State's men) 93

    Article V: Aspects of the Constitution Concerning Money.. 101

    Article VI: Summary.. 115

Part IV: *Liberty Yields While Tyranny Gains – The How* 119

    Article I: Reason.. 127

    Article II: Passion 133

    Article III: Value of Liberty.. 138

Section I: Economics 139

Section II: Liberty As Its Own Enemy 145

Article IV: Maximization of Satisfaction from Another Angle .. 151

Article V: Special Knowledge 159

Article VI: From Instrument to Institution 168

Article VII: Summary 176

Part V: *United States Constitution – Post-1913* 181

Article I: Taxes and the 16th Amendment 183

Section I: Lead up to the 16th Amendment 185

Section II: Effects of the 16th Amendment 202

Article II: The Federal Reserve Act and the United States Monetary System 211

Section I: Structure of the Federal Reserve System 217

Subsection A: Keynes' Reflections 227

Section I (continued): Structure of the Federal Reserve System 240

Section II: Federal Reserve Notes (FRNs) 243

Section III: Creation of "Credit" (or money), and Expansions of the Supply 257

Article III: 17th Amendment 268

Article IV: Synthesis 280

Part VI: *Conclusion* 297

Bibliography 303

Dedicated to the never-ending struggle in pursuit of liberty, no matter how fleeting its attainment may be, and to each teacher, coach, and instructor from whom I have had the privilege of learning.

INTRODUCTION

Humanity's journey through the ages is a never-ending series of human actions and their results, which are followed by subsequent human actions and their results, and so on. The effect of each individual's action differs depending on the conditions at the time he acts. Although the effects are varied and innumerable, one common thread unites them all: each individual seeks one ultimate end, to maximize his satisfaction. This fundamental law of human nature is the cause of every human action.

Because individuals act to maximize their satisfaction, and because governments are constituted by and for individual men and women, governments have the potential to help maximize the satisfaction of all its citizens—defined as the general welfare. However, this outcome is only a potential. A government may choose to maximize the satisfaction of a few, or perhaps only one individual, without regard to the general welfare.[1]

In the case of the government of the United States, the Preamble to the Constitution explicitly states that the ultimate purpose of our government is the general welfare. After the more than two centuries since the federal government's inception,

---

1   General welfare is defined as the opportunity for each and every individual to be secure in their rights to pursue their own path to happiness, or maximize their satisfactions, while not infringing on the opportunities of another individual to do the same.

with the levers of power in the hands of individuals seeking to maximize their satisfaction, it should not be surprising that our government drifted from general welfare to a specific and special welfare. Expecting an institution constituted and managed by men and women to be immune to this fundamental maxim—that each person will act to maximize his own satisfaction—is not rational. Thomas Jefferson understood the concept when he wrote, "[t]he natural progress of things is for liberty to yield and government to gain ground."[2]

This notion introduces the thesis of this book: how three events of 1913 (the 16th Amendment, 17th Amendment, and the Federal Reserve Act [FRA]) transformed the United States' system of governance from one whose end was general welfare to one of specific welfare, where the satisfaction of all was subsumed to the satisfaction of a few. We will explore this thesis by addressing the following three topics:

- Why the United States Government was established (Parts I, II, and III);
- How the end of the United States Government was subtly transformed from one of general welfare to specific welfare (Part IV); and
- What exactly caused it to happen (Part V)

Consider one way the transformation matters. Although the United States recently suffered through a severe recession, another monetary crisis will inevitably occur again in the not-too-distant future. The reason concerns the United States' monetary system and the manner in which the federal government creates currency and credit, or what is understood to be "money." Today

---

[2] THE POLITICAL WRITINGS OF THOMAS JEFFERSON 138 (Edward Dumbauld ed., The Bobbs-Merrill Company, Inc. 1955) (1788).

the United States is the sole creator of the currency it has declared legal tender. Because additions of currency very well may lead to a general increase in prices, those who get access to the new currency first will obtain greater benefits than those who receive access to it later. By the nature of the current system, unless all citizens receive the same amount of new money at the same time, some individuals or groups attain special privileges while others do not, which certainly does not promote the concept of general welfare. Although many individuals may not observe and grasp this concept during periods when the economy is stable—if there is such a time—when monetary crises happen, the monetary authority's actions tend to attract the public's attention. Those who do not receive the newly created money first are more able to recognize the specific privileges and benefits granted by the United States to preferential groups. When these circumstances arise, if the specific privileges are striking enough, then a sufficient number of individuals may recognize the departure from seeking general welfare and may seek redress to return to a system of governance that promotes the general rather than specific welfare.

The idea of promoting the general welfare as espoused in the Constitution's Preamble is still the greatest idea for a system of government ever conceived, and its virtues have not changed. That idea is to promote the general welfare by securing liberty from external and internal threats. External threats are kept at bay by the common defense; internal threats are mitigated through a balancing and diffusing power, which is based on key aspects of constitutional construction. This book's contention is that the 16th Amendment, the 17th Amendment, and the FRA created an imbalance in the federal government, constituting

Introduction

an internal threat that has deprived citizens of general welfare while substituting specific interests and special welfare that have transgressed upon rights and liberty, and cultivated tyranny in their stead.

Over a hundred years have passed since the inception of the three events of 1913, and the elapsed time has obscured the cause-and-effect trail and made it difficult to establish a linkage between those events and the results today. As Thomas Paine stated more than two centuries ago:

> There are certain circumstances, which, at the time of their happening, are a kind of riddles and as every riddle is to be followed by its answer, so those kind of circumstances will be followed by their events, and those events are always the true solution. A considerable space of time may lapse between, and unless we continue our observations from the one to the other, the harmony of them will pass away unnoticed; but the misfortune is, that partly from the pressing necessity of some instant things, and partly from the impatience of our own tempers, we are frequently in such a hurry to make out the meaning of every thing as fast as it happens, that we thereby never truly understand it . . . ."[3]

Despite the challenge, identifying a shift and the cause of such a shift from general welfare to specific welfare is necessary if we are to understand such critical issues as liberty rather than tyranny, and how to break the cycle of monetary crisis after monetary crisis.

---
3   THOMAS PAINE, THE CRISIS 38 (Prometheus Books 2008) (1776).

Understanding this shift begins with acknowledging the basic truth that all humans act to maximize their satisfaction. From this basic, self-evident truth, a logical deduction is that people will inevitably form a government whose duty is to maximize the satisfaction of each individual, and hence the general welfare.

After exploring that basic truth, our examination will next move to the relevant portions of the Constitution prior to 1913 and explain how taxes, the election of senators, and the monetary powers were constructed in a manner to promote the general welfare through a balance and diffusion of power that would protect against internal threats.

At that point, the book will review various tactics that individuals exploit to maximize their satisfactions at the expense of others. These tactics inevitably cause liberty to yield and tyranny to advance, and such tactics include effects such as the 16th and 17th Amendments, along with the FRA. We'll conclude with an explanation of how each of these actions has transformed the purpose of our government from one of general welfare to specific welfare.

Interestingly, the fact that all individuals act to maximize their satisfactions plays an important role in the adage espoused by Mark Twain: that history may not repeat exactly, but it sure does rhyme.[4] Older ideas resurface as the conditions return that make such ideas relevant and significant.[5] As Marcus Aurelius

---

[4] Commonly attributed to Mark Twain. *See* JOSHUA MATZ & LAURENCE TRIBE, UNCERTAIN JUSTICE 257 (Henry Holt and Company, LLC 2014) (citing JOHN ROBERT COLOMBO, *A Said Poem*, *in* NEO POEMS 46 (Sono Nis Press 1970)).

[5] Although by no means a perfect example, note the similar principle expressed by Marcus Aurelius (circa 150 A.D. in MEDITATIONS) and Adam Smith (1776 in THE WEALTH OF NATIONS) concerning what Adam Smith coined the "invisible hand." Aurelius wrote, "We all work together to the same end,

noted, "[s]o always remember these two things. First, that all things have been of the same kind from everlasting, coming round and round again, and it makes no difference whether one will see the same things for a hundred years, or two hundred years, or for an infinity of time."[6] Liberty will not yield indefinitely. Eventually, the tyrannized have nothing left to lose other than their liberty. Somewhere leading up to this point, which is certainly variable depending upon the individual, liberty attains a value that drives the actions of men and women willing to attain it. This constant ebb and flow delivers a never-ending cycle of history, which is in turn driven by the law of nature previously mentioned.

Eventually there will come an event that is the tipping point, which begins the revolution, so to speak. This tipping point swings the pendulum in the other direction as history continues its never-ending rhyme of repetition.

---

some with conscious attention, others without knowing it – just as Heraclitus, I think, says that even people asleep are workers in the factory of all that happens in the world. One person contributes in this way, another in that: and there is room even for the critic who tries to oppose or destroy the production – the world had need for him too." MARCUS AURELIUS, MEDITATIONS 54 (Martin Hammond trans., Penguin Books 2006) (150 A.D.). Now compare Aurelius to Smith in 1776: "He generally, indeed, neither intends to promote the public interest, nor knows how much he is promoting it. By preferring the support of domestic to that of foreign industry, he intends only his own security; and by directing that industry in such a manner as its produce may be of the greatest value, he intends only his own gain, and he is in this, as in many other cases, led by an invisible hand to promote an end which was no part of his intention. Nor is it always the worse for the society that it was no part of it. By pursuing his own interest he frequently promotes that of the society more effectually than when he really intends to promote it." ADAM SMITH, THE WEALTH OF NATIONS 572 (Edwin Cannan ed., Bantam Books, 2003) (1776).

6   MARCUS AURELIUS, MEDITATIONS 14 (Martin Hammond trans., Penguin Books 2006) (150 A.D.).

A pair of scales perfectly poised cannot ponderate on either side; and a man who has no motives to act, will not act at all. Every thing must be at rest which has no force to impel it: but as the last straw breaks the horse's back, or a single sand will turn the beam of scales which hold weights as heavy as the world; so, without doubt, as minute causes may determine the actions of men, which neither others nor they themselves are sensible of.[7]

When the tipping point is reached, an understanding of what caused the current state of affairs is necessary in order to reform the end of government from one of specific welfare to one of general welfare. Inevitably a move to re-establish justice— defined here as an equal application of law to all citizens, while the laws themselves must secure the liberty of each citizen—and the ultimate goal of general welfare is only swinging the pendulum in another direction, but such is the case in human affairs. On that note, we segue into the examination of the causal factors that resulted in a shift from general to specific welfare, and start with an explanation of the basic law of nature that all men and women seek to maximize their own satisfactions.

---

[7]   2 THOMAS GORDON & JOHN TRENCHARD, CATO'S LETTERS 782 (Ronald Hamowy ed., Liberty Fund, Inc. 1995) (c. 1720).

PART I:

MAXIMIZATION OF SATISFACTION – THE WHY

As mentioned, the reason the U.S. Government has transformed from ensuring the general welfare to one of ensuring specific welfare for a few is that humans act to maximize their own satisfaction. This is the basic premise of this book. Because the truth of any premise is critical to ensuring the validity of our argument, we must start with an explanation and validation of our premise, at least to the extent possible because the subject concerns human action and all its associated complicated behavior.

We use "to the extent possible" because human action and the desires that drive it are highly variable and subject to rapid changes. As just one example, passions alone vary greatly especially because each person's passion is expressed differently in force, feeling, or method. Strong passions such as love or hate can radically change a person's actions. Other passions such as grief and joy or hope and fear may cause a person to react the opposite way to what they had done before.

We cannot rightly use the classical scientific method to explain the premise, where we would use induction to formulate a hypothesis, and then use deduction to validate the hypothesis.

With billions of humans and an infinite number of variables, it just isn't possible to test such a hypothesis.[8] Instead, however, the law that all humans act to maximize their satisfactions is a self-evident law in the same manner that the law of identity is self-evident. One doesn't need to use the scientific method to validate 10 equals 10.

Nonetheless, a brief explanation of the scientific method will help to understand why the law that humans seek to maximize their satisfactions will subsequently lead to humans creating governments. Therefore, in the next article we will first review the classical scientific method. Following that, we will explore deduction because it is used later in our analysis to draw various inferences derived from the premise. We will then present examples to show how people maximize satisfaction by either avoiding pain or seeking pleasure. (If while reading Part I the reader becomes satisfied with the explanation of maximization of satisfaction and would like to move forward, please skip to Part II.)

Article I: The "Science" of Human Nature – Induction and Deduction

Science involves specifics and generalizations, created from a constant back and forth between induction and deduction. Induction involves observations of specific effects and working from the effects to a general truth. Deduction involves the opposite: working from a general truth to expected consequences. However, understanding induction and deduction is not

---

[8] For an excellent, in-depth analysis of science and the classical scientific method, see William Stanley Jevons, The Principles Of Science: A Treatise on Logic and Scientific Method (Adamant Media Corporation 3rd ed. reprt. 2008) (1879).

enough. We must cultivate the ability to connect cause and effect, by combining both induction and deduction to accurately predict consequences. In the words of William Stanley Jevons, "[e]xperience gives us the materials of knowledge: induction digests those materials, and yields us general knowledge. When we possess such knowledge, in the form of general propositions and natural laws, we can usefully apply the reverse process of deduction to ascertain the exact information required at any moment."[9]

When considering induction, science would be considered perfect if it were possible to accumulate knowledge from all observations. Because this is not possible, we are forced to rely on imperfect knowledge as David Hume so concisely expressed:

> Mankind are so much the same, in all times and places, that history informs us of nothing new or strange in this particular. Its chief use is only to discover the constant and universal principles of human nature, by showing men in all varieties of circumstances and situations, and furnishing us with materials from which we may form our observations and become acquainted with the regular springs of human action and behaviour. These records of wars, intrigues, factions, and revolutions, are so many collections of experiments, by which the politician or moral philosopher fixes the principles of his science, in the same manner as the physician or natural philosopher becomes acquainted with the nature of plants, minerals, and other external objects, by the experiments which he forms concerning them.[10]

---

9   WILLIAM STANLEY JEVONS, THE PRINCIPLES OF SCIENCE: A TREATISE ON LOGIC AND SCIENTIFIC METHOD pt. 1, at 12 (Adamant Media Corporation 3rd ed. reprt. 2008) (1879).
10   DAVID HUME, AN ENQUIRY CONCERNING HUMAN UNDERSTANDING 78 (Prometheus Books, 1988) (1748).

Hume referenced war in the context of using induction to explain the idea of imperfect induction. If we had knowledge of every cause and effect in every conflict throughout human history, it would be possible to use induction to decipher the law of nature that governs warfare. That is obviously not possible; however, it is possible for people to formulate general truths concerning war. Armed with these truths, a wise commander is able to use them to develop a strategy and associated tactics that bring victory.

Similarly, we may use observations of specific acts and their associated effects to help explain how the named law of nature is universally self-evident. From this general law, one may deduce the theory behind government, or at least the potential for what a government may achieve.

Although self-evident truths do not require testing via a hypothesis, some people may be unable to recognize such self-evident truths. Therefore, a further demonstration will explain why the named law is self-evident. Let us now use observations from today and the past, along with induction, to explain the self-evident nature of this named law where everyone acts to maximize his own satisfaction.

Article II: Maximization of Satisfaction

Approximately 2,300 years ago, Aristotle articulated the same law of human nature: that all men and women act to maximize their satisfaction. He demonstrated that the idea that all people seek happiness, or the maximization of their own satisfaction, is by no means new. In all likelihood, it is a concept that is as old as humanity itself.

Since—to resume—all knowledge and all purpose aims at some good, what is this which we say is the aim of Politics; or in other words, what is the highest of all realizable goods?

As to its name, I suppose nearly all men agreed; for the masses and the men of culture alike declare that it is happiness, and hold that to "live well" or to "do well" is the same as to be "happy."[11]

Aristotle used the term "happiness," which was referenced in the Declaration of Independence with the phrase "in pursuit of happiness." Additionally, the U.S. Constitution's Preamble states that the purpose of government is the general welfare, or in other words, general happiness. In the contexts used here, happiness is synonymous with maximizing satisfaction.

There are instances that may call into question whether the named law is in fact a law because an individual may take actions to maximize his satisfaction when no other person can fathom the reason he did so. What can make such actions so seemingly contradictory are the varying influences behind the decisions to pursue them, such as different means and resources, knowledge, experiences, faculties of reasoning, beliefs, or values. In the most extreme instance, how is it possible that someone with a destructive addiction or compulsion cannot understand that continuing their self-destructive actions will result in their death? This question invokes judgments of reasonability, mental abilities or deficiencies, a person's time preferences, and so on, where the

---

11   ARISTOTLE, NICOMACHEAN ETHICS 3 (F.H. Peters, M.A. trans., Barnes & Noble, Inc. 2004) (350 B.C.E).

sum of all possible forces acting upon a person is never equal to those acting upon another. Make no mistake, however, that each person's actions seek to maximize their satisfaction.

Let's next look at two different methods to maximize satisfaction, or happiness. One means is by satisfying one's pleasures while the other entails avoiding or minimizing pain, which is where we will begin.

Section I: Minimizing Pain

Sigmund Freud describes three categories from where pain originates. "It is much less difficult to be unhappy. Suffering comes from three quarters: from our own body, which is destined to decay and dissolution, and cannot even dispense with anxiety and pain as danger-signals; from the outer world, which can rage against us with the most powerful and pitiless forces of destruction; and finally from our relations with other men."[12]

Freud provides an example of what he labeled the first quarter: humans turning to intoxicants to relieve pain caused by their own bodies. Certainly, some intoxicants combine with natural chemicals in the body to increase pleasure. However, other intoxicants serve to ameliorate our pain. This literally dulls the senses, while at the same time these intoxicants can increase pleasure by creating in our minds a fantasy world that lets us disengage from the pain of the external world around us.[13]

Freud's latter two quarters are very similar: they both involve pain caused by external forces that prove difficult for an individual to control. In an effort to eliminate this pain, we may seek to create peace by extracting ourselves from the pain caused by

---
12   Sigmund Freud, Civilization & Its Discontents 28 (Joan Riviere trans., Martino Publishing 2010) (1930).
13   *Id.* at 30.

interaction with the external world. Taken to an extreme, hermits are examples of people who attempt to wholly separate themselves from the external world in an effort to secure happiness. A less extreme example is a person who tries to find happiness by devoting all his energies to tasks dealing with the material world rather than addressing the challenges of interacting with other humans.[14]

Examining what people do to avoid pain brings to mind an interesting dynamic. Achieving pleasure does not necessarily require an interaction with others while mitigating pain often does, which is why sympathy can be a powerful influence upon others. Sympathy can manifest itself in two ways: it has the potential to alleviate pain and also to produce joy. No wonder why some people choose sympathy as a means to find satisfaction. As Adam Smith noted:

> Sympathy, however, enlivens joy and alleviates grief. It enlivens joy by presenting another source of satisfaction; and it alleviates grief by insinuating into the heart almost the only agreeable sensation which it is at that time capable of receiving.
>
> It is to be observed accordingly, that we are still more anxious to communicate to our friends our disagreeable than our agreeable passions, that we derive still more satisfaction from their sympathy with the former than from that with the latter, and that we are still more shocked by the want of it.[15]

---

14   *Id.* at 32-33.
15   ADAM SMITH, THE THEORY OF MORAL SENTIMENTS 9 (Classic House Books 2009) (1759).

Maximization of Satisfaction – The Why

A common example can further explain this point. Say a person is stopped by a police officer for a traffic violation. The offender perceives the expected ticket as bringing pain, and there are various methods the offender may use to avoid the ticket. One method could involve bribery, and another involves an appeal to passion.

Although illegal, the first method may entail offering something of sufficient value to the officer to cause the officer to ignore his duty. However there may not be enough gold in Fort Knox for the officer to compromise his integrity. Nonetheless, as George Washington succinctly noted, "[f]ew men have the virtue to withstand the highest bidder."[16] That is not to say that all men and women have a price, but as Washington observed, few do not.

The other method would be for the offender to create the circumstances that would allow for the officer to eliminate the expected pain. In this context, the offender is attempting to minimize his pain by hoping the officer will seek pleasure by minimizing the pain of a fellow human. Once again, Adam Smith provides some insight why this tactic bears fruit. "The agreeable passions of love and joy can satisfy and support the heart without any auxiliary pleasure. The bitter and painful emotions of grief and resentment more strongly require the healing consolation of sympathy."[17]

An offender can express his pain by becoming visibly upset through crying or sobbing to appeal to the officer's sense of

---

[16] THE QUOTABLE FOUNDING FATHERS 382 (Buckner F. Melton, Jr. ed., Fall River Press 2008) (citing George Washington in letter to Robert Howe, August 17, 1779).
[17] ADAM SMITH, THE THEORY OF MORAL SENTIMENTS 10 (Classic House Books 2009) (1759).

sympathy. Depending on the officer's sentiments and attitude, this tactic may or may not work. In this scenario, the aim of the offender is to provide an opportunity for the officer to maximize his own satisfaction by alleviating someone else's pain.

One could characterize such an exchange as a win-win situation if only viewed as a situation concerning the two individuals. However, taken in the context of the entire society and the importance of justice, precedence, traffic safety, perceptions of others, and more, it should not be considered as a win-win situation. Regardless, it demonstrates a situation that involves people acting to maximize their satisfactions, whether by minimizing pain or seeking pleasure.

Saul Alinsky, author of *Rules for Radicals,* provides his reflections on the satisfaction that may be attained by relieving the suffering of another. He offers thoughts on how much power and persuasion a person may have over another when considering those who suffer through no fault of their own, such as the young, old, or disabled. Alinsky wrote, "Clarence Darrow put it on more of a self-interest basis: 'I had a vivid imagination. Not only could I put myself in the other person's place, but I could not avoid doing so. My sympathies always went out to the weak, the suffering, and the poor. Realizing their sorrows I tried to relieve them in order that I myself might be relieved.'"[18]

Freud and Alinsky provide a sound foundation to understand the concept of minimizing pain in an effort to maximize satisfactions. Now that we have examined the one category of maximizing satisfaction—through minimizing pain—it is time to investigate the other: by seeking pleasure.

---

18   SAUL ALINSKY, RULES FOR RADICALS: A PRACTICAL PRIMER FOR REALISTIC RADICALS 74 (Vintage Books reprt. 1989) (1971).

Section II: Seeking Pleasure

In this section we will discuss human needs and desires, starting with an examination of how beliefs and culture shape needs and desires. After better understanding our needs and desires, we will then address the two basic methods to fulfill them: either through exchange or through force.

What we ultimately seek through either exchange or force is to attain goods or services to satisfy our needs and desires in an attempt to maximize our pleasure. As previously mentioned, when dealing with human action, there are as many perceived needs and desires as there are individuals. Certainly there is a distinction between needs and desires, where needs would cover those things vital to support life. For simplification within our context, we will use the term "desires" to include both the necessary and the nice-to-have.

Because each person has different beliefs, preferences, and tastes, each person has different desires. Moreover, because each person also has different knowledge, experience, and wisdom, which ultimately shape their faculty of reasoning, each person takes a different action in an attempt to fulfill his or her desires.

However, attempting to understand the cause of human desires is akin to the age-old dilemma of attempting to determine which came first: the chicken or the egg. Is the desire to attain certain things based on belief alone, or does culture create the belief? If culture creates the belief, from where does culture obtain the belief? Culture—as expressed by custom, habit, or ritual—and belief influence one another, and beliefs are critically important in creating desires.

Marcus Aurelius summarized the importance of beliefs

1913: From General To Specific Welfare

perfectly: "Whenever you meet someone, ask yourself first this immediate question: 'What beliefs does this person hold about the good and bad in life?' Because if he believes this or that about pleasure and pain and their constituents, about fame and obscurity, death and life, then I shall not find it surprising or strange if he acts in this or that way, and I shall remember that he has no choice but to act as he does."[19]

Beliefs play a paramount role in shaping human action. If we are to put what drives human action into terms familiar to a military strategist, then beliefs are a center of gravity. The person or group that is able to influence the beliefs of society will also be the person or group who has control. Discussing how to influence a person or group's beliefs will be discussed in Part IV. For now, let us examine desires.

Individuals' actions undertaken to fulfill their desires may be placed into one of two general categories: force or exchange. In the category of force, the ultimate result is that one person gains while the other person loses. If one person desires something that another person possesses and the first person takes it by force, then that person has gained that thing while the other person has been deprived of it. The result is a "win" and a "loss." The common label for such use of force is robbery, even though the means to that end come in many different variations.

Concerning the notion of exchange, not every person maintains exactly the same desire as every other person at every instant in time. If that were the case, exchange would cease to occur. According to Thomas Hobbes, "[f]or if all things were

---

[19]   MARCUS AURELIUS, MEDITATIONS 73 (Martin Hammond, trans., Penguin Books 2006) (150 A.D.).

equally in all men, nothing would be prized."[20] For that matter, the use of coercion through force would cease as well if every person had the exact same desires. The only time an exchange or the use of force occurs is when desires are imbalanced between two actors. Without such imbalances, no one would be acting on their desires and the world as we know it would become static and stagnant. The fact that all people differ in their desires is what generates a dynamic world. If differing desires are so important that they drive all human action, then desires are worthy of a further analysis, especially when discussing the topic of exchange.

Each individual is constantly searching for the means to fulfill his or her desires with an eye towards maximizing their satisfactions.[21] Carl Menger provides an excellent explanation of terms addressing humanity's quest to fulfill its desires. He explains: "Things that can be placed in a causal connection with the satisfaction of human needs we term *useful things*. If, however, we both recognize this causal connection, and have the power actually to direct the useful things to the satisfaction of our needs, we call them *goods*."[22]

---

20   THOMAS HOBBES, LEVIATHAN 39 (Barnes & Noble, Inc. 2004) (1651) (explaining the concept of virtue but applicable in the context used here).

21   Any particular action may be taken as a means to an intermediate end. An action may even be one that seemingly results in a contradiction to our basic premise. A process of foregoing a lesser satisfaction in the shorter-run in order to obtain the ultimate end in the longer-run, or a difference in time preference between individuals, would certainly explain this ostensible contradiction. It is similar to retreating in a single battle as a tactic pursued to achieve the strategic goal of winning the war. A similar example concerns an argument where one contender uses a tactic of conceding a lesser point with the intention of achieving concessions on more substantial points that would lead to winning the argument. Nonetheless, let there be no doubt that each individual does in fact take action to maximize his or her satisfaction.

22   CARL MENGER, PRINCIPLES OF ECONOMICS 52 (James Dingwall & Bert F. Hoselitz trans., Ludwig von Mises Institute reprt. 2007) (1871) (footnotes omitted).

From this definition, we can identify four qualities that a good must possess: it must satisfy a human need; it must possess properties that allow it to be brought into a causal relationship to satisfy this need; humans must be able to recognize this connection; and an individual must have command of the goods to be able to direct them toward fulfilling some need.[23] In this context, a good can be either a tangible object or a service.

Continuing with Menger's reflections on goods, humanity's attempts to satisfy desires with goods would not create conflict if those goods were not scarce. If goods were unlimited in nature, each individual would be able to satisfy his desires to his utmost satisfaction without limiting the satisfactions of any other person. However, that is not always the case. In fact, most goods are not infinite and are therefore scarce. This scarcity has a potential to create conflict when the demand for a particular good exceeds the supply. This is where we first see the necessary role for government. While we will later return to examining a potential role for government, for now let us focus our discussion on maximizing satisfaction via seeking pleasure.

When an individual assigns a cost to attaining each of the available goods, that person must then prioritize those goods in order to maximize his own satisfaction.[24] The desirability of any good is called its value, and the balance between the supply and demand of the good determines its price. Because of goods'

---

23   Id.
24   This point should not be confused with the notion that all seek their self-interest, or in other words, that all are greedy. Some people, or perhaps even most people, rank highly their desire to help others. If that is the case, then those people will undoubtedly rank-order goods and services to fulfill that particular desire's priority. The point is that all seek to maximize their satisfactions, and they do that by prioritizing their desires and using the goods and services in their command to fulfill them in the most economical manner.

differences in value, supply, and demand, this results in a market with different prices for goods.

Every single exchange occurs because one person values what another is holding more than what they themselves are currently holding, and vice versa. Economics is commonly called the study of exchange. However, economics would be more appropriately labeled the science and art of human action. The one certainty in economics is that all individuals act to maximize their satisfactions.

Hopefully this explanation shows how people exchange goods in attempts to fulfill desires and thus maximize their satisfactions. Let us now continue our examination by reviewing reflections from philosophers of the past to provide additional context.

In *The Wealth of Nations*, Adam Smith's reference to an invisible hand is directly related to the concept of each person acting to maximize his satisfaction. He goes on to explain that every individual is part of a family; every family is part of a community or town; every town is part of a county; every county is a part of a state; and every state is part of a nation. Because every individual pursues his own interest (or more to our point, seeks to maximize his satisfaction), that person will be willing to pay the price in a manner that does so. As a person who produces goods will presumably maintain command of those goods, they become his wealth.[25] Because a man or woman is also a part of a larger group, or nation in Smith's sense, their wealth also contributes to the wealth of a nation through a mechanism Smith called an "invisible hand."[26] Though an individual may have no

---
25 See CARL MENGER, PRINCIPLES OF ECONOMICS 109 (James Dingwall & Bert F. Hoselitz trans., Ludwig von Mises Institute reprt. 2007) (1871) (defining wealth as the entire sum of economic goods at a person's command).
26 ADAM SMITH, THE WEALTH OF NATIONS 572 (Edwin Cannan ed., Bantam Books 2003) (1776).

conscious intention of contributing to the wealth of a nation, by attempting to maximize his satisfaction and by a seemingly invisible hand, each person invariably contributes to the wealth of his nation.

Moving on to Jean-Jacques Rousseau's *The Social Contract*, his reflections affirm the self-evident law of nature that all seek to maximize their satisfactions. He wrote, "[t]here is no people on earth the choice of whose pleasures is not decided by opinion rather than nature. Right men's opinions, and their morality will purge itself. Men always love what is good or what they find good [maximize their satisfactions by fulfilling their desires]; it is in judging what is good that they go wrong [the function of reason as noted by Aristotle]. This judgment, therefore, is what must be regulated."[27] Although using different language, Rousseau is expressing the same notion as the fundamental law under examination.

Thomas Jefferson was certainly a wise man, and he too understood this law of nature. Not only that, but he expressed an idea that may be deduced from that law, which we will examine later in Part IV (Liberty Yields While Tyranny Gains). Jefferson wrote: "If once the people become inattentive to the public affairs . . . you and I and Congress and Assemblies, Judges and Governors, shall all become wolves. It seems to be the law of our general nature, in spite of individual exceptions."[28] The reference to wolves evokes my own terminology of maximizing satisfactions.

---

27   Jean-Jacques Rousseau, The Social Contract 99 (G.D. H. Cole trans., BN Publishing 2007) (1762).
28   Albert Jay Nock, Jefferson 112 (The Ludwig von Mises Institute 2007) (1926) (citing Jefferson writing from Paris to Edward Carrington).

Maximization of Satisfaction – The Why

The next author is noteworthy more for what he did not say than for what he did. Saul Alinsky, in *Rules for Radicals*, describes what he labels as "self-interest." He lists figures from history who expressed what he refers to as humanity's inclination for self-interest.

> From the great teachers of Judeo-Christian morality and the philosophers, to the economists, and to the wise observers of the politics of man, there has always been universal agreement on the part that self-interest plays as a prime moving force in man's behavior. The importance of self-interest has never been challenged; it has been accepted as an inevitable fact of life. In the words of Christ, "Greater love has no man than this, that a man lay down his life for his friends." Aristotle said, in *Politics*, "Everyone thinks chiefly of his own, hardly ever of the public interest." Adam Smith, in *The Wealth of Nations*, noted that "It is not from the benevolence of the butcher, the brewer, or the baker that we expect our dinner, but from their regard of their own interest. We address ourselves not to their humanity, but to their self-love, and never talk to them of our own necessities, but of their advantage [1776's version of how to influence people]." In all the reasoning found in *The Federalist Papers*, no point is so central and agreed upon as "Rich and poor alike are prone to act upon impulse rather than pure reason and to narrow conceptions of self-interest . . ." To question the force of self-interest that pervades all areas of political life is to refuse to see man as he is, to see him only as we would like him to be.[29]

---

[29] Saul Alinsky, Rules for Radicals: A Practical Primer for Realistic Radicals 53-54 (Vintage Books reprt. 1989) (1971).

The idea here is subtly yet substantially different from our self-evident premise. What differs is that Alinsky is missing maximization of satisfaction. His reflections focus on "self-interest," and he states that self-interest is "a prime moving force." But while self-interest may be a moving force, the desire to maximize one's satisfaction is in fact *the* moving force.

Alinsky implies in his discussion of self-interest that in cases where someone acts in a manner that benefits another, this action is not done out of self-interest. Therefore, he concludes that self-interest may only be *a* moving force since there are instances where individuals act for the benefit of another. But when viewed from the perspective that *the* moving force of all human actions is to maximize satisfaction, we see the self-evident nature that in all cases, people act to maximize their satisfaction regardless of whether or not their action benefits someone else.

In the instances where one acts to benefit another, the person is still acting to maximize his satisfaction even though the desire driving that action may not be readily apparent. If a person had $20 and gave $10 to another with no exchange of goods, all that we can say with any degree of certainty is that the person gave the money away because he derived more satisfaction from doing so than keeping it.

A passage from Thomas Hobbes' *Leviathan* expresses nearly the same thought concerning maximizing satisfaction. Granted, the language he uses is somewhat different than that used today, but the principle is identical.

> Felicity is a continuall progresse of the desire, from one object to another; the attaining of the former, being still but the way to the later. The cause whereof is, That the

object of mans desire, is not to enjoy once onely, and for one instant of time; but to assure for ever, the way of his future desire. And therefore the voluntary actions, and inclinations of all men, tend, not onely to the procuring, but also to the assuring of a contented life; and differ onely in the way: which ariseth partly from the diversity of passions, in divers men; and partly from the difference of the knowledge, or opinion each one has of the causes, which produce the effect desired.[30]

Indeed, everyone acts to maximize their own satisfactions, but this is manifested in numerous ways due to different desires, knowledge, experience, wisdom, and passions.

Freud also offered thoughts on how maximizing satisfactions (or happiness) is what drives human action:

We will turn, therefore, to the less ambitious problem, what the behavior of men themselves reveals as the purpose and object of their lives, what they demand of life and wish to attain in it. The answer to this can hardly be in doubt: they seek happiness, they want to become happy and to remain so. There are two sides to this striving, a positive and a negative; it aims on the one hand at eliminating pain and discomfort, on the other at the experience of intense pleasures. In its narrower sense the word "happiness" relates only to the last.[31]

---

[30] THOMAS HOBBES, LEVIATHAN 59 (Barnes & Noble, Inc. 2004) (1651).
[31] SIGMUND FREUD, CIVILIZATION & ITS DISCONTENTS 26-27 (Joan Riviere trans., Martino Publishing 2010) (1930).

John Locke also affirmed the law of maximizing satisfaction but in a more concise manner. "Morality is the rule of man's actions for the attaining happiness. For the end and aim of all men being happiness alone, nothing could be a rule or a law to them whose observation did not lead to happiness and whose breach did [not] draw misery after it."[32]

David Hume is equally on point. "The great end of all human industry [action], is the attainment of happiness. For this were arts invented, sciences cultivated, laws ordained, and society modeled [The Declaration of Independence's "pursuit of happiness"], by the most profound wisdom of patriots and legislators."[33]

Emer de Vattel, an authority on natural jurisprudence during the time of Hume and Smith, expressed similar thoughts. "The natural law is the *science of the laws of nature*, of those laws which nature imposes on mankind, or to which they are subject by the very circumstance of their being men; a science, whose first principle is this axiom of incontestable truth- 'The great end of every being endowed with intellect and sentiment, is happiness.'"[34]

Dale Carnegie, in his popular book *How to Win Friends & Influence People* written in 1937, also captures the essence of the premise quite well.

> Every act you have ever performed since the day you were born was performed because you wanted something. How

---
[32] JOHN LOCKE, Morality, in POLITICAL ESSAYS 267 (Mark Goldie ed., Cambridge University Press 1997) (c. 1677-1678).
[33] DAVID HUME, ESSAYS MORAL, POLITICAL AND LITERARY 149 (Henry Frowde reprt. 1904) (1741-42).
[34] EMER DE VATTEL, THE LAW OF NATIONS 69 n.* (Béla Kapossy & Richard Whatmore eds., Liberty Fund, Inc. 2008) (1758).

about the time you gave a large contribution to the Red Cross? Yes, that is no exception to the rule. You gave the Red Cross the donation because you wanted to lend a helping hand; you wanted to do a beautiful, unselfish, divine act. 'Inasmuch as ye have done it unto one of the least of these my brethren, ye have done it unto me.'

If you hadn't wanted that feeling more than you wanted your money, you would not have made the contribution. Of course, you might have made the contribution because you were ashamed to refuse or because a customer asked you to do it. But one thing is certain. You made the contribution because you wanted something.[35][36]

Earlier, we presented several examples that showed how minimizing pain to maximize satisfaction seemingly contradicted the discussed natural law, and we will offer another one here, in this case a person who donated enormous sums of money to charity.

---

[35] DALE CARNEGIE, HOW TO WIN FRIENDS & INFLUENCE PEOPLE 34 (Dorothy Carnegie & Arthur R. Pell, Ph.D. eds., Simon & Schuster 2009).

[36] As an aside, when it comes to the golden rule of human relationships, philosophers of the past may likely have deduced it from our basic premise. As Carnegie wrote, "Philosophers have been speculating on the rules of human relationships for thousands of years, and out of all that speculation, there has evolved only one important precept. It is not new. It is as old as history. Zoroaster taught it to his followers in Persia twenty-five hundred years ago. Confucius preached it in China twenty-four centuries ago. Lao-tse, the founder of Taoism, taught it to his disciples in the Valley of the Han. Buddha preached it on the bank of the Holy Ganges five hundred years before Christ. The sacred books of Hinduism taught it a thousand years before that. Jesus taught it among the stony hills of Judea nineteen centuries ago. Jesus summed it up in one thought – probably the most important rule in the world: 'Do unto others as you would have others do unto you.'" DALE CARNEGIE, HOW TO WIN FRIENDS & INFLUENCE PEOPLE 107 (Dorothy Carnegie & Arthur R. Pell, Ph.D. eds., Simon & Schuster 2009).

How can it be said that such individuals are not acting altruistically for the benefit of others before themselves, as it appears at first sight? Actually, upon closer inspection, a person giving to charity does not invalidate the law. Consider that the marginal utility of $100 is quite insignificant for a billionaire, but $100 may seem like a significant sum of money for a person in possession of only $200. Regardless of the sums involved, whatever the person who gave up such a sum received in exchange was obviously of higher value, regardless of whether it was a tangible object or something abstract. Perhaps the gain was the praise by his peers and the public for his benevolence. On the other hand, the motive may be that as a person ages and approaches death, such acts of charity may be attempts to gain favor with deities in the afterlife, or the person may simply wish to dispose of his estate as he sees fit while he still can.

In any of these cases, we see that when people act to maximize their satisfaction by exchanging things, they value the things offered less than those they receive. We can assert with certainty that the satisfaction gained from whatever was received was of greater value than what was delivered. If that were not the case, then no exchange would occur. Although it may seem that a person who donates a sum of money is seeking to maximize another's satisfaction, upon closer inspection the donor is still maximizing his own. This is not to dispute that a generous person does not act to benefit others. On the contrary, a generous person will act to the advantage of others because this is what maximizes the satisfaction of a person who places a high value on generosity.

In summary, we examined the two general categories under the topic of maximization of satisfaction: minimizing pain and maximizing pleasure. We compared reflections from philosophers of the past with everyday examples, including some seemingly contradictory situations, to help the reader understand the self-evident nature of the fundamental law of human nature.

The fact that people act to maximize their satisfaction is what drives all human action. It also compels humanity to form systems of governance for various reasons as examined in Part II, Article I. Unfortunately, the law that compels individuals to create a system of government eventually will also—through their own susceptibility to the very same natural law—undermine that government. We will now use deduction and the fundamental natural law to discuss the theory behind the formation of government, which is the next topic.

PART II:

RESULT OF OUR PREMISE – GOVERNMENT

It is an accepted truth that something cannot be created from nothing. Men and women must start with something and change its original form into something else that fulfills his or her desires. The proof of this simple truth should be self-evident as well. If people were able to produce something from nothing, there would be no concept of scarcity. After countless millennia, by now humans would have determined how to take advantage of producing something from nothing and fulfilled all their desires. Society would not have recognized a need for government as a means to maximize our happiness since all desires would have been already fulfilled.

Obviously, that is not the case. Because something cannot be produced from nothing, it is not plausible to construct a theory that government existed first and then produced a society, which is defined as a collection of individuals living under its jurisdiction. Instead of government creating society, people within society used the available resources to produce a government by changing the form of those resources into something that would fulfill their desires. In this part, we'll discuss the theory of government, why people constructed it, and what people expected it to accomplish.

Before explaining why humans would construct a government, let's first preview some elements of Part IV (Liberty Yields While Tyranny Gains) before we proceed through Parts II and III.

When it comes to addressing the need for government and what it ought to accomplish, these questions automatically arouse the passions of the people. This response is expected because of the inherent power that people in government wield over those who are not. Moreover, a government implements its power through force rather than through exchange. Therefore, when one group speaks of government doing this or that on their behalf, those who are on the receiving end of the force would naturally object. Unlike the process of exchange, where one can simply abstain from participating, this is not possible when a government uses force to impose its will.

Government uses the law as its instrument of force. As with any source of power, the law may be used for good (in a manner that benefits the general welfare) or bad (which will be examined more closely in an upcoming section).[37] Because the law is

---

[37] Concerning "good" and "bad," one needs to look no further than the intense debate surrounding the question of ratifying the United States Constitution. The Federalists generally sold the idea of ratifying the Constitution based on all of the happiness that such a government would provide (or good). In principle the Anti-Federalists originally were the Federalists, but by a stroke of tactical genius were cast as the Anti-Federalists by the later named Federalists. *See* JACKSON TURNER MAIN, THE ANTI-FEDERALISTS CRITICS OF THE CONSTITUTION 1781-1788 viii (W. W. Norton & Company, Inc. 1974). The Anti-Federalists were generally fearful of the general misery (or bad) that could be caused by a powerful central government, or more precisely, by the people who would seize control of the levers of the governmental structure. As previously mentioned with regards to there being few if any new ideas in this world, just two of the debates at the time concerned what amounted

the source of so much power, individuals may be able to use the government and the law to secure special privileges and advantages for themselves or members of their group. A government potentially has immense power since it can compel hundreds of millions of people to act towards a specific end. As history shows, however, this amassing of power will lead to the dissolution of government.

Once the first instance of special privileges occurs and is allowed to persist, it sets a precedent that will eventually lead to a government's doom. When citizens—the people who grant power to the government—realize that obtaining a position to create law is the means to securing special privileges, and when one combines that with the law of human nature, the question arises of how long it will take before the government creates the conditions that will lead to its demise. In other words, a government's evolution cycles through the conditions in what Thomas Hobbes expressed in *Leviathan* as the original state of nature. The difference is that instead of individual against individual, it becomes individual against individual with an agent of government as the intermediary.

As we examine the potential of what a government can accomplish, we should keep in mind a key point, which is that government is not a morally pristine institution. It is people who construct and manipulate the levers of government, which means the same law of nature applies to those inside the government as

---

to a mandated balanced budget (or whether the United States should have the authority to borrow) and term limits. At the time, the citizens opted for the ability to have an unbalanced budget and no limit on the number of terms (subsequently altered by the 22nd Amendment to the United States Constitution, at least for the President). If the truth be told, when one compares the predictions of the Federalists to the Anti-Federalists, contemporary effects seem to indicate the prescience of the Anti-Federalists.

it does to those on the outside. The result is that the power of the government will be used to secure special privileges for those on the inside.

In light of this, what actions would a government pursue to cultivate its potential of promoting the people's happiness?

ARTICLE I: WHY WE INSTITUTE GOVERNMENTS – THE THEORY

The equal rights of man and the happiness of every individual are now acknowledged to be the only legitimate objects of government.
- Thomas Jefferson[38]

From our law of nature, we may deduce that there exists at least one person who maximizes his satisfaction by putting forth the idea of government. A quote from *Cato's Letters* delivers the point succinctly. "One man, or a few men, have often pretended the publick, and meant themselves, and consulted their own personal interest, in instances essential to its well-being; but the whole people, by consulting their own interest, consult the publick, and act for the publick by acting for themselves:"[39]

Ultimately though, a government's power depends on the consent of the governed. However, history demonstrates that it is not uncommon for a small group to take control of the government and use its power to tyrannize the very citizens who created it.

Such tyranny would not result from a mass of oppressed people acting because they thought they were seeking pleasure. Instead the oppressed would be acting to minimize their pain, or

---

[38] THE POLITICAL WRITINGS OF THOMAS JEFFERSON 60 (Edward Dumbauld ed., The Bobbs-Merrill Company, Inc. 1955) (1823).
[39] 1 THOMAS GORDON & JOHN TRENCHARD, CATO'S LETTERS 271 (Ronald Hamowy ed., Liberty Fund, Inc. 1995) (c. 1720).

so they would believe. Perhaps this group had become apathetic to participation in the governmental process, or perhaps it saw no practical means to resist. For whatever reason, each individual continues on a passive course without any overt resistance. On the other hand, it would be reasonable to assert that the small ruling body is maximizing their satisfaction by seeking pleasure rather than avoiding pain. In a successful dictatorship, once the dictator has achieved the loyalty and submission of enough people, who are acting to maximize their satisfaction, he or she effectively enslaves the remaining members of the state.

Now, let's take another step. Imagine conditions where no individual yet has the means to understand the advantages afforded to each member of a group if they cooperate towards a common goal.

With this imaginary environment in mind, we must first examine the concept of rights and liberty because without an understanding of these two concepts, the point of such imaginary environment will be lost. In this imaginary environment, each individual has, on his or her own authority, all rights. To explain these rights, we turn to Thomas Hobbes and his succinct description of a right: ". . . because RIGHT, consisteth in liberty to do, or to forbeare . . . . "[40] In other words, a right is the liberty to act or not act while liberty is freedom from arbitrary authority.

Rights and liberty are absolutely vital to the understanding of a theory of government as espoused by writers between the years of 1600 and 1800, a period often referred to as "The Enlightenment." This period is important because it had a profound effect on the construction of the United States' system of governance. With an understanding of rights and liberty as

---

40   THOMAS HOBBES, LEVIATHAN 79 (Barnes & Noble, Inc. 2004) (1651).

described above, each individual in our imaginary, government-less environment possesses all of his or her rights. Nevertheless, the ability to exercise these rights is fleeting because another person may easily transgress upon them. "The liberty of one is thwarted by that of another; and whilst they are all equal, none will yield to any, otherwise than by a general consent. This is the ground of all just governments; for violence or fraud can create no right; and the same consent gives the form to them all, how much soever they differ from each other."[41] In this situation, no one is completely secure in his rights, and subsequently no one has any liberty. Moreover, no two people possess equal physical or mental abilities, which will make it even more difficult for those who are below average in either or both of these categories to ever secure their rights and liberty.

Because we are all born with unequal abilities, it is highly unlikely that we will be able to enjoy the full exercise of our rights even as each of us acts to maximize his or her satisfaction. If there is someone who is physically superior and who also derives pleasure from imposing their will on physically weaker men and women, then one can expect that the weaker people will not have an opportunity to fully enjoy their rights.

However, physical strength may be overcome by intellect and cunning, and the physically inferior yet mentally superior are certain to find an advantage. If we remain within our imaginary environment where cooperation has not yet been developed, we may begin to have a sense of what Thomas Hobbes (*Leviathan*),[42] Frederic Bastiat (*The Law*),[43] Karl Marx

---

41   ALGERNON SIDNEY, DISCOURSES CONCERNING GOVERNMENT 30-31 (Thomas G. West ed., Liberty Classics 1990) (1698).
42   THOMAS HOBBES, THE LEVIATHAN 76 (Barnes & Noble, Inc. 2004) (1651).
43   FREDERIC BASTIAT, THE LAW 13-14 (Dean Russell trans., Foundation for Economic Freedom 2d ed. 1998) (1850).

and Frederick Engels (*Economic and Philosophic Manuscripts of 1844 and the Communist Manifesto*),[44] Joseph Schumpeter (*Capitalism, Socialism, and Democracy*),[45] David Hume (*Hume's Political Discourses*),[46] John Locke (*Political Essays*)[47] et al. labeled as "a state of nature," where every individual (or eventually group) is at war with every other individual or group.

If we remove the imaginary restriction, we can then use our law of nature to deduce what might happen. As the physically stronger deprive the weaker of their rights, the mentally superior eventually conclude that cooperating with others for their mutual defense will secure their rights. Taking this thought process one step further, the physically weaker but mentally superior may conclude that their mutual defense could deter future acts, and may even engage in offensive actions against the physically superior. The physically superior could then adopt the tactics demonstrated by the group formed against them. This process continues until we reach conditions similar to a state of nature where each individual is pitted against another. Instead of the original state of nature, this revised process has not just pit individuals against individuals, but also groups against groups. The following excerpt from Hobbes, some 350 years ago, accurately describes the state of nature that evolved when each person strived to maximize his or her satisfaction.

---

[44] KARL MARX & FREDERICK ENGELS, *Communist Manifesto*, in ECONOMIC AND PHILOSOPHIC MANUSCRIPTS OF 1844 AND THE COMMUNIST MANIFESTO 219 (Martin Milligan trans., Prometheus Books 1988) (1847).
[45] JOSEPH A. SCHUMPETER, CAPITALISM, SOCIALISM, AND DEMOCRACY 283 (Harper Perennial Modern Thought 2008) (1942).
[46] DAVID HUME, *Of Political Society*, in HUME'S POLITICAL DISCOURSES 248 (The Walter Scott Publishing Co., LTD n.d.) (1752).
[47] JOHN LOCKE, *First Tract on Government*, in POLITICAL ESSAYS 37 (Mark Goldie ed., Cambridge University Press 1997) (1660).

From this equality of ability, ariseth equality of hope in the attaining of our Ends. And therefore if any two men desire the same thing, which neverthelesse they cannot both enjoy, they become enemies; and in the way to their End, (which is principally their owne conservation, and sometimes their delectation only,) endeavor to destroy, or subdue one an other. And from hence it comes to passe, that where an Invader hath no more to feare, than an other mans single power; if one plant, sow, build, or possesse a convenient Seat, others may probably be expected to come prepared with forces united, to dispossesse, and deprive him, not only of the fruit of his labour, but also of his life, or liberty. And the Invader again is in the like danger of another. . . .

Hereby it is manifest, that during the time men live without a common Power to keep them all in awe, they are in that condition which is called Warre; and such a warre, as is of every man, against every man. For WARRE, consisteth not in Battell onely, or the act of fighting; but in a tract of time, wherein the Will to contend by Battell is sufficiently known: and therefore the notion of *Time,* is to be considered in the nature of Warre; as it is in the nature of Weather. For as the nature of Foule weather, lyeth not in a showre or two of rain; but in an inclination thereto of many dayes together: So the nature of War, consisteth not in actuall fighting; but in the known disposition thereto, during all the time there is no assurance to the contrary. All other time is PEACE. . . .

It may seem strange to some man, that has not well weighed these things; that Nature should thus dissociate, and render men apt to invade, and destroy one another: and he may therefore, not trusting to this Inference, made from the Passions, desire perhaps to have the same confirmed by Experience. Let him therefore consider with himselfe, when taking a journey, he armes himselfe, and seeks to go well accompanied; when going to sleep, he locks his dores; when even in his house he locks his chests; and this when he knows there bee Lawes, and publike Officers, armed, to revenge all injuries shall bee done him; what opinion he has of his fellow subjects, when he rides armed; of his fellow Citizens, when he locks his dores; and of his children, and servants, when he locks his chests. Does he not there as much accuse mankind by his actions, as I do by my words? But neither of us accuse mans nature in it. The Desires, and other Passions of man, are in themselves no Sin. No more are the Actions, that proceed from those Passions, till they know a Law that forbids them: which till Laws be made they cannot know: nor can any Law be made, till they have agreed upon the Person that shall make it.[48]

Hopefully, this examination of the state of nature adequately explains the rationale for a theory of government, and why people take pains to create such institutions to maximize their satisfactions. Over time, people realized that all have an opportunity for rights, but if no one is secure in them then none have any semblance of liberty. Therefore, in an effort to maximize their

---

48   THOMAS HOBBES, LEVIATHAN 76-77 (Barnes & Noble, Inc. 2004) (1651).

satisfaction, men and women created government as the means to secure through force, as paradoxical as that may seem, rights and liberty towards *the* end of promoting the general welfare. "But if governments arise from the consent of men, and are instituted by men according to their own inclinations, they did therein seek their own good; for the will is ever drawn by some real good, or the appearance of it."[49]

From the time of Plato to Thomas Jefferson, various authors have expressed the same basic theory. As Jefferson noted, "it is to secure our just rights that we resort to government at all."[50] On another occasion, he further explained, "[t]he equal rights of man and the happiness of every individual are now acknowledged to be the only legitimate objects of government."[51] Before reviewing some of these author's reflections, let us continue discussing the theory of government. More specifically, we will examine what advantages a government may provide towards promoting the general welfare.

As Hobbes stated, in such a state of nature there is no supreme man-made law

". . . till they have agreed upon the Person that shall make it."[52] There is certainly the natural law upon which each individual acts to maximize his or her satisfaction. From this law springs the law of the market, where the populace determines the rules of the market by either buying or abstaining from the exchange

---

49 ALGERNON SIDNEY, DISCOURSES CONCERNING GOVERNMENT 49 (Thomas G. West ed., Liberty Classics 1990) (1698).
50 Edward Dumbauld, *Introduction* to THE POLITICAL WRITINGS OF THOMAS JEFFERSON xxvi (Edward Dumbauld ed., The Bobbs-Merrill Company, Inc. 1955) (citing letter to d'Ivernois, February 6, 1795. *Works*, VIII, 165).
51 THE POLITICAL WRITINGS OF THOMAS JEFFERSON 60 (Edward Dumbauld ed., The Bobbs-Merrill Company, Inc. 1955) (1823).
52 THOMAS HOBBES, LEVIATHAN 77 (Barnes & Noble, Inc. 2004) (1651).

of goods and services. Yet again, however, this quickly reverts right back where we began. The strong deprive the weak of their rights until the time when a sufficient number of the weak unite against the strong.

Given enough experience, people begin to ponder if this constant struggle for achieving our desires is the best way of living that we may hope to achieve. What if there was a way to stop allocating resources from the need to constantly defend what you possessed? What if, instead of expending them for defense, we could use the time and resources for achieving other satisfactions? What if there was a system that society could construct that would secure everyone's rights? Would this not be something that the vast majority of people would agree in order to satisfy their desires, which in this case we define as the general welfare?[53]

The answer is yes, and the means to achieve this general welfare would be some form of government. To see this notion succinctly encapsulated, let's look no further than the Declaration of Independence:

> We hold these truths to be self-evident, that all men are created equal [although most certainly not equal in physical or mental abilities], that they are endowed by their Creator with certain unalienable Rights, that among these are Life, Liberty and the pursuit of Happiness.--That to **secure these rights** [emphasis added], Governments are instituted among Men, deriving their just powers from

---

[53] The term "vast" is used since all of humanity has different preferences and desires. As noted, some derive pleasure from pain, as contradictory as that may appear. Nonetheless, if someone were to maximize their satisfaction by maximizing their pain, then one will expect that person to act accordingly.

the consent of the governed,--That whenever any Form of Government becomes destructive of these ends, it is the Right of the People to alter or to abolish it, and to institute new Government, laying its foundation on such principles and organizing its powers in such form, as to them shall seem most likely to effect their Safety and Happiness.[54]

Jefferson did not discover or articulate a new idea: that a government's sole end is to promote the general welfare, or happiness, which is the result of securing the rights and liberty of the citizens. Arguably, his expression of this idea is perhaps the most eloquent. Nonetheless, he was not the only one, and to capture the reflections of every philosopher who expressed this idea would be tedious and redundant. However, reviewing the thoughts of some of the great thinkers of the past is appropriate to our understanding of the idea.[55]

Beginning with the Greeks, Plato is an excellent example of someone who expressed the need of people to promote their general happiness through some system of governance:

---

54 THE DECLARATION OF INDEPENDENCE para. 2 (U.S. 1776).
55 It must be noted that truth does not depend on the number of people who believe it to be true, nor does it depend on the length of time that a belief was held. If that were not the case, we may still believe that the Sun revolved around the Earth, and that the Earth was flat. Thankfully, appeals to experience, observation, logic, and reason overturned those erroneous beliefs. An appeal to an expert can be the source of a logical fallacy if such an appeal is used incorrectly. However, I use the thoughts of historical philosophers as a means to demonstrate the reason why people in the past chose to construct governments – nothing more. Their thoughts are based on their experiences and observations. Perhaps the future will show that there is a better reason to construct a government. Until that time, my appeal to the thoughts of those from the past is the best means at my disposal to demonstrate that governments in theory have been, and are, constructed for the general happiness of all.

'I think,' I said, 'that we shall find our reply if we stick to the path we have been pursuing, and say that, though it would not in fact be in the least surprising if our Guardians were very happy indeed, our purpose in founding our state was not to promote the particular happiness of a single class, but, so far as possible, of the whole community. Our idea was that we were most likely to find justice in such a community, and similarly injustice in a really badly run community, and in light of our findings be able to decide the question we are tying to answer. We are therefore at the moment trying to construct what we think is a happy community by securing the happiness not of a select minority, but of the whole.'[56]

He goes on to say,

'None the less, it is only right to repeat again what I said then: if any Guardian looks for happiness in a way unworthy of his status, if he tires of the restraint and security of the ideal life we have drawn for him, and is impelled by some senseless and extravagant idea of happiness into using his power to appropriate the community's wealth – well, he will learn the wisdom of Hesiod's saying that the half is more than the whole.'[57]

Plato wrote this in his attempt to explain the necessary steps to reform the Greek government in the 4th century B.C.E. His

---

56   PLATO, THE REPUBLIC 126 (Betty Radice ed., Desmond Lee trans., Penguin Books 2d rev. ed. reprt. 1987) (c. 380 B.C.E.).
57   PLATO, THE REPUBLIC 192 (Betty Radice ed., Desmond Lee trans., Penguin Books 2d rev. ed. reprt. 1987) (c. 380 B.C.E.).

words provide evidence of his understanding of the purpose—or "end"—of government.

In the following two excerpts, Aristotle does not use the explicit language of "general welfare." In fact, when they are taken separately, it may be more difficult to see his reference to government's end being the general welfare. However, when the two excerpts are placed together and read as a whole, then we may easily recognize the underlying principle.

> Now that we have discussed the several kinds of virtue and friendship and pleasure, it remains to give a summary account of happiness, since we assume that it is the end of all that man does. . . .[58]

> But all kinds of association or community seem to be, as it were, parts of the political community or association of citizens. For in all of them men join together with a view to some common interest [general welfare], and in pursuit of some one or other of the things they need for their life. But the association of citizens seems both originally to have been instituted and to continue for the sake of common interest; for this is what legislators aim at, and that which is for the common interest of all is said to be just.[59]

Because all people act to maximize their individual satisfaction, it follows that happiness is a common interest and pursuit of all. What each person defines as happiness and the means chosen to reach it will certainly differ, but the end itself will be

---
[58] ARISTOTLE, NICOMACHEAN ETHICS 215 (F.H. Peters, M.A. trans., Barnes & Noble, Inc. 2004) (350 B.C.E).
[59] Id. at 172-73.

common to all. It is upon this common interest that a group of people may form a government whose end is to promote their general welfare.

While Jean-Jacques Rousseau did not explicitly use "general welfare," his reflections are even closer to supporting that exact phrase than Aristotle's.

> The first and most important deduction from the principles we have so far laid down is that the general will alone can direct the State according to the object for which it was instituted, *i.e.* the common good: for if the clashing of particular interests made the establishment of societies necessary [from the state of nature discussed previously], the agreement of these very interests made it possible. The common element in these different interests is what forms the social tie; and, were there no point of agreement between them all, no society could exist. It is solely on the basis of this common interest that every society should be governed.[60]

In a manner similar to Rousseau, St. Thomas Aquinas did not explicitly use "general welfare," but he expressed the same sentiment when he uses the phrase "common good."

"Now the end of law is the common good; because as Isidore says (*Etym.* V. 21) that *law should be framed, not for any private benefit, but for the common good of all the citizens.*"[61]

---

60   JEAN-JACQUES ROUSSEAU, THE SOCIAL CONTRACT 25 (G.D. H. Cole trans., BN Publishing 2007) (1762).
61   ST. THOMAS AQUINAS, ON LAW AND JUSTICE: EXCERPTS FROM SUMMA THEOLOGICA 1017 (Neil H. Alford et al. eds., Leslie B. Adams, Jr. spec. ed. reprt. 1988) (1485).

Result of Our Premise – Government

John Locke influenced the thoughts of those who created our government, and it is not surprising that his ideas, if not the same language, are included in our founding documents such as the Declaration of Independence and the United States Constitution. His ideas provide a clear and understandable progression of the theory of government that results in government's ultimate end: general welfare. We can readily see in his writing what others previously expressed: a government that secures rights and liberty may lift people out of a state of nature, which thus promotes the general welfare.

Locke noted, "[f]or, if men could live peaceably and quietly together, without uniting under certain laws, and entering into a commonwealth, there would be no need at all of magistrates or polities [forerunner to Madison's quip on government being unnecessary if men were angels], which are only made to preserve men in this world from the fraud and violence of one another; so that what was the end of erecting of government ought alone to be the measure of its proceeding."[62] He then adds, "[a]nd I think it will easily be granted that the making of laws to any other end but only for the security of the government and protection of the people in their lives, estates, and liberties, i.e. the preservation of the whole, will meet with the severest doom at the great tribunal . . . ."[63]

In reference to the magistrate, Locke stated, ". . . since in truth a magistrate is set above a people that governs them for this reason, that he may provide for the common good and the general welfare; he holds the helm so that he may guide the ship into harbour and not on to the rocks."[64]

---

[62] JOHN LOCKE, *An Essay on Toleration, in* POLITICAL ESSAYS 135 (Mark Goldie ed., Cambridge University Press 1997) (1660).
[63] *Id.* at 142.
[64] JOHN LOCKE, *Second Tract on Government, in* POLITICAL ESSAYS 61 (Mark Goldie ed., Cambridge University Press 1997) (1660).

Lastly, Locke affirmed these same sentiments in his treatise on civil government. "The great and chief end, therefore, of men uniting into commonwealths, and putting themselves under government, is the preservation of their property; to which in the state of Nature there are many things wanting."[65]

Hugo Grotius, circa 1625, acknowledged the same sentiments. In his examination of the lawfulness of war, he stated, "[f]or the end of society is to form a common and united aid to preserve to every one his own. Which may easily be understood to have obtained, before what is now called property was introduced."[66]

Algernon Sidney, circa 1698, described his understanding of the theory of government in the following manner:

> The weakness in which we are born, renders us unable to attain this good of ourselves: we want help in all things, especially in the greatest. The fierce barbarity of a loose multitude, bound by no law, and regulated by no discipline, is wholly repugnant to it: Whilst every man fears his neighbour, and has no other defence than his own strength, he must live in that perpetual anxiety which is equally contrary to that happiness, and that sedate temper of mind which is required for the search of it. The first step towards the cure of this pestilent evil, is for many to join in one body, that everyone may be protected by the united force of all; and the various talents that men possess, may by good discipline be rendered useful to the whole; as the meanest piece of wood or stone being placed by a

---

[65] JOHN LOCKE, THE SECOND TREATISE ON CIVIL GOVERNMENT 70 (Prometheus Books 1986) (1690).
[66] HUGO GROTIUS, ON THE LAW OF WAR AND PEACE 16 (Kessinger Publishing reprt. (1625).

wise architect, conduces to the beauty of the most glorious building. But every many bearing in his own breast affections, passions, and vices that are repugnant to this end, and no man owing any submission to his neighbour; none will subject the correction or restriction of themselves to another, unless he also submit to the same rule.[67]

Thomas Gordon, writing in the 1720s under the pseudonym Cato and a significant influence on the American Revolutionaries, wrote in *Cato's Letters*:

What is the public, but the collective body of private men, as every private man is a member of the public? And as the whole ought to be concerned for the preservation of every private individual, it is the duty of every individual to be concerned for the whole, in which himself is included. . . . In truth, our whole worldly happiness and misery (abating for accident and diseases) are owing to the order or mismanagement of government; and he who says that private men have no concern with government, does wisely and modestly tell us, that men have no concern in that which concerns them most . . . .[68]

Perhaps even more to the point concerning the reason for the formation of governments, Gordon wrote, "[m]en are so far from having any views purely publick and disinterested, that government first arose from every man's taking care of himself;

---

[67] ALGERNON SIDNEY, DISCOURSES CONCERNING GOVERNMENT 83 (Thomas G. West ed., Liberty Classics 1990) (1698).
[68] 1 THOMAS GORDON & JOHN TRENCHARD, CATO'S LETTERS 271 (Ronald Hamowy ed., Liberty Fund, Inc. 1995) (c. 1720).

and government is never abused and perverted, but from the same cause."⁶⁹ As mentioned previously, the people's desire to maximize their satisfactions not only produces but also destroys governments, as Mr. Gordon expressed in the above passage.

Adam Smith, in his *The Theory of Moral Sentiments*, agreed with the notion that the end of government is the general welfare of all. "All constitutions of government, however, are valued only in proportion as they tend to promote the happiness of those who live under them. This is their sole use and end."⁷⁰

Interestingly, both of Smith's works (*The Wealth of Nations* and *The Theory of Moral Sentiments*) were published prior to the U.S. Constitution (1776 and 1759, respectively). Not only that, but sections of the Constitution bear a striking resemblance to the words and ideas in Smith's words. It appears that the Founders wholeheartedly agreed with him when they established an interdependent governmental system designed to overtly keep specific interests at bay.

Mr. Abel Parker Upshur, a former Judge of the General Court of Virginia, United States Secretary of the Navy, and United States Secretary of State, wrote circa 1840 what he labeled as a review of Justice Joseph Story's *Commentaries on the Constitution*. Upshur intended to express the importance of the States in the role of our government, which will be examined in Part III, Article IV. We mention that excerpt now because of his reference to the end of government, which is found towards the end of the citation. "In venturing upon so bold a step [declaring their independence], congress acted precisely as they did in all other cases, in the name of the States whose representatives they

---

69   *Id.* at 280.
70   ADAM SMITH, THE THEORY OF MORAL SENTIMENTS 194 (Classic House Books 2009) (1759).

were, and with a full reliance that those States would confirm whatever they might do for the general good."[71]

We must also include a passage from *The Federalist* where it addresses the theory of government. As Madison stated, "[i]t is too early for politicians to presume on our forgetting that the public good, the real welfare of the great body of the people, is the supreme object to be pursued; and that no form of government whatever, has any other value, than as it may be fitted for the attainment of this object. Were the plan of the convention adverse to the public happiness, my voice would be, reject the plan."[72]

From all these excerpts it should be apparent that governments established with the end of providing the general happiness or welfare are not new by any means. In fact, this general idea is likely as old as humanity itself. Unfortunately, the same law that provided for the creation of a government is the same one that tends towards its abuse and dissolution. The next section reviews a theory of government structured to prevent its demise.

ARTICLE II: NECESSARY RESTRAINT

We have determined the natural law that all men act to maximize their satisfaction. From this, we then determined that an important means to further a people's happiness is to institute a society with a sovereign, governing body whose end is promoting the general welfare.

---

[71] ABEL PARKER UPSHUR, A BRIEF INQUIRY INTO THE TRUE NATURE AND CHARACTER OF OUR FEDERAL GOVERNMENT: BEING A REVIEW OF JUDGE STORY'S COMMENTARIES ON THE CONSTITUTION OF THE UNITED STATES 26-27 (Kessinger Publishing) (1868).

[72] THE FEDERALIST No. 45, at 256 (James Madison) (George Stade ed., Barnes & Noble, Inc. 2006).

1913: From General To Specific Welfare

In a state of nature, all had equal rights, but no one was secure in them or their liberty. Therefore, in order to ensure that all remain secure in their rights and liberty, and the resulting general welfare, some means are necessary to achieve the end.

Some means must obviously provide the power necessary to defend against external threats against the peace and security of society. However, those entrusted with the power to defend against such attacks are also subject to the same law of human nature. If there is no restraint placed upon this power, it is an invitation for abuse by those who exploit others as a means to further their special privilege, or welfare, at the expense of liberty for the rest of society. To preserve the liberty and general welfare, it is paramount that restraints are put in place to ensure the power granted to the central government is limited to accomplish its intended purpose and nothing more.

Adam Smith discussed the principle of a balance of power with regards to a force used to prevent external threats.

> As it is only by means of a well-regulated [note similar language to the 2nd Amendment of the U.S. Constitution] standing army that a civilized country can be defended; so it is only by means of it, that a barbarous country can be suddenly and tolerably civilized. A standing army establishes, with an irresistible force, the law of the sovereign through the remotest provinces of the empire, and maintains some degree of regular government in countries which could not otherwise admit of any.... Men of republican principles have been jealous of a standing army as dangerous to liberty. It certainly is so, wherever the interest of the general and that of the principal officers are not

necessarily connected with the support of the constitution of the state. The standing army of Caesar destroyed the Roman republic. The standing army of Cromwel turned the long parliament out of doors.[73]

To the point of a standing army, Smith noted: "A militia, however, in whatever manner it may be either disciplined or exercised, must always be much inferior to a well-disciplined and well-exercised standing army."[74]

Seemingly well aware of Smith's observations, our Founders struck a balance between a militia and a standing army in that they provided for both. The militia was intended to be well-regulated, or disciplined, and comprised of the people,[75] whereas the standing army required funds to be appropriated for no more than two years at one time.[76] By this construction, the idea is to provide for the common defense from external threats with a militia and standing army. Internal threats, such as by a person or group who intended to use a standing army as a force to transgress the rights of the people, were to be thwarted by the militia. Additionally, the potential internal threat of an ever-expanding standing army was to be checked by limiting appropriations to no more than two years. Purposefully, the two-year restriction coincided with the length of the term for members of the House of Representatives, where all bills of revenue must originate. In light of the Founders' restraint upon the government, which is perhaps overlooked, the Founders' wisdom and knowledge of human nature remain impressive to this day.

---

73 ADAM SMITH, THE WEALTH OF NATIONS 898 (Edwin Cannan ed., Bantam Books 2003) (1776).
74 *Id.* at 890.
75 U.S. CONST. amend. II.
76 U.S. CONST. art. I, § 8, cl. 12.

1913: From General To Specific Welfare

If one begins with the natural law that all will act to maximize their satisfaction, then one can predict what will occur if there are no safeguards in place to prevent the power of the government from being used for unintended purposes. The power granted to a sovereign body is too tempting for an enterprising person or group. When a group is able to seize the center of gravity with no limitations on its power, the results are not difficult to predict: absolute arbitrary authority, or more ominously—tyranny.

Let's dwell on an economic analogy that is useful in illuminating what will occur under an unrestrained government. Because all act to maximize happiness in their everyday lives, this may manifest itself in the market with a desire to buy low and sell high. This is the basic principle of trading goods for gain: buy low and sell high. Similarly, a person wants others to buy goods and services *from* him at the highest price while he wants others to sell *to* him at the lowest price. Now imagine what would happen if some entity were granted the power to buy low and sell high into perpetuity with no restraint (see Part V, Article II for examination of the Federal Reserve System). With such power, it is inevitable that it would eventually be used for personal or specific welfare.

The situation devolves to something even more dangerous to general welfare when enough people exploit the power of creating government statutes to secure various special privileges.[77] When this process has run its course, the society will effectively revert back to Hobbes' state of nature. Each group has secured their own special interest so that they can sell high and buy low;

---

77   The term "statute" is used instead of law to highlight the following point. The term "law" should be reserved for legislation that secures rights and liberty. In the sense used above, the statues are the opposite of law as they are creating tyranny. When one's rights are secured, then liberty follows.

however, every other group has done the same. The end result is that in order to do any business, one must navigate through a tangle of statutes. This alone creates substantial costs for all conducting transactions. Instead of promoting the general welfare, widespread misery and destitution will spread under an absolute arbitrary authority. In response, the people agitate for action as individuals attempt to secure more favorable statutes from the legislators, and in the case of our example with no restraints, there would seemingly be no means to halt such a tightening spiral.

Nonetheless, eventually this spiral ceases when it becomes apparent that these conditions are not addressing the happiness of the people. Even worse, the amount of time that has passed from the root cause to the manifestation of the symptoms may be so great that it prevents a discovery of the root cause. The challenge is to create a system of government that maximizes the amount of time between the inception of the root cause and the point where the circumstances revert to a state of nature.

Returning to governmental restraints, a natural one is placed on men and women, especially those in governing positions, by the threat of public censure. However, because public censure is fleeting and dependent on the volatile passions and opinions of the people, such censure may not be enough of a deterrent to rein in the abuses of government officials. Additionally, if these officials have the ability to project sufficient force and the will to use it, public censure may very well become irrelevant. When the governing entity is willing to use force to punish those attempting censure, how many people will risk incurring such punishments? Without restraints on the governing entity, natural law will lead towards a consolidation of power.

1913: From General To Specific Welfare

No matter what restraints are set in place, someone will find a way to circumvent them, and these cycles can take decades to develop because the process is dynamic and evolutionary. So what is another method, besides censure, that can prevent a deterioration of the general welfare?

The best method available to act as a restraint on humanity's natural tendency to maximize its satisfaction is to incorporate the very same law of nature in the structure of government: pit ambition against ambition; special interest against special interest; greed against greed. One can achieve a balance of power by utilizing this strategy. The balance of power serves as a mechanism to check power against power, and ensure an environment that fosters the general welfare instead of facilitating the devolution of government into one that promotes special welfare. From the writings of the Founders themselves, it's apparent that the Founders recognized this fundamental law of human nature and so established a balance of power when they constituted our United States government.

Alexis de Tocqueville eloquently summarized the principle of a balance of power as applied to a government.

> There is a second means of diminishing the action of authority: this does not consist of stripping society of some of its rights, or paralyzing its efforts, but of dividing the use of its forces among several hands; of multiplying officials while allocating to each of them all the power he needs to do what he is destined to execute. One encounters peoples whom this division of social powers can also bring to anarchy; by itself, however, it is not anarchic. In partitioning authority in this way, it is true, one renders

its action less irresistible and less dangerous, but one does not destroy it.[78]

The U.S. Constitution employs various methods to partition authority exactly as de Tocqueville described in the quoted material above. In the remainder of this work, we will deal with only three methods: taxes, election of the senate, and the power over legal tender and currency. The overturning of these three checks on power in 1913 and its effects are discussed in detail in Part V. For now, we'll review the U.S. Constitution prior to 1913 and begin with the Preamble.

---

[78] ALEXIS DE TOCQUEVILLE, DEMOCRACY IN AMERICA 67 (Harvey C. Mansfield & Delba Winthrop eds. & trans., The University of Chicago Press, LTD. 2002) (1835).

PART III:

UNITED STATES CONSTITUTION PRE-1913

We the People of the United States, in Order to form a more perfect Union, establish Justice, insure domestic Tranquility, provide for the common defence, promote the general Welfare, and secure the Blessings of Liberty to ourselves and our Posterity, do ordain and establish this Constitution for the United States of America.[79]

Locke provides clear thoughts on the importance of a preamble in the context of legislation, or in the case of the U.S. Constitution, the Supreme Law itself.

The preamble of a statute being always accounted an excellent key to open the meaning of the purview. And therefore though the body or purview of the statute may seem very large, referring all to the discretion of the court, yet 'tis very well known that discretion according to interpretation of law is not an extravagant liberty or licence to do what they please; but their proceedings are to be limited and bounded within the rule of law and reason.

---

79 U.S. Const. pmbl.

Discretion being a faculty of discerning *per legem quid sit justum*, and not to be guided by will or private affection because *talis discretio discretionem confundit*.[80] And there can be no better guide to their discretion in this case than the preamble of the statute.[81]

Justice Joseph Story, in 1833, also provided specific insight into the meaning and importance of the Preamble to our Constitution. Although his chapter on the subject of the Preamble is worth reading in its entirety, only short portions are included here.

The importance of examining the preamble, for the purpose of expounding the language of a statute, has been long felt, and universally conceded in all juridical discussions. It is an admitted maxim in the ordinary course of the administration of justice, that the preamble of a statute is a key to open the mind of the makers, as to the mischiefs which are to be remedied and the objects which are to be accomplished by the provisions of the statute. We find it laid down in some of our earliest authorities in the common law, and civilians are accustomed to a similar expression, *cessante legis proemio, cessat et ipa lex*.[82] Probably it has a foundation in the expression of every code of written law, from the universal principle of interpretation, that the well and intention of the legislature are to be regarded

---

[80] This definition, and the Latin tags, follow Coke's INSTITUTES (Part II) and his REPORTS. 'What would be just according to law'; 'Such discretion confounds discretion.'
[81] JOHN LOCKE, *Selecting the Grand Jury*, in POLITICAL ESSAYS 284 (Mark Goldie ed., Cambridge University Press 1997) (1681).
[82] Bac. Abrig. Statute I.; 2 Plowden, R. 369; 1 Inst. 79.

and followed. It is properly resorted to where doubts or ambiguities arise upon the words of the enacting part; for if they are clear and unambiguous, there seems little room for interpretation, except in cases leading to an obvious absurdity, or to a direct overthrow of the intention expressed in the preamble.

There does not seem any reason why, in a fundamental law or constitution of government, an equal attention should not be given to the intention of the framers, as stated in the preamble. And accordingly we find that it has been constantly referred to by statesmen and jurists to aid them in the exposition of its provisions....[83]

And here we must guard ourselves against an error which is too often allowed to creep into the discussions upon this subject. The preamble never can be resorted to to enlarge the powers confided to the general government or any of its departments. It cannot confer any power *per se*; it can never amount, by implication, to an enlargement of any power expressly given. It can never be the legitimate source of any implied power, when otherwise withdrawn from the Constitution. Its true office is to expound the nature and extent and application of the powers actually conferred by the Constitution, and not substantively to create them. For example, the preamble declares one object to be, "to provide for the common defence." No one can doubt that this does not enlarge the powers of Congress to pass any measures which they may deem useful for the

---

[83] *See* Chisholm v. Georgia, Chief Justice Jay's opinion, 2 Dall. 419.

common defence.[84] But suppose the terms of a given power admit of two constructions, the one more restrictive, the other more liberal, and each of them is consistent with the words, but is, and ought to be, governed by the intent of the power; if one would promote and the other defeat the common defence, ought not the former, upon the soundest of principles of interpretation, to be adopted? Are we at liberty, upon any principles of reason or common-sense, to adopt a restrictive meaning which will defeat an avowed object of the Constitution, when another equally natural and more appropriate to the object is before us? Would not this be to destroy an instrument by a measure of its words, which that instrument itself repudiates?[85]

In other words, the Preamble provides the purpose, *or mission statement*, of the U.S. Constitution. Actions taken to implement the enumerated powers must be in accordance with the general means expressed in the Preamble. If statutes are enacted to implement an enumerated, or specific, power but do not fall under one of the general means expressed in the Preamble (or worse, are contradictory), then the statute should never be considered lawful.

With these thoughts in mind, let us now turn to the words of the Preamble. We may deduce from the Preamble all the means that are *necessary* to achieve the end of government, or general welfare. In other words, general welfare requires liberty,

---

84 Yet, strangely enough, this objection was urged very strenuously against adoption of the *Constitution*; 1 Elliot's Debates, 293, 300.
85 1 JOSEPH STORY, COMMENTARIES ON THE CONSTITUTION OF THE UNITED STATES 338-40 (Thomas M. Cooley ed., The Lawbook Exchange, LTD. 4th ed. 2008) (1873).

and liberty is built of four components: 1) law that ensures one's rights are secure from internal attack; 2) a common defense for security against external attack; 3) justice, or the application of such law equally to all; and 4) domestic tranquility.

The Preamble could've been written so that its logical flow is more readily apparent: "We, the People of the United States, in order to form a more perfect Union whose end is the General Welfare, do ordain and establish this Constitution for the United States of America to secure our rights and blessings of liberty for ourselves and our posterity, establish justice, provide for the common defense, and ensure the domestic tranquility. " Although this version perhaps would more clearly articulate the general means provided to attain the end, the current Preamble is certainly more eloquent and definitely sufficient.

Taking the Preamble as a mission statement, it must then describe the what, when, how, where, why, and who. In the Preamble, we can readily identify each of these items.

The "what" is as discussed previously: to promote the general welfare. General welfare in this sense is based on the ultimate end that all humans seek to achieve: a maximization of satisfaction. As Emer de Vattel, a writer who influenced the ideas of the mid-1700s and the Constitution, noted: "[i]n the act of association, by virtue of which a multitude of men form together a state or nation, each individual has entered into engagements with all, to promote the general welfare; and all have entered into engagements with each individual, to facilitate for him the means of supplying his necessities, and to protect and defend him."[86]

The "when" is obviously further defined in the body of the

---

86   EMER DE VATTEL, THE LAW OF NATIONS 86 (Béla Kapossy & Richard Whatmore eds., Liberty Fund, Inc. 2008) (1758).

Constitution. However, this leads us to discuss the "Union." It's worthy to note that in creating a Union, the intent was to create a perpetual Union. Our forefathers intentionally omitted a termination date of the government because the Union was constituted to exist as long as it promoted the general welfare, the end of any society seeking to maximize its happiness. At a minimum, this sentiment dovetails with the idea expressed by Jefferson in the Declaration of Independence: "[t]hat whenever any Form of Government becomes destructive of these ends [securing rights to life, liberty, and pursuit of happiness], it is the Right of the People to alter or abolish it, and to institute new Government, laying its foundation on such principles and organizing its powers in such form, as to them shall seem most likely to effect their Safety and Happiness."[87]

"Where" is self-evident: the United States of America.

The next aspect is "why," and the reason is found and explained in the Declaration of Independence. In addition, the preceding section on the theory of government and the people's need to seek happiness also explains the "why." The colonists believed that their contemporary system of government at the time was not the best means to provide for their general welfare. After many years of much debate, they decided that the Constitution was the best means to their desired end.

There is much more to the "who" than just the explicit words written in the Preamble. Explicitly, the "who" is "We, the people of the United States...."[88] However, the language in the originally approved Preamble provided: "We, the people of the States of New Hampshire, Massachusetts, Rhode Island and Providence

---

87 THE DECLARATION OF INDEPENDENCE para. 2 (U.S. 1776).
88 U.S. CONST. pmbl.

Plantations, Connecticut, New York, New Jersey, Pennsylvania, Delaware, Maryland, Virginia, North Carolina and Georgia, do ordain, declare and establish the following constitution, for the government of ourselves and our posterity."[89] Upon unanimous adoption of the Preamble and the U.S. Constitution, the documents were sent to the committee of five to " . . . revise the style of, and arrange the article agreed to by the house; which passed in the affirmative."[90] It was this committee that produced the Preamble as written in the ratified Constitution of today, with one exception: instead of "to establish justice . . ." it today states "establish justice."[91]

Because the committee of five was charged with only revising the wording versus altering the substance of the adopted Preamble, the two versions essentially conveyed the same idea. One explanation for the change may be related to the method for ratification. Because only nine states were necessary for ratification, there existed a chance that states named in the Preamble might never join the Union. More than likely, the committee attempted to sidestep such a dilemma by simplifying the words to "We, the People of the United States . . ."[92] At the time, it probably seemed quite innocuous. However, over time it has proved to be quite significant.

Today, whether recognized or not by the people who are governed by it, the change in language is vitally important. Many governmental leaders, members of the media, academics, etc.

---

89   ABEL PARKER UPSHUR, A BRIEF INQUIRY INTO THE TRUE NATURE AND CHARACTER OF OUR FEDERAL GOVERNMENT: BEING A REVIEW OF JUDGE STORY'S COMMENTARIES ON THE CONSTITUTION OF THE UNITED STATES 51 (Kessinger Publishing) (1868) (citing 1 Elliot's Debates, 255).
90   Id. (citing 1 Elliot's Debates, 324).
91   Id. at 52.
92   Id.

refer to our Union as a democracy versus a republic. The language "We the People" is cited as evidence. Spreading democracy has even become a keystone in our foreign policy, even though what the Constitution guarantees is a republic. The change of the Preamble, from the original to the current version along with the 17th Amendment, had a profound impact on nullifying one of three important restraints to maintain a balance of power: the power of the states as an integral check on the power of the central government. We will expand on the critical influence of the 17th Amendment on the United States Senate in Part III, Article IV. For now, it's important to note the influence that a seemingly irrelevant change of words at the time had on the understanding of the most important document used to construct any system of governance—its constitution.

The "how" is expressed as one principle with two components. The one principle is through liberty, or freedom from arbitrary authority. The two components are protection from both external and internal threats. The protection from external threats is accomplished by the means of providing for the common defense. The protection from internal threats begins with securing individual rights and the subsequent liberty for ourselves and our posterity, provided through a balance of power within the government.

Internal liberty is provided by securing individual rights, which requires an establishment of justice.[93] However, justice is

---

93   Aristotle defines justice as one of two ways. First, justice is that which is in accordance with the law while the other definition is one of fairness or equity. Therefore, ". . . we apply the term just to whatever tends to produce and preserve the happiness of the community, and the several elements of that happiness." ARISTOTLE, NICOMACHEAN ETHICS 91 (F.H. Peters, M.A. trans., Barnes & Noble, Inc. 2004) (350 B.C.E). The Preamble uses justice in both of these senses.

dependent upon law, and without a fair application of law, justice is impossible. If legislation transgresses individual rights, then the legislation is not actually "law," and justice is impossible. However, when legislation secures rights and liberty, it is considered "law." Only when law is applied equally to all, then there may be an establishment of justice. "By the establishment of liberty, a due distribution of property and an equal distribution of justice is established and secured. As rapine is the child of oppression, justice is the offspring of liberty, and her handmaid; it is the guardian of innocence, and the terror of vice...."[94]

Because St. Thomas Aquinas provided such an insightful description of the relation of rights, liberty, and justice, his reflections are included here. "Now the proper matter of justice consists of those things that belong to our intercourse with other men, as shall be shown further on (A. 2). Hence the act of justice in relation to its proper matter and object is indicated in the words, *Rendering to each one his right*, since, as Isidore says (*Etym.* x), *a man is said to be just because he respects the rights (jus) of others.*"[95]

John Locke also provided a compelling explanation of the relationship of rights, liberty, and justice, and it is included because his writings greatly influenced the Declaration of Independence.[96]

---

94   1 THOMAS GORDON & JOHN TRENCHARD, CATO'S LETTERS 436 (Ronald Hamowy ed., Liberty Fund, Inc. 1995) (c. 1720).
95   ST. THOMAS AQUINAS, ON LAW AND JUSTICE: EXCERPTS FROM SUMMA THEOLOGICA 1435 (Neil H. Alford et al. eds., Leslie B. Adams, Jr. spec. ed. reprt. 1988) (1485).
96   "Great mistakes in the ruling part, many wrong and inconvenient laws, and all the slips of human frailty will be borne by the people without mutiny or murmur. But if a long train of abuses, prevarications, and artifices, all tending the same way, make the design visible to the people, and they cannot but feel what they lie under, and see whither they are going, it is not to

By drawing upon his keen grasp of human nature, Locke explained that laws are necessary to describe the free actions of man. From the perspective of the peoples within a state, laws are a means to the end of happiness. "Every one as he is bound to preserve himself, and not to quit his station willfully, so by the like reason, when his own preservation comes not in competition, ought he as much as he can to preserve the rest of mankind, and not unless it be to do justice on an offender, take away or impair the life, or what tends to the preservation of the life, the liberty, health, limb, or goods of another."[97]

The "preservation of the life, the liberty, health, limb, or goods of another" should also be familiar because the Declaration of Independence used words similar to Locke's. Thomas Jefferson said, ". . . all men are created equal, that they are endowed by their Creator with certain unalienable Rights, that among these are Life, Liberty and the pursuit of Happiness.--That to secure these rights, Governments are instituted among Men. . . ."[98] The Declaration of Independence, essentially a declaration of war unless our independence was granted, describes the basic belief that is the bedrock of the union of the states. All men and women seek happiness, and the path to obtain this happiness is through securing rights and the liberty that logically follows.

---

be wondered that they should then rouse themselves. . . ." JOHN LOCKE, THE SECOND TREATISE ON CIVIL GOVERNMENT 121 (Prometheus Books 1986) (1690). Compare that to The Declaration of Independence: "But when a long train of abuses and usurpations, pursuing invariably the same Object evinces a Design to reduce them under absolute Despotism, it is their right, it is their duty, to throw off such Government, and to provide new Guards for their future security." THE DECLARATION OF INDEPENDENCE para. 2 (U.S. 1776).

97   JOHN LOCKE, THE SECOND TREATISE ON CIVIL GOVERNMENT 10 (Prometheus Books 1986) (1690).

98   THE DECLARATION OF INDEPENDENCE para. 2 (U.S. 1776).

Locke argued that establishing justice was based on compliance with laws that are used to create liberty.

There is another item from the Preamble that is related to liberty from internal threats. If justice has been established due to the implementation and enforcement of laws that are used to secure rights and liberty, then a consequence of this process is peace and prosperity, or "insuring the domestic Tranquility."[99] Another aspect of this phrase addressed standardizing and centralizing issues that were a source of contention among the states.

Alexander Hamilton, in *The Federalist Number 7* (concerning war among the states and its particular causes), listed three general areas that were a source of strife and acrimony: territorial disputes, debts, and commercial disputes.[100] If the new government successfully regulated these concerns among the states, then such action would produce domestic tranquility—at least between the states if not within any particular state.

The last phrase of the Preamble that needs explanation is: "in Order to form a more perfect Union."[101] Article III of the Articles of Confederation provides insight into the decision to use this phrase:

> The said states hereby severally enter into a firm league of friendship with each other, for their common defence, the security of their Liberties, and their mutual and general welfare, binding themselves to assist each other, against all force offered to, or attacks made upon them, or any of them, on account of religion, sovereignty, trade, or any other pretence whatever.[102]

---

99 U.S. Const. pmbl.
100 The Federalist No. 7 (Alexander Hamilton).
101 U.S. Const. pmbl.
102 Articles of Confederation of 1781, art. III.

The Articles of Confederation already established a union of sorts, but this union was defined as a "firm league." It had the same end (general welfare) along with the same general means to that end (securing of liberty). Advocates of the Constitution claimed that the government of the United States of America created by the Articles of Confederation lacked the authority to achieve its end.[103] As such, the delegates to the Constitutional Convention were charged with making the appropriate changes to grant the newly formed government the authority to achieve the end of general welfare. By using the phrase "a more perfect Union," it likely softened the resistance from those who preferred the Articles of Confederation. The phrase implied that the Articles were perfect, but the Constitution would be "more perfect." Certainly the choice of the phrase was purely rhetorical; it was, however, of very significant meaning.

"Perfect" may be better understood by considering it as "progress." In the classical sense of the word, progress means forward movement toward the desired goal.

The end of the Articles of Confederation was the same as that of the Constitution: general welfare. However, the means to do so as provided in the former were perceived to be lacking by some, e.g., the Federalists. The Constitution sought to remedy the problems of the Articles of Confederation by providing the necessary means to promote the general welfare. In this manner, the Constitution would "form a more perfect Union."

Aquinas and Hume expressed this same understanding of "perfect." As Aquinas wrote, "In things ordained to an end, there is perfect goodness when a thing is such that it is sufficient in itself to conduce to the end: while there is imperfect goodness

---

103   THE FEDERALIST No. 1 (Alexander Hamilton).

when a thing is of some assistance in attaining the end, but is not sufficient for the realization thereof."[104] Hume chose the following language to express the meaning of perfect: "Every work of art has also a certain end or purpose for which it is calculated; and is to be deemed more or less perfect, as it is more or less fitted to attain this end."[105]

Emer de Vattel brilliantly stated the meaning of perfect in relation to a government.

> The *perfection* of a nation is found in what renders it capable of obtaining the end of civil society; and a nation is in a perfect state, when nothing necessary is wanting to arrive at that end. We know that the perfection of a thing consists, generally, in the perfect agreement of all its constituent parts to tend to the same end. A nation being a multitude of men united together in civil society, - if in that multitude all conspire to attain the end proposed in forming a civil society, the nation is perfect; and it is more or less so, according as it approaches more or less <5> to that perfect agreement. In the same manner its external state will be more or less perfect, according as it concurs with the interior perfection of the nation.
>
> The *end* or *object* of civil society is to procure for the citizens whatever they stand in need of, for the necessities, the conveniences, the accommodation of life, and, in general,

---

104 ST. THOMAS AQUINAS, ON LAW AND JUSTICE: EXCERPTS FROM SUMMA THEOLOGICA 1026 (Neil H. Alford et al. eds., Leslie B. Adams, Jr. spec. ed. reprt. 1988) (1485).
105 DAVID HUME, ESSAYS MORAL, POLITICAL AND LITERARY 246 (Henry Frowde reprt. 1904) (1741-42).

whatever constitutes happiness, - with the peaceful possession of property, a method of obtaining justice with security, and, finally a mutual defence against all external violence.

It is now easy to form a just idea of the perfection of a state or nation: -every thing in it must conspire to promote the ends we have pointed out.

In the act of association, by virtue of which a multitude of men form together a state or nation, each individual has entered into engagements with all, to promote the *general welfare* [emphasis added]; and all have entered into engagements with each individual, to facilitate for him the means of supplying his necessities, and to protect and defend him.[106]

He explains further: "[t]he perfection of a state, and its aptitude to attain the ends of society, must then depend on its constitution: consequently the most important concern of a nation that forms a political society, and its first and most essential duty towards itself, is to chuse the best constitution possible, and that most suitable to its circumstances. When it makes this choice, it lays the foundation of its own preservation, safety, perfection, and happiness: - it cannot take too much care in placing these on a solid basis."[107] When one views the phrase "in order to form a more perfect Union" from the context of de Vattel's writings, it makes crystal-clear the meaning of the phrase—and

---

106   EMER DE VATTEL, THE LAW OF NATIONS 86 (Béla Kapossy & Richard Whatmore eds., Liberty Fund, Inc. 2008) (1758).
107   *Id.* at 92.

for that matter the meaning of the Preamble and the entire Constitution.[108]

So we see, the Preamble is the very mission statement for our entire system of government. It provides the purpose for government (maximization of satisfaction, or general welfare) with the general means to that end: liberty from external and internal threats along with justice based on laws whose purpose is to attain the intermediate end of liberty, while domestic tranquility is a natural result when these general means are achieved. When we view the Preamble in the context of the entire Constitution, it is easier to see that the rest of the document becomes the specific means, which are used to achieve the general means of securing rights and liberty, which are used to achieve the ultimate end of general welfare.

This structure allows for a debate of specific means and intermediate ends through the use of logic and reason. As we shall soon discuss, if the end or general means are no longer considered when debating legislation, the nature of the debate changes.

---

[108] Adam Smith expressed his thoughts on the duties of a government with regards to promoting the general welfare by securing rights and liberty from external and internal attacks. Moreover, he expressed essentially the same principles upon which the Constitution was created: the Preamble states the ultimate end and general means to be used while the body expresses the particulars to be used. "According to the system of natural liberty, the sovereign has only three duties to attend to; three duties of great importance, indeed, but plain and intelligible to common understandings: first, the duty of protecting the society from the violence and invasion of other independent societies [from external threats]; secondly, the duty of protecting, as far as possible, every member of the society from the injustice or oppression of every other member of it, or the duty of establishing an exact administration of justice [from internal threats]; and thirdly, the duty of erecting and maintaining certain public works and certain public institutions, which it can never be for the interest of any individual, or small number of individuals, to erect and maintain [specific means to achieve ultimate end]. . . ." ADAM SMITH, THE WEALTH OF NATIONS 874 (Edwin Cannan ed., Bantam Books 2003) (1776).

Oftentimes today, political debate centers on how much currency should be spent (one million, ten million, one billion, or today even trillions) to accomplish some task versus whether the means under consideration are even authorized. Debating whether the means are authorized should avail itself to utilizing reason, e.g., does this proposed action secure the rights and subsequent liberty of all, and hence the general welfare? However, when debating how much currency should be spent, the logical end is not so much whether it is authorized, but whether it should be 100 billion or perhaps one trillion. What is too often missed in such debate is that some person or group will receive the new currency before others, which is by definition special versus general welfare. The point being, debating whether the means are authorized is a legitimate one attempting to determine if proposed actions are constitutional. A debate over how much should be spent very well may be one concerning a subject that is beyond the authority granted to the central government and is beyond the authority of the Constitution from the beginning.

A better way to frame a political debate concerning constitutional issues is to first ask whether the particular task falls under the general means of protecting an individual's liberty. If it is determined that such a task does not contradict the general means, then the debate may move to discussions concerning the degree by which these means are applied. When issues are debated in this manner, there is a definite answer concerning the question of whether the central government has the authority to take a proposed action (see Part III, Article II for a further examination of restraints that are necessary). When there is no restraint via a requirement to fall under the general means of protecting individual liberty, there is essentially no limit to the number of topics that may be subject to debate, as seen in today's contemporary political climate.

Now that we've reviewed the Preamble—the Constitution's mission statement—and discussed the end—or goal—of government, let's now turn to an examination of the Constitution itself and its enumerated powers.

Article I: Enumerated, Specific Powers

After the Preamble, the rest of the Constitution provides the specific means to accomplish the end of general welfare. Article I, Section 8 provides a listing of the powers granted to the federal government. The enumerated powers are listed first as they appear in the Constitution and then according to each of the general means as listed in the Preamble.

> *1.) The Congress shall have Power To lay and collect Taxes, Duties, Imposts and Excises, to pay the Debts and provide for the common Defence and general Welfare of the United States; but all Duties, Imposts and Excises shall be uniform throughout the United States;*
>
> *2.) To borrow Money on the credit of the United States;*
>
> *3.) To regulate Commerce with foreign Nations, and among the several States, and with the Indian Tribes;*
>
> *4.) To establish an uniform Rule of Naturalization, and uniform Laws on the subject of Bankruptcies throughout the United States;*

5.) To coin Money, regulate the Value thereof, and of foreign Coin, and fix the Standard of Weights and Measures;

6.) To provide for the Punishment of counterfeiting the Securities and current Coin of the United States;

7.) To establish Post Offices and post Roads;

8.) To promote the Progress of Science and useful Arts, by securing for limited Times to Authors and Investors the exclusive Right to their respective Writings and Discoveries;

9.) To constitute Tribunals inferior to the supreme Court;

10.) To define and punish Piracies and Felonies committed on the high Seas, and Offenses against the law of Nations;

11.) To declare War, grant Letters of Marque and Reprisal, and make Rules concerning Captures on Land and Water;

12.) To raise and support Armies, but no Appropriation of Money to that Use shall be for a longer Term than two Years;

13.) To provide and maintain a Navy;

14.) To make Rules for the Government and Regulation of the land and naval Forces;

15.) To provide for calling forth the Militia to execute the Laws of the Union, suppress Insurrections and repel Invasions;

1913: From General To Specific Welfare

16.) To provide for organizing, arming, and disciplining, the Militia, and for governing such Part of them as may be employed in the Service of the United States, reserving to the States respectively, the Appointment of the Officers, and the Authority of training the Militia according to the discipline prescribed by Congress;

17.) To exercise exclusive Legislation in all Cases whatsoever, over such District (not exceeding ten Miles square) as may, by Cession of particular States, and the Acceptance of Congress, become the Seat of Government of the
United States, and to exercise like Authority over all Places purchased by the Consent of the Legislature of the State in which the Same shall be, for the Erection of Forts, Magazines, Aresenals, dock-Yards and other needful Buildings; - And

18.) To make all laws which shall be **necessary and proper** *[emphasis added] for carrying into Execution the foregoing Powers, and all other Powers vested by this Constitution in the Government of the United States, or in any Department or Officer thereof.*[109]

If we group the enumerated powers according to the general means of the Preamble, we see how each of the enumerated are based upon those codified in the Preamble. The method of grouping begins with securing liberty from external attack and is followed by the power to make law. Law is used as the means to secure the intermediate aim of liberty, and the rule of law establishes justice. From justice follows domestic tranquility. The

---
109 U.S. Const. art. I, § 8, cl. 1-18 (numbers added for organization).

numbering system is only used to keep track of the powers; in the following listing, the number "1" does not correspond to the same number "1" above.

Liberty from External Attack

1.) To provide for organizing, arming, and disciplining, the Militia, and for governing such Part of them as may be employed in the Service of the United States, reserving to the States respectively, the Appointment of the Officers, and the Authority of training the Militia according to the discipline prescribed by Congress;

2.) To define and punish Piracies and Felonies committed on the high Seas, and Offenses against the law of Nations;

3.) To declare War, grant Letters of Marque and Reprisal, and make Rules concerning Captures on Land and Water;

4.) To raise and support Armies, but no Appropriation of Money to that Use shall be for a longer Term than two Years;

5.) To provide and maintain a Navy;

6.) To make Rules for the Government and Regulation of the land and naval Forces;

7.) To provide for calling forth the Militia to execute the Laws of the Union, suppress Insurrections and repel Invasions;

Secure Liberty through Legislation
(granting power to make law)

8.) *To exercise exclusive Legislation in all Cases whatsoever, over such District (not exceeding ten Miles square) as may, by Cession of particular States, and the Acceptance of Congress, become the Seat of Government of the United States, and to exercise like Authority over all Places purchased by the Consent of the Legislature of the State in which the Same shall be, for the Erection of Forts, Magazines, Aresenals, dock-Yards and other needful Buildings; - And*

9.) *To make all laws which shall be necessary and proper for carrying into Execution the foregoing Powers, and all other Powers vested by this Constitution in the Government of the United States, or in any Department or Officer thereof.*

Establish Justice

10.) *To constitute Tribunals inferior to the supreme Court;*
As discussed earlier, domestic tranquility was dependent on easing three areas of contention: territorial disputes, debt, and commerce. Because the topic of territorial disputes is outside the focus of our discussion, we'll keep our attention on debt and commerce. Because money plays such a critical role in the creation of debt (and likewise, credit), and because money is one of the principal topics of our discussion (indirectly through the Federal Reserve Act), we will use the word "money" in place of "debt." Below are the enumerated powers of money and commerce, grouped respectively.

Ensure Domestic Tranquility
Money:

11.) To establish an uniform Rule of Naturalization, and uniform Laws on the subject of Bankruptcies throughout the United States;

12.) To coin Money, regulate the Value thereof, and of foreign Coin, and fix the Standard of Weights and Measures;

13.) To provide for the Punishment of counterfeiting the Securities and current Coin of the United States;

14.) The Congress shall have Power To lay and collect Taxes, Duties, Imposts and Excises, to pay the Debts and provide for the common Defence and general Welfare of the United States; but all Duties, Imposts and Excises shall be uniform throughout the United States;

15.) To borrow Money on the credit of the United States;

Commerce:

16.) To regulate Commerce with foreign Nations, and among the several States, and with the Indian Tribes;

17.) To establish Post Offices and post Roads;

18.) To promote the Progress of Science and useful Arts, by securing for limited Times to Authors and Investors the exclusive Right to their respective Writings and Discoveries;

As to the phrase that was struck through, "*To establish a uniform Rule of Naturalization,*" while naturalization may be considered a subject other than commerce, it is included in the commerce section since it more resembles this subject (regulating the flow of labor into the United States) than any of the others.

Nearly all of the powers granted in Section 8 fit neatly into one of the general means outlined in the Preamble. However, at first it seems there is a glaring lack of means to secure liberty from internal threats. Upon closer inspection, however, liberty from internal threats is secured explicitly by the "necessary and proper" clause. When discussing this clause in *The Federalist*, "necessary" is discussed extensively when compared to "proper."[110] Therefore, a better explanation of "proper" is warranted, using an example not mentioned in the Preamble. Of course, the following discussion is not the Supreme Court's interpretation of the Constitution. Nonetheless, it is a quite logical interpretation of the Constitution's body combined with its Preamble, or mission statement.

The Constitution logically provides this security by requiring bills to be tested against the Preamble to see if the bills secure rights and liberty, and ultimately promote the general welfare. If bills are prohibited from granting special privileges, then the people are secure from internal threats.

As noted, the Constitution was intended to form "a more perfect Union." The Articles of Confederation placed an explicit restriction on the general government: "Each state retains its sovereignty, freedom, and independence, and every Power, Jurisdiction and right, which is not by this confederation expressly delegated

---

[110] *See, e.g.*, THE FEDERALIST NO. 44, at 251-53 (James Madison) (George Stade ed., Barnes & Noble, Inc. 2006).

to the United States, in Congress assembled."[111] This clause created much contention between the states and the general government. It restricted the general government in such a manner that enfeebled it, and the states consistently challenged the lawfulness of legislation passed by the United States. The Constitution sought to rectify this problem. The Preamble, *combined* with the body of the Constitution, would have provided ample security from internal threats and an overreaching general government.

Perhaps the Constitution would have been considered more ideal had it omitted "necessary and proper" altogether. At the time, the Founders opted for a positive granting of powers without the restriction of those "expressly delegated." Their attempt to provide a restriction, although vehemently opposed by the Anti-Federalists, was through the necessary and proper clause.

Interestingly, James Madison expressed the same notion concerning the need of the necessary and proper clause, but in relation only to the enumerated powers themselves and not in relation to the general means provided in the Preamble. "Had the constitution been silent on this head, [omitting the 'necessary and proper' clause] there can be no doubt that all the particular powers requisite as means of executing the general powers, would have resulted to the government, by unavoidable implication."[112] What is missing is the applicability of each enumerated power to the general means in the mission statement. The "necessary" aspect is readily apparent. The important restriction follows from the "proper" aspect. "Proper" not only applies to each listed power; just as importantly, it also applies to the general means and ultimate end. Without using the Preamble as the test

---

111 ARTICLES OF CONFEDERATION of 1781, art. II.
112 THE FEDERALIST No. 44, at 252 (James Madison) (George Stade ed., Barnes & Noble, Inc. 2006).

for applicability, the "proper" portion of "necessary and proper" is essentially meaningless.[113]

To further amplify the need for security from internal threats, a discussion of the Bill of Rights is necessary. Both Federalists and Anti-Federalists were concerned with restraining the power that would be granted to the new federal government. Some of the Anti-Federalists desired a Bill of Rights to ensure the security of liberty from the centralization of powers while some of the Federalists argued that such a Bill of Rights was not necessary.[114] They claimed the Constitution was in practicality a Bill of Rights in itself. The only powers authorized were those enumerated, and there was no need for a continued explication of restrictions. In fact, the Federalists insisted that any Bill of Rights would implicitly give more powers to the general government.[115] By listing those rights that were not delegated to the general government, any rights that were not specifically listed would be implicitly granted to the general government. We can see the dilemma facing both the Federalists and the Anti-Federalists. However, the Federalists feared the Constitution would not be ratified without a Bill of Rights. The compromise was a Bill of Rights that included the 9th and 10th Amendments, which prevented the potential of implicitly granting more powers to the general government than those explicitly enumerated.

---

113   See GARY LAWSON & GUY I. SEIDMAN, *Necessity, Propriety, and Reasonableness, in* THE ORIGINS OF THE NECESSARY AND PROPER CLAUSE 120-43 (Cambridge University Press 2010).
114   3 THE COMPLETE ANTI-FEDERALIST 33 (Herbert J. Storing, ed., The University of Chicago Press 1981); *see also* 4 THE COMPLETE ANTI-FEDERALIST 47-48 (Herbert J. Storing, ed., The University of Chicago Press 1981).
115   THE FEDERALIST NO. 84, at 474 (Alexander Hamilton) (George Stade ed., Barnes & Noble, Inc. 2006).

Amendment IX: The enumeration in the Constitution, of certain rights, shall not be construed to deny or disparage others retained by the people.[116]

Amendment X: The powers not delegated to the United States by the Constitution, nor prohibited by it to the States, are reserved to the States respectively, or to the people.[117]

The "necessary and proper" clause and the Bill of Rights were the more specific means to secure the blessings of liberty from internal threats. More accurately, together they were intended to provide a way to counter the law of human nature. The clause is not only applicable to each specifically enumerated power but also to the general means embodied in the Preamble. The application of the clause to those general means is the next subject for discussion.

Article II: "Necessary and Proper" Applied

"[W]herever a general power is given, every particular power necessary for doing so is included."[118] A truer observation could not be stated. Although we have already examined the necessary and proper clause in relation to both the specific and general means, we will examine the necessary and proper clause against one of the actual enumerated powers in relation to the Preamble. We will use as an example the clause dealing with post offices and post roads. When establishing a post road, it is necessary to have land available for laying the road. However, a problem

---

116 U.S. Const. amend. IX.
117 U.S. Const. amend. X.
118 The Federalist No. 44, at 253 (James Madison) (George Stade ed., Barnes & Noble, Inc. 2006).

arises as portions of the countryside were already settled. From a strict definition of "necessary" and a strict application of the Constitution, a post road may be established without having any utility for the connection of post offices. From the perspective of the necessity of the road, there is no requirement to have it constructed so that it runs along the shortest distance between two points. Nonetheless, the "proper" portion of the clause is what prevents building a 100-mile road between two points that are only 10 miles apart. Moreover, the "proper" portion of the clause has a dual purpose: one in relation to the enumerated power and the other in relation to the general means of the Preamble.

In relation to the enumerated power, "proper" refers to its appropriateness or suitability. In the narrow view of this enumerated power, the end is to connect post offices for the efficient distribution of postage.

In relation to the general means of securing liberty from internal threats, in this case, "proper" also has a pertinent application. In order to connect two post offices in the most direct manner, a road may cross through private property. If the general government were to construct such a road without appropriate agreement and compensation, then the liberty of that property owner would be violated. The means chosen to accomplish the end of the enumerated power would have been contradictory to the general means. The conflict between the two would have resulted in defeating the ultimate end: general welfare.

So far we have explored the more obvious restraints on the powers of the general government, or those that are explicitly mentioned. Now let's focus on the more obscure restraints, or those that are the result of interactions of various principles. More specifically, we will examine the restraints that are intertwined with taxes, money, and the powers of the states. These three restraints are the crux of our argument, which is to show how three actions in 1913 eviscerated these restraints, which attempted to ensure general versus specific welfare. The ratification of the 16th and 17th Amendments and the passage of the Federal Reserve Act forever altered the end of the government of the United States of America from one of general welfare to one of specific welfare. Effectively, since that time the United States has been transformed into a venue used to legally exploit one person for the benefit of another. The actual process is quite concealed and intricate. Accomplished in a variety of ways, the process may manifest itself in privileges bestowed on one group at the expense of another and in exchange for the votes of the former. Based on the theory of government expressed by philosophers throughout the ages, this return to a state of nature is the very thing that governments are constituted to prevent. However, keeping in mind the fundamental law of nature, it should not be too surprising that history often repeats itself.

Article III: Taxes

I like the power given the legislature to levy taxes, and for that reason solely approve of the greater House being chosen by the people directly. For though I think a House chosen by them will be very illy qualified to legislate for the Union, for foreign nations, etc., yet this evil does not weigh against the good of preserving inviolate the fundamental principle that the people are not to be taxed but by representatives chosen immediately by themselves. - Thomas Jefferson[119]

---

119   The Political Writings of Thomas Jefferson 140 (Edward Dumbauld ed., The Bobbs-Merrill Company, Inc. 1955).

Based on the natural law that all act to maximize their satisfactions, it should not be surprising that some people will seek to use the power of government to secure for themselves a method to tax others to pay for what they desire. The manifestation of this law of nature concerning government and taxation is expressed in the phrase "taxation without representation."

It is accepted as common wisdom that taxation without representation was a significant contributing factor that led to the Revolutionary War. When the Founding Fathers secured their independence, they took great care to prevent a repeat of tyranny through taxation without representation. The process of making taxation reliant upon representation prevents one group with political power from preying upon another group who lacks it. It is a means to secure rights, liberty, and the general welfare, and *The Federalist* provides an excellent explanation behind the fundamental concept of taxation in the Constitution, discussing various methods to either promote or constrain liberty.

Alexander Hamilton, in *The Federalist Number 30*, describes how the Articles of Confederation lacked the required power to collect needed revenue for emergencies, present and future, and to pay the debts of the confederacy. He goes on to declare that money is a crucial principle of a state whereby money enables the state to perform its most essential operations. "A complete power, therefore, to procure a regular and adequate supply of revenue, as far as the resources of the community will permit, may be regarded as an indispensable ingredient in every constitution."[120] The important point from Hamilton's quote is his argument that any constitution creating a government must

---

120   THE FEDERALIST NO. 30, at 159 (Alexander Hamilton) (George Stade ed., Barnes & Noble, Inc. 2006).

have adequate provisions to provide a secure source of revenue to fulfill its obligations. "From a deficiency in this particular, one of two evils must ensue; either the people must be subjected to continual plunder, as a substitute for a more eligible mode of supplying the public wants, or the government must sink into a fatal atrophy, and in a short course of time perish."[121]

An overriding concern during the drafting of the Constitution was how to secure revenue to sustain government, yet secure it in a manner that protected the people's liberty and ensured the sovereignty of each state. Hamilton's reflections, especially the last sentence of the following quote, provide a summary of the restraint intended to be imposed: direct taxation and its tie to representation.

> I repeat here what I have observed in substance in another place, that all observations, founded upon the danger of usurpation, ought to be referred to the composition and structure of the government, not to the nature and extent of its powers. The state governments, by their original constitutions, are invested with complete sovereignty. In what does our security consist against usurpations from that quarter? Doubtless in the manner of their formation, and in a due dependence of those who are to administer them upon the people.[122]

For our purposes, the important principle to be gleaned from this passage—with regards to simultaneously securing both governmental revenue and liberty—is that those who administer

---

[121] *Id.*
[122] THE FEDERALIST No. 31, at 167 (Alexander Hamilton) (George Stade ed., Barnes & Noble, Inc. 2006).

our government must be *dependent* on the people for the prime source of government revenue versus the people being dependent on the government for their revenue.

For this purpose the founders of the Constitution made a compromise that resulted in the central government having essentially plenary powers of taxation, with the taxes on state exports as the only exception. Such complete powers were considered critical because any government duly constituted must have the necessary powers of taxation to continue to function. Without this power, whenever an unexpected and substantial external threat arose, a government's need for revenue would be so paramount that it would be forced to either risk being destroyed or possibly conquered by an external aggressor; or resort to unconstitutional acts to acquire the needed revenue.[123] Either option would inevitably nullify the liberties discussed in the Preamble.

Direct and Indirect Taxes

Ultimately, the Constitution granted all powers of taxation (except as noted above and with certain concurrent powers among the States) to the federal government, divided between the two broadest subdivisions: direct and indirect taxes. The only stipulations placed on the government were that capitation[124] (or other direct) taxes had to be apportioned in the

---

123   *See* THE FEDERALIST NO. 30, at 159-62 (Alexander Hamilton) (George Stade ed., Barnes & Noble, Inc. 2006).
124   Concerning capitation and direct taxes Justice Joseph Story noted: "[i]t is clear that capitation taxes, or, as they are more commonly called, poll-taxes, that is, taxes upon the polls, heads, or persons of the contributors, are direct taxes, for the Constitution has expressly enumerated them as such." 1 JOSEPH STORY, COMMENTARIES ON THE CONSTITUTION OF THE UNITED STATES 680 (Thomas M. Cooley ed., The Lawbook Exchange, LTD. 4th ed. 2008) (1873) (citing 2 Smith's Wealth of Nations, B. 5, ch. 2, art. 4; The Federalist, No. 36; 2 Elliot's Debates, 209).

same manner as the representatives of the people in the House of Representatives;[125] while indirect taxes (duties, imposts, and excises) had to be uniform throughout the United States.[126] This tax system was one based on taxation with representation. Through a combination of direct and indirect taxes, with their respective restrictions, the rights and liberty of the citizens were secure while the central government had the power to raise sufficient revenue for any potential emergencies. Because the delicate balance between revenue, liberty, and taxes was, and still is, dependent upon direct and indirect taxes, a further examination of the two is warranted.

A capitation or direct tax is distinctly different from an indirect tax. The former is unavoidable while the latter may be avoided, or shifted to another party.[127] This unavoidable characteristic of a capitation, along with the requirement to have them apportioned based on a state's representation in the House, provided a substantial, although by no means absolute, protection for liberty as it restrained the representatives from imposing any inordinate direct tax.

If an exorbitant tax was instituted, the constituents of each representative had a timely process to seek a redress for their

---

125 U.S. CONST. art. I, § 9, cl. 4.
126 U.S. CONST. art. I, § 8, cl. 1.
127 Of course, there is a significant relationship between liberty and taxation. Liberty is freedom from arbitrary authority. If citizens are to be taxed - or have taken from them what was produced by their mind or body - and have liberty at the same time, then they must have a say in how they will be taxed. If not, an arbitrary authority will tax them, at least from the perspective of each individual. Certainly arbitrary authority is quite the opposite of liberty. The idea of taxation with liberty is accomplished by having direct taxes, or those one cannot avoid, be apportioned based on one's representation. Although there is still an arbitrary element involved, the proportional link was, and still is, the best method in existence at least from the perspective of people being united in some type of governing system.

grievance every two years via election of their representative. Moreover, they would theoretically know the source for the painful tax (the representative they previously elected). On the other hand, an onerous indirect tax could be avoided by abstaining from purchasing that particular good or service, providing immediate feedback to the Congress through a reduction in revenue initially sought via the tax. Consequently, the original constitutional structure for direct and indirect taxes invariably limited government spending to an amount supportable by the productive capacity and consent of their constituents. The distinction between these two types of taxes and their specific, constitutional regulations is critical.

The Wealth of Nations, first published in 1776 by Adam Smith, provides more insight into the logic of taxation, representation, and liberty.[128] "The impossibility of taxing the people, in proportion to their revenue, by any capitation, seems to have given occasion to the invention of taxes upon consumable commodities [indirect, or excises, imposts, and duties]. The state not knowing how to tax, directly and proportionably, the revenue of its subjects, endeavours to tax it indirectly by taxing their expen[s]e, which, it is supposed, will most cases be nearly in proportion to their revenue. Their expen[s]e is taxed by taxing the consumable commodities upon which it is laid out."[129] This passage from Smith explains what is meant by the term "indirect," and what Smith understood the advantages of such a tax to be. The next category to further explore is the direct tax.

---

128   Notably, nowhere does the Constitution expressly mention indirect taxes; instead, it is the logical distinction for the remaining portion of taxes excluding those that are direct.

129   ADAM SMITH, THE WEALTH OF NATIONS 1102 (Edwin Cannan ed., Bantam Books 2003) (1776).

Because direct taxes (capitation or poll tax) may be so oppressive, it is worthwhile to read the thoughts of Alexander Hamilton from *The Federalist*.

> As to poll taxes, I, without scruple, confess my disapprobation of them; and though they have prevailed from an early period in those states, which have uniformly been the most tenacious of their rights, I should lament to see them introduced into practice under the national government. But does it follow, because there is a power to lay them, that they will actually be laid? Every state in the union has power to impose taxes of this kind; and yet in several of them they are unknown in practice. Are the state governments to be stigmatized as tyrannies, because they possess this power? If they are not, with what propriety can the like power justify such a charge against the national government, or even be urged as an obstacle to its adoption? As little friendly as I am to the species of imposition, I still feel a thorough conviction, that the power of having recourse to it, ought to exist in the federal government. There are certain emergencies of nations, in which expedients, that in the ordinary state of things ought to be forborn, become essential to the public weal. And the government, from the possibility of such emergencies, ought ever to have the option of making use of them. The real scarcity of objects in this country, which may be considered as productive sources of revenue, is a reason peculiar to itself, for not abridging the discretion of the national councils in this respect.[130]

---

[130] THE FEDERALIST No. 36, at 192-93 (Alexander Hamilton) (George Stade ed., Barnes & Noble, Inc. 2006) (footnote omitted).

Hamilton was attempting to assuage the fears of giving the new government the authority to institute a direct tax *only* for exigencies (levied with apportionment). His argument said nothing of the power to levy such tax permanently and capriciously without accountability through apportionment.

As mentioned, the designers of the Constitution had devised a means to accomplish a direct tax that did not conflict with liberty. The solution was that any direct tax had to be apportioned according to the census, which would also determine the number of representatives in the House, while indirect taxes had to be uniform throughout.

Direct taxation by representation was an ingenious safeguard invoked in an attempt to secure liberty. House members were to be elected every two years, and the House was the only branch of Congress that could originate bills of revenue even though the Senate could make amendments to said bills. Therefore, if a state with the largest delegation of representatives was seeking large sums of money in the form of a direct tax, they would need to not only take that proportional amount from their constituents, they would be required to seek re-election from those same constituents within at least two years. This system, by design, was a natural check on the power to levy direct taxes. Constituents would not only have a fairly expeditious redress within two years via elections, but they also would know precisely who to hold accountable for any undesired taxes. At the time of the drafting of the Constitution, imagine the near impossibility of achieving its ratification with a direct tax that could be levied without any regard to the constituents' representation. Such a construction likely would have had little chance of ratification. Unfortunately, as will be explained in Part V, Article I, that is exactly how the Constitution is applied today.

Continuing with direct taxation, no one is more careful with his or her own money, and no one is more careless than with that of another. Direct taxation according to representation is a means of ensuring that an individual spends his or her own money and not that of another. The following quotations from *Cato's Letters* are added for context and to further illuminate the issue. "The only secret therefore in forming a free government, is to make the interests of the governors and of the governed the same, as far as human policy can contrive. Liberty cannot be preserved any other way. Men have long found, from the weakness and depravity of themselves and one another, that most men will act for interest against duty, as often as they dare. So that to engage them to their duty, interest must be linked to the observance of it, and danger to the breach of it."[131] This passage underscores the natural law that all men and women act to maximize their satisfactions, and to restrain this inclination we must pit self-interest against itself. In government, an intrinsic way to achieve this is to link the spending of money to the taking of money through apportionment of direct taxes. "When the deputies [representatives] thus act for their own interest, by acting for the interest of their principals [constituents]; when they can make no law but what they themselves, and their posterity, must be subject to; when they can give no money, but what they must pay their share of; . . . their principals may then expect good laws, little mischief, and much frugality."[132]

Apportionment of direct taxes was certainly an important restraint upon the general government to secure against internal threats to liberty. Even still, many Anti-Federalists were

---

[131] 1 THOMAS GORDON & JOHN TRENCHARD, CATO'S LETTERS 417 (Ronald Hamowy ed., Liberty Fund, Inc. 1995) (c. 1720).
[132] *Id.* at 418.

vehemently opposed to any sort of authority for direct taxes.[133] Their fears were based on a solid understanding of human nature. The constitutional attempt to assuage that fear was to link direct taxes to representation, but as we will examine, the 16th Amendment negated that restraint and, in combination with the 17th Amendment and the Federal Reserve Act, did eventually undermine liberty. On that note, we'll look at how the security of liberty was to be provided by senators elected by the states.

Article IV: Senators of the States (Statesmen, or State's men)

'The voice of the people is the voice of God'. Surely, we have been taught by a most unhappy lesson how doubtful, how fallacious this maxim is, how productive of evils, and with how much party spirit and with what cruel intent this ill-omened proverb has been flung wide lately among the common people. – John Locke[134]

And if I should undertake to say, there never was a good government in the world, that did not consist of the three simple species of monarchy [president], aristocracy [senate] and democracy [house], I think I might make it good. – Algernon Sidney[135]

---

133   See Jackson Turner Main, The Anti-Federalists Critics of the Constitution 1781-1788 144-46 (W. W. Norton & Company, Inc. 1974); see also 2 The Complete Anti-Federalist 118, 390 (Herbert J. Storing, ed., The University of Chicago Press 1981); 3 The Complete Anti-Federalist 162 (Herbert J. Storing, ed., The University of Chicago Press 1981); 5 The Complete Anti-Federalist 222-23 (Herbert J. Storing, ed., The University of Chicago Press 1981).
134   John Locke, *Essays on the Law of Nature V*, in Political Essays 106 (Mark Goldie ed., Cambridge University Press 1997) (1660) (footnote omitted).
135   Algernon Sidney, Discourses Concerning Government 166 (Thomas G. West ed., Liberty Classics 1990) (1698).

The purpose of establishing different houses of legislation is to introduce the influence of different interests or different principles.
- Thomas Jefferson[136]

The heart of the Senate's power to secure internal liberty springs from the principle of a balance of power. In the case of the United States Senate, it is a balance of power between the people (the House of Representatives) and the Executive (the President). A brief history of England's political system during feudalism, specifically the relationship between Parliament and the king, provides a better understanding of the historical significance of this principle.

During the period when feudalism was dismantled, the English royalty rose to achieve substantial power. The barons, or nobles, were at a disadvantage and joined together to advance their interests against the royalty, similar to a modified state of nature as previously described by Hobbes. The combination of barons proved to be insufficient, and the barons sought assistance from the common people.

> To give the needful authority to any act of general government, the concurrence of both [king and nobles] was essential; and hence parliaments, elsewhere only occasional, were in England habitual. But the natural state of these rival powers was one of conflict; and the weaker side, which was usually that of the barons, soon found that it stood in need of assistance.... As they [barons] had been obliged to combine for the sake of their own defence, so they found

---

136   THE POLITICAL WRITINGS OF THOMAS JEFFERSON 103 (Edward Dumbauld ed., The Bobbs-Merrill Company, Inc. 1955).

themselves under the necessity of calling in the people in aid of their coalition.[137]

A balance of power between the king, the nobility, and the people provided the basis for England's (now the United Kingdom's) House of Lords and House of Commons. The House of Commons is representation for the people while the House of Lords is representation for the nobility. "From its origin, royalty was real; while feudality ultimately grouped itself into two masses, one of which became the high aristocracy; the other, the body of the commons. Who can mistake, in this first travail of the formation of the two societies, in these so different characteristics of their early age, the true origin of the prolonged difference in their institutions and in their destinies?"[138]

The colonists brought the concepts of these institutions and the principle of a balance of power with them to the New World. The Founders recognized that the public was more susceptible to passion and emotion than the nobility, or the wealthy landowners, who were generally understood to be more educated and logical. The passions of the common people could easily be harnessed, but they were often used for ends destructive to the society.

Royalty, on the other hand, wielded great power, which stemmed from their position, lands, and money. The people were in constant fear of royalty's power turning against them at the whim of the king or queen. The nobility secured a vital link between the two. Compared to the common person, the nobility

---

137 JOHN STUART MILL, DISSERTATIONS AND DISCUSSION: POLITICAL, PHILOSOPHICAL, AND HISTORICAL 357 (William V. Spencer reprt. 1864) (citing Essais, p. 419).
138 *Id.* at 359.

had an independent source of wealth, their land, which tied their livelihood to both royalty and the commoners and so allowed them to mediate between the two. "Each [the commons and the nobility] was essential, and equally essential, in achieving the equilibrium in government that brings tranquility and happiness to all; but any of them, released from the counter-pressures of the others, would degenerate – into a tyranny, or into a self-aggrandizing oligarchy, or into an anarchic democracy destructive, in the end, to liberty as well as to property."[139]

The House of Commons, the House of Lords, and the king or queen are forerunners to our House of Representatives, the Senate, and the Executive branch, respectively. The latter institutions have different names, but the basic essence of them is essentially the same. Not only that, but the principle of a balance of power is inherent in the United States' structure as well. Bernard Bailyn noted the dangers to liberty if any of the institutions became too powerful. As we shall later discuss, the effect of changing the source of representation in the Senate in 1913 drastically altered the balance of power in the general government. For now, we will further expand on the principle of a balance of power before returning specifically to the Senate, which acts as a balance between the people and the executive.

A balance of power is similar in nature to Madison's phrase of pitting ambition versus ambition.[140] A balance of power serves to check the other's influence.

As de Vattel stated in *The Law of Nations*, "[b]ut force of arms is not the only expedient by which we may guard against

---

139   BERNARD BAILYN, THE IDEOLOGICAL ORIGINS OF THE AMERICAN REVOLUTION 274 (The Belknap Press of Harvard University Press 1967).
140   THE FEDERALIST NO. 51, at 288 (James Madison) (George Stade ed., Barnes & Noble, Inc. 2006).

a formidable power. There are other means, of a gentler nature, and which are at all times lawful. The most effectual is a confederacy of the less powerful sovereigns [de Vattel is referring to states, but the principle is valid with regards to the Senate], who, by this coalition of strength, become able to hold the balance against that potentate whose power excites their alarms. Let them be firm and faithful in their alliance; and their union will prove the safety of each."[141]

John Trenchard in *Cato's Letters* provides his reflections on the importance of nobility's (or the U.S. Senate's) role in a balance of power. Although he does not specifically mention it, it may likely be assumed that the balance of power is due to underlying interests that are represented, which are due to the method of election.

> Now it seems to me, that the great secret in politicks is, nicely to watch and observe this fluctuation and change of natural power, and to adjust the political to it by prudent precautions and timely remedies, and not put nature to the expence of throws and convulsion to do her own work . . . Suppose, for example, a limited monarchy, which cannot subsist without a nobility: If the nobles have not power enough to balance the great weight of the people, and support the crown and themselves, it is necessary to take some of the richest of the commoners into that order; if they have more power than is consistent with the dependence upon their monarch, it is right to create no more, but to let those already created expire and waste by degrees, till they become a proper balance. . . ."[142]

---

141   Emer de Vattel, The Law of Nations 496 (Béla Kapossy & Richard Whatmore eds., Liberty Fund, Inc. 2008) (1758).
142   2 Thomas Gordon & John Trenchard, Cato's Letters 610 (Ronald Hamowy ed., Liberty Fund, Inc. 1995) (c. 1720).

Justice Story, extracting from Mr. Pitkin's history of an argument between Mr. John Adams and Mr. Roger Sherman, included Mr. Sherman's points on the subject of the role of the Senate and its importance.

> It appears to me that the senate is the most important branch in the government for the aid and support of the executive, for securing the rights of the individual States, the government of the United States, and the liberties of the people....
>
> The senators, being chosen by the legislatures of the States, and depending on them for re-election, will naturally be watchful to prevent any infringement of the rights of the States. And the government of the United States being federal, and instituted by a number of sovereign States for the better security of their rights, and advancement of their interests, they may be considered as so many pillars to support it, and by the exercise of the State governments, peace and good order may be preserved in the places most remote from the seat of the federal government, as well as at the centre.
>
> I believe this will be a better balance to secure the government than three independent negatives would be."[143]

Adam Smith too notes the importance of a balance of power among states, and how it greatly contributes to a state's general

---

[143] 2 Joseph Story, Commentaries on the Constitution of the United States 346-47 n. 2 (Thomas M. Cooley ed., The Lawbook Exchange, LTD. 4th ed. 2008) (1873) (citing 2 Pitkin's Hist. p. 285-91).

peace and tranquility. Although at the time he was not particularly referring to what would become the sovereign states of America, he expressed the same principle. "The most extensive public benevolence which can commonly be exerted with any considerable effect, is that of the statesmen, who project and form alliances among neighboring or not very distant nations, for the preservation either of, what is called, the balance of power, or of the general peace and tranquility of the states within the circle of their negotiations."[144] In a sense, ratification of the Constitution placed each state in a balance of power among the other states. Moreover, the method of election for the Senate provided a means for the states to exert their influence and power to counterbalance that of the people and the executive. Because it was felt that the common people were more susceptible to passions and emotions than the nobles, the Founders were likely counting on the men of the states to counter the passions of the people and the ambition of the executive.

Because Justice Story so eloquently summarized the importance of the Senate, a fairly lengthy passage of his is included below.

> Whatever basis, therefore, is assumed for one branch of the legislature, the antagonist basis should be assumed for the other. If the House is to be proportional to the relative size and wealth and population of the States, the Senate should be fixed up an absolute equality as the representative of **State sovereignty** [emphasis added] . . . The equal vote allowed in the Senate is, in this view, at once a constitutional

---

[144]   ADAM SMITH, THE THEORY OF MORAL SENTIMENTS 244 (Classic House Books 2009) (1759).

recognition of the sovereignty remaining in the States and an instrument for the preservation of it. It guards them against (what they meant to resist, as improper) a consolidation of the States into one simple republic; and, on the other hand, the weight of the other branch counterbalances an undue preponderance of State interests, tending to disunion. . . .

If each branch is substantially framed upon the same plan, the advantages of the division are shadowy and imaginative; the visions and speculations of the brain, and not the waking thoughts of statesmen or patriots. It may be safely asserted that, for all the purposes of liberty, and security, of stable laws and of solid institutions, of personal rights, and of the protection of property, a single branch is quite as good as two, if their composition is the same and their spirits and impulses the same. Each will act as the other does; and each will be led by the same common influence of ambition or intrigue or passion to the same disregard of the public interests, and the same indifference to, and prostration of, private rights.[145]

As noted by Justice Story, an important element of the balance of power was the method of election for the Senators. If the members of both branches of Congress are acting on behalf of the same people, then there is no balancing of interests. The Senate likely will, in the long run, become susceptible to the passion of the people in the same manner as the House, and there

---

[145] 1 Joseph Story, Commentaries on the Constitution of the United States 502 (Thomas M. Cooley ed., The Lawbook Exchange, LTD. 4th ed. 2008) (1873) (citations omitted).

will be no balance between the power of the executive and the power of the people.

In closing, recognize that the representation of the states in the federal legislature was expected to be an important balance of power, especially in light of the omission of the phrase "expressly delegated." Nevertheless, much like the structure of the tax system, this restraint was erased in 1913. To further expand our understanding of the impact of that action, our next subject is the crucial topic of money.

ARTICLE V: ASPECTS OF THE CONSTITUTION CONCERNING MONEY

In an advanced society, with a robust division of labor and extensive indirect exchange, money becomes a substitute for most goods and services available for purchase. Money's value may be divided into two categories: 1) the value due to its direct use, or use-value; or 2) the value based upon what it may be exchanged for, or exchange-value. In the case of paper money, its use-value is likely close to zero and so nearly all of the value of paper money is because of its exchange-value. Regardless of whether money has use- or exchange-value, it is a symbol that represents access to nearly anything.

When viewed from this perspective, money is an important item to have in your command. Therefore, it's accurate to state that the person or group who commands the creation of new quantities of money or its symbols, or who commands the value of those symbols, will be extremely powerful.

As Washington said, "[f]ew men have virtue to withstand the highest bidder."[146] This is testament to Washington's

---

146   THE QUOTABLE FOUNDING FATHERS 382 (Buckner F. Melton, Jr. ed., Fall River Press 2008) (citing George Washington in letter to Robert Howe, August 17, 1779).

understanding of human nature: all people act to maximize their satisfactions. In addition, that statement demonstrates his understanding of the power of money. If there is a price to be negotiated, the only limitation is attaining enough units of money to meet that price. If we have the ability to create new units with seemingly no limitation, then there is obviously no limit on the ability to control people by acting upon their satisfactions.

Let's examine each center of power (the people, the States, and the federal government) concerning the monetary powers granted to them by the Constitution prior to 1913. Then we'll explore how the three centers of power act upon each other, and how they serve as restraints. By acting as restraints, all three centers of power promote the general welfare by securing rights and liberty, yet avoid the consequences of yielding too much power held by any one person or group.

At this point, it's worth noting the rights of the King of England concerning monetary powers as described by Sir Matthew Hale in *An Analysis of the Civil Part of the Law*, circa the early 1600s. The following passage is taken from "Section V: Concerning the king's rights of dominion or power of empire."

Seventhly, in relation to the regulation of trade and commerce.

1. His right of { Coining new monies, Authenticating foreign coin. . . .

3. His right in instituting and regulating the instruments of publiccommerce, with respect to

1913: From General To Specific Welfare

Undue { Weights.
        Measures.

Excessive prices, &c.[147]

The Constitution recognized this very same practice, but granted those powers to the Congress as follows:

To coin Money, regulate the Value thereof, and of foreign Coin, and fix the Standard of Weights and Measures;[148]

To provide for the Punishment of counterfeiting the Securities and current Coin of the United States;[149]

To borrow Money on the credit of the United States;[150]

To establish... uniform Laws on the subject of Bankruptcies throughout the United States;[151]

Beginning with the first clause, which is strikingly similar to the privileges of the king circa the early 1600s, its entirety is best understood by reviewing the language used in the Coinage Act of 1792.

---

147   SIR MATTHEW HALE, *The Analysis of the Law*, in THE HISTORY OF THE COMMON LAW OF ENGLAND: AND AN ANALYSIS OF THE CIVIL PART OF THE LAW 10 (6th ed. reprt. 1820) (1713).
148   U.S. CONST. art I, § 8, cl. 5.
149   U.S. CONST. art I, § 8, cl. 6.
150   U.S. CONST. art I, § 8, cl. 2.
151   U.S. CONST. art I, § 8, cl. 4.

... That there shall be from time to time struck and coined at the said mint, coins of gold, silver, and copper, of the following denominations, values, and descriptions, viz. EAGLES – each to be of the value of ten dollars or units, and to contain two hundred and forty-seven grains and four eights of a grain of pure, or two hundred and seventy grains of standard gold. ... DOLLARS OR UNITS – each to be of the value of a Spanish milled dollar as the same is now current, and to contain three hundred and seventy-one grains and four sixteenth parts of a grain of pure, or four hundred and sixteen grains of standard silver.[152]

The Coinage Act of 1792 and the plain language of the Constitution leave no doubt as to the meaning of the phrase "to coin money."

The excerpt provides that the federal government is granted authority to strike and produce coins; to regulate the value by defining the composition of each of the units or dollars; to regulate the value of foreign coins by defining the United States dollar in relation to the Spanish-milled dollar as well as in relation to a specified weight of silver. The Act later specifies that the officers of the mint will by their best endeavors ensure the coins meet the specified standards and measures.

The next clause in the Constitution grants the authority to punish the counterfeiting of the coin or securities of the United States. To explain the advantages of counterfeiting, let's assume that a dollar is defined as 100 grains of fine silver. A counterfeiter then uses the silver from one coin to make two counterfeit

---

152   Coinage Act of 1792, ch. 16, § 9, 1 Stat. 246 (repealed 1982), *available at* http://memory.loc.gov/cgi-bin/ampage?collId=llsl&fileName=001/llsl001.db&recNum=369.

coins that each contain 50 grains of silver, combined with cheap metals to match the weight and volume of the original coin and struck in a manner to pass as legitimate.

Discounting whatever costs are associated in producing the counterfeited coin, the counterfeiter now has double the purchasing power he previously had. The counterfeiter secures great advantage by this deception, yet the disadvantage done to other people is great as well. As we shall examine in an upcoming section (Part IV, Article III, Section I), a flourishing division of labor and extensive indirect exchange are key ingredients to a society with rapidly expanding wealth (the command of goods to satisfy needs).[153][154] A mechanism that provides for indirect exchange is money, and for such a system to thrive, we have to trust the quality and certification of money. Without this trust, then the indirect exchange may cease altogether and commerce will grind to a halt. For this reason the Constitution granted the authority to the general government to punish counterfeiters of the coin.[155]

---

153   See CARL MENGER, PRINCIPLES OF ECONOMICS 109 (James Dingwall & Bert F. Hoselitz trans., Ludwig von Mises Institute reprt. 2007) (1871) (defining wealth as the entire sum of economic goods at a person's command).

154   JOHN LOCKE, THE SECOND TREATISE ON CIVIL GOVERNMENT 28-30 (Prometheus Books 1986) (1690) (describing how the concept of money is a key ingredient to increasing wealth).

155   For some historical perspective, de Vattel included in his THE LAW OF NATIONS a passage from Boizard's TREATISE ON COIN concerning the practice of counterfeiting coin, or money. "The kings [of France] had recourse to this strange expedient in cases of urgent necessity: but they saw its injustice. – The same author, speaking of the debasement of coin, or the various modes of reducing its intrinsic value, says – 'Those expedients are but rarely resorted to, because they give occasion to the exportation or melting down of the good specie, and to the introduction and circulation of foreign coin, - raise the price of every thing, - impoverish individuals, diminish the revenue, which is paid in specie of inferior value, - and sometimes put a total stop to commerce. This truth has been so well understood in all ages, that those princes, who

The same principle holds true concerning the securities of the United States, which is also a part of the same clause. Keep in mind that the securities refer to the debt instruments that are the result of the enumerated power of borrowing, which is the third clause. The reference to the securities of the United States is wholly different from the bills of credit reference in Article I, Section 10 of the Constitution. Moreover, the distinction between bills of credit and debt securities is important because Federal Reserve Notes, which are used as currency, are effectively bills of credit. Therefore, a brief aside is warranted to explain what a bill of credit is.

James Madison's thoughts on bills of credit are somewhat lengthy, but they are included here for an insight concerning bills of credit, coining of money, and securities created as a result of borrowing. His excerpt is in the context of the prohibition of states emitting bills of credit. However, if it is recognized that the structure of the Constitution only grants authority to the United States through enumerated powers, then the lack of an enumerated power is the same as a prohibition. The principle of enumerated powers becomes even clearer when one considers that emitting bills of credit was listed as an enumerated power in an early draft of the Constitution, but it was subsequently stricken from the final document. Therefore, through such an omission, the Constitution prohibits the emitting bills of credit.[156] Noteworthy in Madison's excerpt is the link between bills of credit and paper money found in the first few lines of the quotation below.

had recourse to one or other of these modes of debasing the coin in difficult times, ceased to practise it the moment the necessity ceased to exist.'" EMER DE VATTEL, THE LAW OF NATIONS 143 n.* (Béla Kapossy & Richard Whatmore eds., Liberty Fund, Inc. 2008) (1758).

156   See 1 EDWIN VIERA, Jr., PIECES OF EIGHT: THE MONETARY POWERS AND DISABILITIES OF THE UNITED STATES CONSTITUTION 141-43 (RR Donnelly & Sons, Inc. 2d rev. spec. ed. 2011).

1913: From General To Specific Welfare

The extension of the prohibition to bills of credit, must give pleasure to every citizen, in proportion to his love of justice, and his knowledge of the true springs of public prosperity. The loss which America has sustained since the peace, from the pestilent effects of paper money on the necessary confidence between man and man; on the necessary confidence in the public councils; on the industry and morals of the people, and on the character of republican government, constitutes an enormous debt against the states, chargeable with this unadvised measure, which must long remain unsatisfied; or rather an accumulation of guilt, which can be expiated no otherwise than by a voluntary sacrifice on the altar of justice, of the power which has been the instrument of it. In addition to these persuasive considerations, it may be observed, that the same reasons which show the necessity of denying to the states the power of regulating coin, prove, with equal force, that they ought not to be at liberty to substitute a paper medium, in the place of coin. Had every state a right to regulate the value of its coin, there might be as many different currencies as states; and thus, the intercourse among them would be impeded; retrospective alterations in its value might be made, and thus the citizens of other states be injured, and animosities be kindled among the states themselves. The subjects of foreign powers might suffer from the same cause, and hence the union be discredited and embroiled by the indiscretion of a single member.[157] No one of these

---

[157] This "evil" expressed by Madison is what essentially occurs today among global states. Each state, state's central bank, or central bank loosely associated with a state, sets the price of their currency by setting the interest rate, which is in effect setting the price of money. As stated earlier, there are no new ideas or principles, only different means and tactics dressed up in new language.

mischiefs is less incident to a power in the states to emit paper money, than to coin gold or silver. The power to make any thing but gold and silver a tender in payment of debts, is withdrawn from the states, on the same principle with that of issuing a paper currency.[158]

Because coining money, borrowing money, and printing paper currency were as contested then as they are today, it is worth including Justice Joseph Story's reflections on bills of credit as well. He quotes the same passage from *The Federalist* as noted just prior so it will not be repeated here. The entire chapter by Justice Story concerning Article I, Section 10 of the Constitution is highly instructive concerning money as defined in the Constitution. Only selected passages are included here, although the entire chapter is recommended for review for the insights it provides into the role of money in the Constitution and a society.

> At last the continental bills became of so little value, that they ceased to circulate; and, in the course of the year 1780, they quietly died in the hands of their possessors. Thus were redeemed the solemn pledges of the national government! Thus was a paper currency, which was declared to be equal to gold and silver, suffered to perish in the hands of persons compelled to take it; and the very enormity of the wrong made the ground of an abandonment of every attempt to redress it! . . . But the history of paper-money, without any adequate funds pledged to

---

[158] THE FEDERALIST NO. 44, at 249 (James Madison) (George Stade ed., Barnes & Noble, Inc. 2006).

redeem it, and resting merely upon the pledge of the public faith, has been in all ages and in all nations the same. It has constantly become more and more depreciated; and in some instances has ceased, from this cause, to have any circulation whatsoever, whether issued by the irresistible edict of a despot, or by the more alluring order of a republican Congress. . . .[159]

It would seem to be obvious that, as the States are expressly prohibited from coining money, the prohibition would be wholly ineffectual if they might create a paper currency and circulate it as money. But, as it might become necessary for the States to borrow money, the prohibition could not be intended to prevent such an exercise of power, on giving to the lender a certificate of the amount borrowed, and a promise to repay it.

What, then, is the true meaning of the phrase "bills of credit," in the Constitution? In its enlarged and perhaps in its literal sense, it may comprehend any instrument by which a State engages to pay money at a future day (and, of course, for which it obtains a present credit), and thus it would include a certificate given for money borrowed. But the language of the Constitution itself, and the mischief to be prevented, which we know from the history of our country, equally limit the interpretation of the terms. The word "emit" is never employed in describing those contracts by which a State binds itself to pay money at a future

---

[159] 2 JOSEPH STORY, COMMENTARIES ON THE CONSTITUTION OF THE UNITED STATES 223-24 (Thomas M. Cooley ed., The Lawbook Exchange, LTD. 4th ed. 2008) (1873) (citations omitted).

day, for services actually received, or for money borrowed for present use. Nor are instruments, executed for such purposes, in common language denominated "bills of credit." To emit bills of credit conveys to the mind the idea of issuing paper intended to circulate through the community, for its ordinary purposes, as money, which paper is redeemable at a future day. This is the sense in which the terms of the Constitution have been generally understood. The phrase (as we have seen) was well known, and generally used to indicate paper currency issued by the States during their colonial dependence. During the war of our revolution, the paper currency issued by Congress was constantly denominated, in the acts of that body, bills of credit; and the like appellation was applied to similar currency issued by the States. The phrase had thus acquired a determinate and appropriate meaning. At the time of the adoption of the Constitution, bills of credit were universally understood to signify a paper medium intended to circulate between individuals, and between government and individuals, for the ordinary purposes of society.[160]

The passages from Justice Story and James Madison provide an excellent summary what constitutes bills of credit,[161] and why

---

160   2 JOSEPH STORY, COMMENTARIES ON THE CONSTITUTION OF THE UNITED STATES 225-26 (Thomas M. Cooley ed., The Lawbook Exchange, LTD. 4th ed. 2008) (1873).

161   Not to be left out of the explanation of bills of credit, Adam Smith provided his reflections on them as well. "The government of Pennsylvania, without amassing any treasure, invented a method of lending, not money indeed, but what is equivalent to money, to its subjects. By advancing to private people, at interest, and upon land security to double the value, paper bills of credit to be redeemed fifteen years after their date, and in the mean time made transferrable from hand to hand like bank notes, and declared by act

the Constitution explicitly prohibited the states from emitting them while implicitly prohibiting the federal government from emitting them. After that brief aside, let us continue with the monetary powers of the federal government.

The last enumerated power to investigate concerning money and the federal government is bankruptcy. Predicting the future is an imperfect art. When it comes to predicting future costs and future sales prices, which ultimately contribute to determining profits and losses, even the most adept businessman can make mistakes. However, for those entrepreneurs willing to risk their capital, there is the potential for large profits. What drives the entrepreneur is providing a product that satisfies a need for a large number of citizens that in turn delivers an appropriate profit. When this situation occurs throughout society, it becomes a means to promoting the general welfare as more and more citizens have their desires fulfilled.

In the case of draconian bankruptcy laws, there would be more risk placed on the entrepreneur. With an increased risk and potentially fewer entrepreneurs, fewer products would be offered, which means many desires would go unfulfilled. While many entrepreneurs would continue, the point is that a lack of bankruptcy law, or worse, tyrannical bankruptcy laws, would stifle risk-taking and invention, which would reduce the general happiness of the citizenry, from the perspective of unmet needs and desires.

---

of assembly to be a legal tender in all payments from one inhabitant of the province to another, it raised a moderate revenue, which went a considerable way towards defraying an annual expence of about 4,500*l.* the whole ordinary expence of that frugal and orderly government. . . . The same expedient was upon different occasions adopted by several other American colonies: but, from want of this moderation, it produced, in the greater part of them, much more disorder than conveniency." ADAM SMITH, THE WEALTH OF NATIONS 1036-37 (Edwin Cannan ed., Bantam Books 2003) (1776).

By granting the authority for bankruptcy with the federal government, although not prohibited to the states, it allows for standardized bankruptcy laws throughout the republic. This enumerated power will ensure that bankruptcy laws are necessary and proper to ensure domestic tranquility and secure the blessings of liberty to promote the general welfare. Granting the power of bankruptcy to the general government does all of this, and brings closure to our discussion of money and the general government.

The next topic concerns the states' powers associated with money—or rather, powers prohibited to the states—as provided in Article I, Section 10 of the Constitution dealing with money and the states. "No State shall enter into any Treaty, Alliance, or Confederation; grant Letters of Marque and Reprisal; **coin Money; emit Bills of Credit; make any Thing but gold and silver Coin a Tender in Payment of Debts** [emphasis added]. . . ."[162]

It is evident that the states are prohibited from coining money and establishing money in the form of paper. The last clause in bold deserves more attention. It prohibits making anything but gold and silver coin a tender, or offer, in payments of debts. It does not mandate that a state must make something legal tender for all its citizens. Instead it only mandates that if a state makes a tender, or offer, to pay a debt, it must be a silver or gold coin. The silver or gold coin would presumably be one that was either coined in a U.S. Mint or declared as currency by the Congress.[163]

---

162   U.S. Const. art. I, § 10, cl. 1.
163   Interestingly, the Constitution does not specify "in payment of *its* Debts." It is reasonable, based on the language of the Constitution, that a State may pass legislation that makes gold or silver coin a legal offer for any debt within its jurisdiction. Obviously, the states today make debt payments in Federal Reserve notes, which are redeemable in lawful money. As we will

1913: From General To Specific Welfare

This is the only section of the Constitution dealing with money and the states, and it brings us to the final topic of the moment, that of money and the people.

Based on the construction of the Constitution, the topic of money and the people is best addressed by reviewing the powers granted to the general government and those prohibited to the states. If the powers were granted to the general government, that power resides there. If it was not granted to the general government and was not prohibited to the states, then it resides with the states. If the power was not granted to the general government and was prohibited to the states, then those remaining powers of money reside with the people.

To determine what powers of money the people retain, let's begin with the general government. It has the power to coin money, regulate its value and that of foreign coin, fix the standard of weights and measures, provide for the punishment of counterfeiting, and the power to borrow. These are the only powers concerning money granted to the general government. The states are prohibited from coining money; emitting any substitute in the form of a bill of credit; and if a state chooses to make anything legal tender for the payments of only debts, it must be of gold or silver coin. Because the United States government was not granted authority to emit bills of credit, notwithstanding subsequent decisions by the United States Supreme Court, and because the states are prohibited from the same, the authority to do so is naturally retained by the people. Additionally, the people have the constitutional authority to create bills of exchange and

---

examine in Part V, Article II, Section II, at present the only redeemable lawful money that is coin is not gold or silver. Therefore, the states offer to pay their debts in a manner that is unequivocally not in compliance with the plain language of the Constitution.

debt securities in whatever form created by mutual and lawful consent. If their state of residence has declared gold and silver coin a legal tender in the payment of *all* debts, then a creditor is obligated to accept legal tender from the debtor unless otherwise specified per mutual agreement. If the exchange resulted in no extension of credit, then either party may use whatever medium of exchange each agreed to use.

Concerning the issue of "legal tender," the federal government is not granted the authority to establish what is a legal offer, or tender. On the other hand, states may only make gold and silver a tender through legislative acts. From a contractual and constitutional standpoint, the people retain the authority to enter into exchange agreements in whatever medium the parties may choose. As mentioned, if a state has declared gold or silver a legal tender for all debts, then the creditor is legally obligated to accept such legal tender, barring any binding agreement for settlement with other means prior to assuming the debt.

To summarize the pre-1913 constitutional monetary situation, the various money powers that were delegated or retained acted as a natural balance of power to ensure that the federal government, the states, and the people did not become dominant over each other. The states were dependent on the federal government to coin money and regulate its value. The federal government was dependent upon the states in that the states could declare gold and silver coin as legal tender, seemingly barring the federal government from declaring bills of credit to be legal tender. Because the states would have to abide by the laws they helped to create, it would be reasonable to expect that states would not create legislation that would be contrary to their interest. Finally, both governments were dependent upon the people. If the people lacked trust in either their state's or the federal government's actions, they were not obligated to use gold or silver coined by the general government, excluding transactions that established debt obligations (although they presumably would need to obtain some coin in order to pay taxes). If the states lacked faith in the general government, they did not have to declare the gold and silver coined by the general government as legal tender. Nonetheless, a state was, and is, constitutionally required to pay its debts in gold or silver coin. This balance of power secured internal liberty as a means to the end of general welfare.

So far, we have reviewed the pre-1913 construction of the money powers delegated to the general government and retained by either the states or the people. We have also examined the powers of direct taxation and representation of the states in the Senate prior to 1913. We have discussed how in each area there was a balance of power to provide for the security of internal liberty. Before beginning an examination of why the law of nature—that all people act to maximize their satisfaction—will result in liberty yielding to tyranny, we will summarize the relationships and interaction between taxation, money, and the representation of the States in the Senate prior to 1913, and how together they were a critical link to securing liberty from internal threats.

ARTICLE VI: SUMMARY

The power to raise revenue (taxation) resided in the House of Representatives, while the Senate could propose amendments to the bills from the House or simply concur. More specifically, direct taxes had to be apportioned based on the representation of the people in the House. The Founders understood the need for plenary powers of raising revenue because of the potential of an external force that could threaten the existence of the republic.

On one hand, Hamilton advocated granting the general government plenary powers of taxation. On the other hand, he recognized the onerous nature of a direct, or poll tax. "As to poll taxes, I, without scruple, confess my disapprobation of them; and though they have prevailed from an early period in those states,[164] which have uniformly been the most tenacious of their rights, I should lament to see them introduced into practice under the national government. But does it follow, because there is a power to lay them, that they will actually be laid?"[165] Because the Constitution required apportionment of direct taxes, the apportionment served as a balance of power. The federal government could levy direct taxes, but the representatives in the House were required to stand before their constituents every two years for re-election. The people would have a redress for their grievances of high taxes in a relatively short period of time.

The states were represented in Congress through the Senate. A state would be required to levy their portion of the direct tax in accordance with their number of representatives in the House. For example, if the total sum of the direct tax was $1M and the State of New York had 20 percent of the representatives in the House, then the State of New York was required to raise $200,000 for their portion. How the state raised that sum was at the discretion of the state. Direct taxes have the potential to raise high revenues, and the states with the most representation were required to pay the most. This method of raising direct

---

164 THE FEDERALIST NO. 36, at 192 n.* (the New England States) (Alexander Hamilton) (George Stade ed., Barnes & Noble, Inc. 2006).
165 Id. at 192.

taxes certainly had the potential to create contention between the general government and the states with the most representation, but that was a compromise between the need for large revenues in the case of an emergency and to maintain liberty from internal threats. The reason for the significant taxes had to be understood and accepted by those required to pay the largest portions. If the reason was not legitimate in their eyes, the people had the power to elect other representatives who would eliminate the tax.

Also, the distribution of the money powers provided another restraint on power. The general government could only coin money and regulate its value. The Constitution did not specify what would be required in payment of taxes, but the logical means would be the coins the general government minted. The states were not obligated to declare gold and silver coin tender for payments of debt within their state, but they had the authority to do so. However, the states were constitutionally obligated to pay their debts in either gold or silver coin. The people did not have to hold the general government's coin except to pay a tax. At the time, the most prevalent taxes were expected to be indirect and could be avoided by choosing not to purchase the goods that required such taxation.

The Constitution provided for the apportionment of taxes, state representation in the Senate, and the money powers to serve as checks against internal threats to liberty. The elimination of one of those areas may not have been sufficient to upset the balance of power, but the elimination of all three in 1913 certainly did. It changed the very end of the Constitution from one of general welfare to specific welfare. Instead of the government being a servant of the people, the people became servants of the government and the entities creating the currency.

Keeping in mind these observations as to why governments are constituted, let's turn our attention back to the law of nature that people act upon to maximize their satisfaction. Analyzing this law and its effects will explain how liberty will always yield while tyranny gains. Once we understand why and how this happens, we may then analyze and comprehend what caused liberty to yield within the context of our Constitution with the ratification of the 16th and 17th Amendments and the enactment of the Federal Reserve Act.

PART IV:

LIBERTY YIELDS WHILE TYRANNY GAINS – THE HOW

Thus it is that liberty is almost every where lost: Her foes are artful, united, and diligent: Her defenders are few, disunited, and unactive. And therefore we have seen great nations, free, happy, and in love with their own conditions, first made slaves by a handful of traitors, and then kept so by a handful of soldiers. - Thomas Gordon in *Cato's Letters*[166]

The body politic, like the human body, begins to die from its birth, and bears in itself the causes of its destruction. - Jean Jacques Rousseau[167]

It can never be too often repeated that the time for fixing every essential right on a legal basis is while our rulers are honest and ourselves united. From the conclusion of this war we shall be going downhill. - Thomas Jefferson[168]

---

[166] 2 THOMAS GORDON & JOHN TRENCHARD, CATO'S LETTERS 706 (Ronald Hamowy ed., Liberty Fund, Inc. 1995) (c. 1720).
[167] THE QUOTABLE FOUNDING FATHERS 135 (Buckner F. Melton, Jr. ed., Fall River Press 2008) (citing JEAN-JACQUES ROUSSEAU, THE SOCIAL CONTRACT, III).
[168] THE POLITICAL WRITINGS OF THOMAS JEFFERSON 38 (Edward Dumbauld ed., The Bobbs-Merrill Company, Inc. 1955).

Although not a perfect analogy, a government can be considered similar to a human body. Just as the human body begins to wither and die upon birth, as soon as a government is established, the same force that created it begins to divert the government from its intended aim and toward its eventual demise. It is difficult to conceive a government founded upon the consent of the governed whose explicit aim was to favor one group over another. Even so, in the long run, such diversion of favors is exactly what will occur.

How is it possible that the very instrument used to secure individual rights—liberty—and the subsequent general welfare can be subverted to undermine each of them? Moreover, how is it possible that such actions can be taken and remain unnoticed by the people who pay to support it? We have already touched on the answer to the first, and it springs from the law of human nature that all act to maximize their satisfactions. To clarify how it is possible, let's provide some historical perspective and reflections on the subject, beginning with a summary given by Frederic Bastiat.

> Self-preservation and self-development are common aspirations among all people. And if everyone enjoyed the unrestricted use of his faculties and the free disposition of the fruits of his labor, social progress would be ceaseless, uninterrupted, and unfailing.

> But there is also another tendency that is common among people. When they can, they wish to live and prosper at the expense of others. This is no rash accusation. Nor does it come from a gloomy and uncharitable spirit. The annals of

history bear witness to the truth of it: the incessant wars, mass migrations, religious persecutions, universal slavery, dishonesty in commerce, and monopolies. This fatal desire has its origin in the very nature of man – in that primitive, universal, and insuppressible instinct that impels him to satisfy his desires with the least possible pain [or maximize his or her satisfaction].

Man can live and satisfy his wants only be ceaseless labor; by the ceaseless application of his faculties to natural resources. This process is the origin of property.

But it is also true that a man may live and satisfy his wants by seizing and consuming the products of the labor of others. This process is the origin of plunder.[169]

Besides our fundamental law of nature, the idea of liberty alone creates a significant hurdle for itself. If a society is based on liberty, it allows for members of the society to advocate for change that could lead to a despotic government. (See Part IV, Article III, Section II). As Milton Friedman noted: "[o]ne feature of a free society is surely the freedom of individuals to advocate and propagandize openly for a radical change in the structure of the society – so long as the advocacy is restricted to persuasion and does not include force or other forms of coercion. It is a mark of the political freedom of a capitalist society [more properly a society that secures rights and liberty] that men can openly advocate and work for socialism."[170]

---

169 FREDERIC BASTIAT, THE LAW 5-6 (Dean Russell trans., Foundation for Economic Freedom 2d ed. 1998) (1850).
170 MILTON FRIEDMAN, CAPITALISM AND FREEDOM 16 (The University of Chicago Press 40th Anniversary ed. 2002).

Bastiat and Friedman are not alone to note the natural tendency for liberty to yield while tyranny reigns. Rousseau too reflects on the topic. "As the particular will acts constantly in opposition to the general will, the government continually exerts itself against the Sovereignty. The greater this exertion becomes, the more the constitution changes; and, as there is in this case no other corporate will to create an equilibrium by resisting the will of the prince, sooner or later the prince must inevitably suppress the Sovereign and break the social treaty. This is the unavoidable and inherent defect which, from the very birth of the body politic, tends ceaselessly to destroy it, as age and death end by destroying the human body."[171]

Lord Kames, circa 1778, echoes the theme of Part IV. (In the following passage, the original text used an "f" in place of an "s." For ease of reading, we have replaced the "f" with an "s" placed in brackets as so: from progrefs to progre[s]s.)

> In the progre[s]s from maturity to a declining [s]tate, a nation differs widely from an individual. Old age puts an end to the latter; there are many cau[s]es that weaken the former; but old age is none of them, if it be not in a metaphorical [s]ense. Riches, [s]elfi[s]hne[s]s, and luxury, are the di[s]ea[s]es that weaken pro[s]perous nations: the[s]e di[s]ea[s]es, following each other in a train, corrupt the heart, dethrone the moral [s]ense, and make an anarchy in the [s]oul: men [s]tick at no expence to purcha[s]e plea[s]ure; and they [s]tick at no vice to [s]upply that expence.[172]

---

171   JEAN-JACQUES ROUSSEAU, THE SOCIAL CONTRACT 69 (G.D. H. Cole trans., BN Publishing 2007) (1762).
172   4 LORD HENRY HOME KAMES, SKETCHES OF THE HISTORY OF MAN 131-32 (A. Strahan & T. Cadell reprt. 1783).

1913: From General To Specific Welfare

Concerning the natural law, the following two perspectives are from the debates surrounding ratification of the Constitution. The first is from a Federalist, Mr. John Jay, and the second is from an Anti-Federalist. John Jay expressed the same sentiments articulated up to this point: the natural tendency is for people to seek a maximization of their own satisfactions. However, the process often changes the government from one whose end is general welfare to one of specific welfare; in other words, the tendency is for tyranny to gain ground. As Jay stated after the Revolution, "the spirit of private gain expelled the spirit of public good, and men became more intent on the means of enriching and aggrandizing themselves than of enriching and aggrandizing their country."[173]

The Impartial Examiner, the pen name for an anonymous Anti-Federalist, brilliantly summarized the principle of liberty yielding to tyranny. Because of its eloquence, a lengthy passage is included here.

> It requires no great degree of knowledge in history to learn what dangerous consequences generally result from large and extensive powers. Every man has a natural propensity to power; and when one degree of it is obtained, *that* seldom fails to excite a thirst for more: - an higher point being gained, still the soul is impelled to a farther pursuit. Thus step by step, in regular progression, she proceeds onward, until the lust of domination becomes the ruling passion, and absorbs all other desires. When any man puts himself under the influence of such a passion, it is natural for

---

173   1 The Complete Anti-Federalist 99 n.17 (Herbert J. Storing, ed., The University of Chicago Press 1981) (citing Ford, Pamphlets 70-71).

him to seek after every opportunity, and to employ every means within reach, for obtaining his purpose. . . . Hence, should it not be a *maxim,* never to be forgotten – that a free people ought to intrust no set of men with powers, that may be abused without controul, or afford opportunities to designing men to carry dangerous measures into execution, without being responsible for their conduct? . . .

It is next to impossible to enslave a people immediately after a firm struggle against oppression, while the sense of past injury is recent and strong. But after some time this impression naturally wears off; - the ardent glow of freedom gradually evaporates; - the charms of popular equality, which arose from the *republican plan,* insensibly decline; - the pleasures, the advantages derived from the new kind of government grow stale through use. Such declension in all these vigorous springs of action necessarily produces a supineness. The altar of liberty is no longer watched with such attentive assiduity; - a new train of passions succeeds to the empire of the mind; - different objects of desire take place: - and, if the nation happens to enjoy a series of prosperity, [then] voluptuousness, excessive fondness for riches, and luxury gain admission and establish themselves – these produce venality and corruption of every kind, which open a fatal avenue to bribery. Hence it follows, that in the midst of this general contageon a few men – or one – more powerful than all others, industriously endeavor to obtain all authority; and by means of great wealth – or embezzling the public money, - perhaps totally subvert the government, and erect a system of aristocratical or monarchic tyranny in its room. What ready means for this *work of evil* are numerous standing armies, and the disposition of the great revenue of the United States! Money can purchase soldiers; - soldiers can produce money; and both together can do any thing."[174]

The Impartial Examiner indeed provided quite an answer to the question of the effects of natural law. The other question posed was how such a person or small group of people would be able to accomplish such a transformation of the purpose of government without interference by the people.

John Lord Somers provides his thoughts to answer this question in his book examining the power and duty of grand juries in England. Once again, the "f"'s have been substituted with an "[s]."

"Few men at fir[s]t [s]ee the danger of little changes in fundamentals; and tho[s]e who de[s]ign them, u[s]ually act with [s]o much craft, as be[s]ides the giving [s]pecious rea[s]ons, they take great care that the true rea[s]on [s]hall not appear. Every de[s]ign therefore of changing the con[s]titution ought to be mo[s]t warily ob[s]erved, and timely oppo[s]ed. Nor is it only in intere[s]t of the people, that [s]uch fundamentals [s]hould be duly guarded, for who[s]e benefit they were at fir[s]t [s]o carefully laid, and whom the judges are [s]worn to [s]erve; but of the king too, for who[s]e [s]ake tho[s]e pretend to act, who would [s]ubvert them."[175]

---
174   5 THE COMPLETE ANTI-FEDERALIST 187-88 (Herbert J. Storing, ed., The University of Chicago Press 1981) (footnote omitted).
175   JOHN LORD SOMERS, THE SECURITY OF ENGLI[S]HMEN'S LIVES: OR THE TRUST, POWER AND DUTY OF GRAND JURIES OF ENGLAND 78 (Kessinger Publishing reprt. n.d.) (1681).

Even though he recorded his thoughts circa 1681, his reflections on human nature are still just as valid today as they were then.[176] Moreover, he provides a sound explanation as to how such a process may occur without many citizens sounding an alarm. Most of Part IV expands on the general means that men and women employ to have the power of government secure their own privileges, despite what efforts may be used to prevent exactly that.

We have already examined the various ways to balance the powers of government. A successful republican government[177]—success being defined as providing general welfare for all—requires an understanding of law, economics, philosophy, history, and other disciplines. Not only do the governors require knowledge and wisdom of these disciplines to achieve success, but also the governed require the same, which is not the case for a non-republican type of government.

---

176   de Vattel expressed similar thoughts in the 1700s. "Sudden revolutions strike the imaginations of men: they are detailed in history; their secret springs are developed. But we overlook the changes that insensibly happen by a long train of steps that are but slightly marked. It would be rendering nations an important service, to sh[o]w from history, how many states have thus entirely changes their nature, and lost their original constitution. This would awaken the attention of man-kind: - impressed thenceforward with this excellent maxim (no less essential in politics than in morals), *prinipiis obsta** - they would no longer shut their eyes against innovations, which, though inconsiderable in themselves, may serve as steps to mount to higher and more pernicious enterprises." EMER DE VATTEL, THE LAW OF NATIONS 93 (Béla Kapossy & Richard Whatmore eds., Liberty Fund, Inc. 2008) (1758) (resist the first advances).

177   Republic and democracy are similar in their roots but vastly different in structure. Republic has roots of res and publica meaning a public thing while democracy has roots of demos and kratos meaning the power of the people. Both are founded on the principle of the people being the sovereign makers of law. However, in a democracy the people directly create law while in a republic their representatives do.

Two examples of non-republican governments are those that have used either religion or the rule of one. These two forms of government, theocracy and monarchy, require their subjects to possess little, if any, knowledge or wisdom of the various disciplines mentioned. On the contrary, they only require submission and obedience. In the case of a theocracy, the laws are immutable edicts from God. The same principle is true of a monarchy except the laws are from the king (who may claim authority from God to rule). In a republic, representatives from the people comprise the government. As the laws are subject to change based on the demands of the people with their representatives acting as agents, both the people and their agents require knowledge, experience, and wisdom if these changes are to benefit the general welfare. In other words, a republic requires a comprehension and application of reason, which is the subject of the following article.

ARTICLE I: REASON

If there be any among us who would wish to dissolve this Union or to change its republican form, let them stand undisturbed as monuments of the safety with which error of opinion may be tolerated, where reason is left free to combat it. - Thomas Jefferson[178]

The most important faculty required of the governed and the governors in a republican government is the ability to reason. The ability to reason is critical because it is the cornerstone of determining cause and effect. If the end of government is the general welfare, then it is incumbent on both parties to discern

---

178 THE POLITICAL WRITINGS OF THOMAS JEFFERSON 42-43 (Edward Dumbauld ed., The Bobbs-Merrill Company, Inc. 1955).

what actions will achieve the end and what actions will run contrary to the end. "A traveler whose end is the most beautiful path will look for other considerations and will test suggestions occurring to him on another principle than if he wishes to discover the way to a given city. *The problem fixes the end of thought* and *the end controls the process of thinking*."[179]

If we are going to apply reason in an endeavor to achieve an end, we must possess the general and specific knowledge relevant to that particular discipline. "The distinction between information and wisdom [or reason as used in our examination] is old, and yet requires constantly to be redrawn. Information is knowledge which is merely acquired and stored up; wisdom is knowledge operating in the direction of powers to the better living of life [achieving a particular end]."[180] Not only that, but we must be able to trace out all of the intended and unintended consequences.[181] Aristotle provides insight on the faculty of reason and its relationship to knowledge and wisdom.

> The wise man, then, must not only know what follows from the principles of knowledge, but also know the truth about those principles. Wisdom, therefore, will be the union of [intuitive] reason with [demonstrative] scientific knowledge, or scientific knowledge of the noblest objects with its crowning perfection, so to speak, added to it. . . .
>
> Prudence, on the other hand, deals with human affairs, and with matters that admit of deliberation: for the prudent

---

179   JOHN DEWEY, HOW WE THINK 11 (Barnes & Noble Publishing, Inc. 2005) (1910).
180   Id. at 43.
181   M. FREDERIC BASTIAT, ESSAYS ON POLITICAL ECONOMY 49-52 (G. P. Putnams & Sons 3rd ed. reprt. 1874).

man's special function, as we conceive it, is to deliberate well; but no one deliberates about what is invariable, or about matters in which there is not some end, in the sense of some realizable good. But a man is said to deliberate well (without any qualifying epithet) when he is able, by a process of reasoning or calculation, to arrive at what is best for man in matters of practice.

Prudence, moreover, does not deal in general propositions only, but implies knowledge of particular facts also; for it issues in action, and the field of action is the field of particulars.

This is the reason why some men that lack [scientific] knowledge are more efficient in practice than others that have it, especially men of wide experience; for if you know that light meat is digestible and wholesome, but do not know what meats are light, you will not be able to cure people so well as a man who only knows that chicken is light and wholesome.[182]

Reason then, in a system of governance where law is subject to change, is a requisite for the governed as well as the governors. It is not sufficient to know that the end is general welfare. It is not sufficient to know that the general means to that end are securing rights and liberty, establishing justice, and domestic tranquility. Both the governors and the governed must understand the relationship between the end and the means; and for this, they must understand:

---

182   ARISTOTLE, NICOMACHEAN ETHICS 122-24 (F.H. Peters, M.A. trans., Barnes & Noble, Inc. 2004) (350 B.C.E).

- the law of human nature;
- the concept of a balance of power, not only in the short term but also in the long term;
- the power of passion over reason; and
- the consequences of setting a precedent contrary to a principle; and to do this they must possess general and particular knowledge of the disciplines mentioned.

Sadly, that may be too much to expect of any people. A cynical view is that it is better to govern through fear, superstition, and with an iron fist. Ben Franklin understood the enormous responsibilities and expectations of the citizens of the United States. "In these sentiments, sir, I agree to this Constitution, with all its faults, if they are such; because I think a General Government necessary for us, and there is no form of government, but what may be a blessing to the people if well administered; and believe further, that this is likely to be well administered for a course of years, and can only end in despotism, as other forms have done before it, when the people shall become so corrupted as to need despotic government, being incapable of any other."[183]

When Franklin emerged from the Constitutional Convention, he was asked, "Well, doctor, what have we got, a republic or a monarchy?" He replied, "A republic, if you can keep it."[184] Franklin certainly understood the need for an educated citizenry and understood human nature. If the people failed to apply reason when deliberating whether the means will secure the rights and liberty of all, then expecting general welfare would be unwarranted.

---

183   THE QUOTABLE FOUNDING FATHERS 47 (Buckner F. Melton, Jr. ed., Fall River Press 2008) (citing Ben Franklin, Speech at the Constitutional Convention, September 17, 1787).
184   *Id.* at 48 (citing Franklin's answer to Mrs. Powell's question, which was recorded by Joseph McHenry).

1913: From General To Specific Welfare

When Alexis de Tocqueville wrote *Democracy in America* in 1835, he made the generalization that Americans of that era certainly did use their faculty of reason, which was and is necessary with a government such as that described in the Constitution. "If I go still further and seek among these diverse features the principal one that can sum up almost all the others, I discover that in most of the operations of the mind, each American calls only on the individual effort of his reason."[185] Should we ask if today's citizens apply reason, or conversely, passion, when deliberating on the means to be used to achieve the end? Perhaps even more importantly, is the question whether they believe the end of government is, or should be, either general or specific welfare?

Reason is meaningless if there is no end, and people are constantly applying reason in order to achieve some outcome in the future. "The only immediate utility of all sciences, is to teach us, how to control and regulate future events by their causes."[186] Because people's ability to reason involves using means that will achieve an end, we should always keep the end in sight when deliberating on the appropriate means. The Preamble describes the end and it lists the general means; the rest of the Constitution is the specific means. The people and their representatives must possess the requisite knowledge, and more importantly, the wisdom concerning numerous topics if they intend to direct the government in a manner that will achieve the end they desire.

The faculty of reason was and is a cornerstone for ensuring the general welfare for ourselves and our posterity. The loss of

---

185 ALEXIS DE TOCQUEVILLE, DEMOCRACY IN AMERICA 403 (Harvey C. Mansfield & Delba Winthrop eds. & trans., The University of Chicago Press, LTD. 2002) (1835).
186 DAVID HUME, AN ENQUIRY CONCERNING HUMAN UNDERSTANDING 72 (Prometheus Books, 1988) (1748).

reason in the deliberation of legislation is sure to hasten the loss of security from internal threats to liberty. As we shall examine, enterprising individuals or groups seeking specific welfare through the instrument of government will do so by getting the people to avoid reason and instead rely on passion and emotion.

Before exploring passion, we must make a distinction between it and reason. An individual acts on his or her passions, as passions drive needs and desires. A passion can be viewed as either advantageous or disadvantageous depending on whether such passion is fulfilled in moderation or to excess. When a passion has run its course to an extreme, it becomes a vice. Considering that virtue is the moderation of passions in such a manner that the passions are advantageous to a society, we then know that reason has reined in the passionate.

If the Constitution is sound it will provide the means to achieve its end, but only if both governors and the governed are well versed in the faculty of reason. As both are human, both are susceptible to letting passions override reason. The governors may at times need to apply reason and deny the pleas of the people, while at other times the people must apply reason and refuse to re-elect the governors. If either party loses reason, the general welfare will be diverted to specific welfare. If both parties lose reason, then the entire government will be lost. It is on that note that we now turn to an investigation of human nature and its passions so that we may fully comprehend Jefferson's intention when he wrote, "[t]he natural progress of things is for liberty to yield and government to gain ground."[187]

---

[187] THE POLITICAL WRITINGS OF THOMAS JEFFERSON 138 (Edward Dumbauld ed., The Bobbs-Merrill Company, Inc. 1955) (citing Jefferson's letter to Edward Carrington, Paris, May 27, 1788).

ARTICLE II: PASSION

And were every pa[ss]ion equally entitled to gratification, man would be utterly unqualified for [s]ociety: he would be a [s]hip without a rudder, obedient to every wind, and moving at random without any ultimate de[s]tination. The faculty of rea[s]on would make no oppo[s]ition; for were there no [s]en[s]e of wrong, it would be rea]s]onable to gratify every de[s]ire that harms not ourselves. . . . Lord Henry Home Kames[188]

At this point, a continued discussion of passion may appear to be unrelated and irrelevant to our thesis: that three actions accomplished in 1913 altered the end of government from general to specific welfare. From the point of view of "why" it happened, that may be true. However, from the point of view of "how," the importance of passions is absolutely material. It is humanity's susceptibility to passion that plays a pivotal role in the transition from general to specific welfare, and this susceptibility was key in the ratification of the 16th and 17th Amendments and the enactment of the Federal Reserve Act. To understand how this happened, we must discuss what tactics were available and likely used to bring about this transformation.

A primary distinction between reason and passion is that passion lacks calculation. The raw emotion driving passion focuses on immediate fulfillment, and future results are of little, if any, consequence. In contrast, reason uses the scientific method (induction and deduction as explained earlier) to determine laws or rules that will allow for the prediction of future results.

Because the application of the Constitution is dependent

---

[188]   4 Lord Henry Home Kames, Sketches of the History of Man 53 (A. Strahan & T. Cadell reprt. 1783).

upon reason (enumerated powers as the specific means circumscribed by the general means in the Preamble to achieve the end of a general maximization of satisfaction), an appeal to passions is ultimately a way to circumvent the Constitution's balance of power. To understand this, it is important to investigate our passions and their effects in greater detail. David Hume's *Treatise on Human Nature* is the source into our initial investigation of passion. Let's continue with an examination of the influence of relations, which provides a powerful force to the passions.

Hume noted there are three types of relations that determine the force of an idea or passion: resemblance, contiguity, and cause and effect. We will focus on the relation of cause and effect.

Cause and effect is an important relation due to the expectations created by the impression or idea of an object whose presence will bring about some result. Take the famous example of Pavlov's dogs and the ringing of a bell being associated with food.[189] The dogs' expectations had been shaped by the routine of a ringing bell followed by the offer of food. With enough repetitions, the dogs began to salivate upon the ringing of the bell even without observing the food. The sound of a ringing bell became related to a passion through the cause and effect relationship.

The association of a bolt of lightning with a clap of thunder is another example of a powerful relationship showing cause and effect between two events. Lightning and thunder are often associated with storm clouds so that when we see dark clouds we presume they are storm clouds, and so we feel anxiety as we anticipate the crash of lightning and thunder.

Understanding the power of cause and effect is important

---

[189]   *See Classical conditioning*, WIKIPEDIA, https://en.wikipedia.org/wiki/Classical_conditioning (last visited Nov. 25, 2016).

because of the potential advantages for those who have special knowledge of these relationships over those who do not. The advantages due to this special knowledge are not new. An understanding of passions as a special knowledge dates back at least to Plato.[190] We will examine the topic of special knowledge in Part IV, Article V, which deals with people maximizing satisfactions through the use of such knowledge. For now, let us continue with why relations are important to the subject of this book.

The 16th Amendment weakened the taxation relationship between the citizens and their representative, with regards to what was taken and who was most responsible for taking it. The 17th Amendment at the time of ratification seemingly appealed to strengthen the relationship between the people and their Senator. However, such a relation was not a significant concern when choosing the method of electing Senators. In fact, the method of election was intended to diminish the relationship between the Senate and the people while it strengthened the relationship between the states and their Senator. Lastly, the Federal Reserve Act ostensibly intended to prevent economic crises, or to minimize the passion of pain perceived by the people when such crises occurred. As the monetary system evolved to its present condition, the ability of the central government to secure purchasing power, by creating more currency through complex and obscure methods, has obfuscated the relation between how much purchasing power is being taken from the people and who is taking it.

As originally constructed, the relations described above concerning the three events of 1913 were intended to be strong

---

190   See PLATO, THE REPUBLIC 155-56 (Betty Radice ed., Desmond Lee trans., Penguin Books 2d rev. ed. reprt. 1987) (c. 380 B.C.E.) (noting how reason provides resistance to desires from passions).

and readily apparent. Instead, these three events obscured the relation between them. Because relations have such an important impact on the power of passions, which in turn has such an important influence on human action, that explains why our examination of relations and passions is fundamental in understanding our premise. Let's leave behind examining relations and move to another aspect of passions: sympathy.

When examining how each person acts to maximize his satisfaction, we discovered that people either seek to attain pleasure or minimize pain. The notion of sympathy primarily concerns one person attempting to alleviate the pain of another. Because we all act to maximize our satisfactions, it is only logical that a person acting out of sympathy is trying to relieve another's pain in order to maximize his own pleasure. Therefore, sympathy has a double relation between pain and pleasure, and as such, it is a significantly powerful passion. As Adam Smith noted, "[a]s the person who is principally interested in any event is pleased with our sympathy, and hurt by the want of it, so we, too, seem to be pleased when we are able to sympathize with him, and to be hurt when we are unable to do so. We run not only to congratulate the successful, but to condole with the afflicted; and the pleasure which we find in the conversation of one whom in all the passions of his heart we can entirely sympathize with, seems to do more than compensate the painfulness of that sorrow with which the view of his situation affects us."[191]

Generally speaking, people are more inclined to have sympathy for someone who suffers through no fault of his own, at least in the mind of the observer. The infirmities that come

---

191   ADAM SMITH, THE THEORY OF MORAL SENTIMENTS 10 (Classic House Books 2009) (1759).

with old age affect the passions much more than afflictions that befall one through self-harm such as drug abuse. Additionally, some may tend to have more sympathy for the indiscretions of the young because of their lack of knowledge and experience. Because sympathy is such a powerful passion, invoking the plea to help the old, young, or mentally or physically handicapped is a persuasive tool to use in order to convince others to act according to your desires.

We have considered reason and passion as well as the relationship between the two. The slight detour was necessary because our Constitution's longevity was based on a reliance on reason to balance the sway of our passions. Even though the use of reason is a requirement to ensure the general welfare, the fundamental law of nature concerning the maximization of satisfaction makes it quite likely that some people will seek to maximize their own satisfaction by securing special welfare for themselves versus general welfare for all. Madison certainly understood this principle: "[i]f men were angels, no government would be necessary. If angels were to govern men, neither external nor internal controls on government would be necessary. In framing a government which is to be administered by men over men, the great difficulty lies in this: you must first enable the government to control the governed; and in the next place oblige it to control itself."[192] That is another way of asking: how does one create an entity powerful enough to repel against all foreign attacks, yet weak enough to ensure it does not become what it was intended to prevent?

On that note, we will proceed to why the trend towards

---

192   THE FEDERALIST NO. 51, at 288 (James Madison) (George Stade ed., Barnes & Noble, Inc. 2006).

specific welfare (or special interests in today's language) was inevitable. By that same token, it is also inevitable that eventually there will be a return to a government based on general welfare, even though the same tendency toward specific welfare will begin once again. In our quest to understand the causes of this never-ending swinging pendulum, our next topic is the economics of liberty, an important requirement for the production of goods and services. But as we will see, liberty becomes complicit in its own demise.

ARTICLE III: VALUE OF LIBERTY

[W]hereas I dare affirm that all that was ever desirable, or worthy of praise and imitation in Rome, did proceed from its liberty, grow up and perish with it. . . . – Algernon Sidney[193]

But if all this be false, absurd, bestial, and abominable, the principles that necessarily lead us to such conclusions are so also; which is enough to sh[o]w, that the strength, virtue, glory, wealth, power, and happiness of Rome proceeding from liberty, did rise, grow, and perish with it. – Algernon Sidney[194]

Whilst liberty continued, it was the nurse of virtue; and all the losses suffered in foreign or civil wars, were easily recovered: but when liberty was lost, valour and virtue was torn up by the roots, and the Roman power proceeding from it, perished. – Algernon Sidney[195]

---

193   ALGERNON SIDNEY, DISCOURSES CONCERNING GOVERNMENT 144 (Thomas G. West ed., Liberty Classics 1990) (1698).
194   *Id.* at 149.
195   *Id.* at 161.

Section I: Economics

Words and their syntax are crucial because they serve as the means through which we communicate our perceptions to others.[196] However, words—especially when presenting complex ideas—can have their meanings distorted, whether intentionally or unintentionally. For us to avoid this confusion, we will first review and/or define several key terms prior to discussing the economics of liberty. Although some of these terms and their concepts have already been examined, we will expand on them for a better understanding of the value of liberty. By the time we have completed our brief review, the pivotal role of liberty in and on our economy will be better understood.

Beginning with a discussion of the term "good," it is not necessary that a good actually fulfill a human need. All that is necessary is that humans believe that there exists a causal relation between a good and the fulfillment of a desire (making need and desire synonyms for our purposes). Nonetheless, "[t]hings that can be placed in a causal connection with the satisfaction of human needs we term *useful things*. If, however, we both recognize this causal connection, and have the power actually to direct the useful things to the satisfaction of our needs, we call them *goods*."[197] There are four requisites for a thing to become a good:

---

[196] "That this is so, and that men in framing different complex ideas, and giving them names, have been much governed by the end of speech in general (which is a very short and expedite way of conveying their thoughts one to another), is evident in the names which in several arts have been found out and applied to several complex ideas of modified actions belonging to their several trades. . . ." John Locke, An Essay Concerning Human Understanding Book I-II 245 (Adamant Media Corporation reprt. 2006) (c. 1690).

[197] Carl Menger, Principles of Economics 52 (James Dingwall & Bert F. Hoselitz trans., Ludwig von Mises Institute reprt. 2007) (1871).

1. A human need (or desire).
2. Such properties that render the thing capable of being brought into a causal connection with the satisfaction of this need.
3. Human knowledge of this causal connection.
4. Command of the thing sufficient to direct it to the satisfaction of the need.[198]

If any one of these requisites is no longer met, then the good loses its significance and reverts back to a "thing."

Let's now discuss the distinction between an economic good and a non-economic good. Economic goods are those whose ". . . requirements [demand for] are larger than the available quantity."[199] Because of this shortage or scarcity, people seek to economize those goods through the following four methods (paraphrasing Menger):

1. Have access to every unit of a good when needed.
2. Conserve its useful properties.
3. Satisfy their more important desires that an economic good can fulfill while forgoing lesser desires.
4. Obtain the greatest result with a given quantity.[200]

On the other hand, non-economic goods are those whose demand is less than the quantity available. Paraphrasing Menger, take the following as an example. Imagine a village that requires 100 gallons of water per day, and a natural spring that provides a minimum of 1,000 gallons per day. Water in this case is a

---

198	Id. at 52.
199	Id. at 94.
200	Id. at 95.

non-economic good because its supply exceeds the demand and so its price is essentially not calculable. It is certainly a good as it satisfies the requirements necessary to be a good (try living without water), but it is not an economic good.[201][202]

The next term to define is "wealth." Simply put, wealth is the entire sum of all economic goods at an individual's command.[203]

The last term to define is "value," and its definition draws upon Aristotle's observation concerning the relationship between wisdom, and cause and effect, or knowing what it is that will fulfill a desire. Value then, is ". . . the importance that individual goods or quantities of goods attain for us because we are conscious of being dependent on command of them for the satisfaction of our needs."[204] Now that goods (both economic and non-economic), wealth, and value have been defined, it is time to turn our attention to the economics of liberty, a topic that encompasses consumption goods and higher-order goods.

Goods of the lowest order are those that directly satisfy the basic needs of people—such as bread for example—and we call such a good a "consumption" good. If not for consumption goods, none of the higher-order goods would exist.

As people continuously seek to maximize their satisfactions, one method to achieve this is by employing the savings from our current production in a manner that will serve to facilitate future production, and we call these savings "capital."[205]

---

201   *Id.* at 98.
202   It is possible, and often occurs, that items that were once non-economic goods become economic goods, and vice versa. The cause of a change in category is due to either an increase in requirements or a decrease in the supply.
203   *Id.* at 109.
204   *Id.* at 115.
205   It should be noted that consumption and capital are two distinct

Capital is defined as a higher-order good, and there is another particular aspect of higher-order goods that we must note: that complementary goods exist within the same order. Menger provides an excellent example of the significance of complementary goods.

> Let us assume, for instance, that an economizing individual possesses no bread directly, but has at his command all the goods of second order necessary to produce it. There can be no doubt that he will nevertheless have the power to satisfy his need for bread. Suppose, however, that the same person has command of the flour, salt, yeast, labor services, and even all the tools and appliances necessary for the production of bread, but lacks both fuel and water. In this second case, it is clear that he no longer has the power to utilize the goods of second order in his possession for the satisfaction of his needs, since bread cannot be made without fuel and water, even if all the other necessary goods are at hand. Hence the goods of second order will, in this case, immediately lose their goods-character with respect to the need for bread, since one of the four prerequisites for the existence of their goods-character (in this case the fourth prerequisite) is lacking.[206]

Among all the higher-order goods, a missing complementary good obviates the need for the other similar complementary

---

concepts. Besides turning savings into capital, one may also use savings for consumption. Moreover, savings may at one point be transformed into capital while the capital may still later be turned into a consumption good. When one begins to consume capital, however, one is no longer producing wealth but is instead consuming it.
206   *Id.* at 59.

goods of that order. Following the progression from a consumption good to the highest-order good related to it, each order is dependent for its "goods" quality on the order below it. As an example, if a person loses command of third-order goods, then the fourth-order goods lose their character as goods. This point makes the three quotations from Algernon Sidney at the beginning of this section especially relevant, for in 1698 Sidney was essentially stating the same thing.

When we look at liberty in ancient Rome, we see that liberty was a requisite, a lower-order good, while the civilization of Rome was a higher-order good used to secure that selfsame liberty. When liberty was destroyed, the value of Rome as a state and civilization was lost as well. With this in mind, it is interesting to observe how the same ideas and consequences continue to be replayed throughout history.

Not surprisingly, Sidney is not the only person to mention the importance of liberty. The following passage from *Cato's Letters* also explains how liberty was a complementary economic good during Roman times.

> This prodigious progress of the Romans in learning had no other cause than the freedom and equality of their government. The spirit of the people, like that of their state, breathed nothing but liberty, which no power sought to control, or could control. The improvement of knowledge, by bringing no terror to the magistrates, brought no danger to the people. Nothing is too hard for liberty; that liberty which made the Greeks and Romans masters of the world, made them masters of all the learning in it: And, when their liberties perished, so did their learning.[207]

---

[207] 2 THOMAS GORDON & JOHN TRENCHARD, CATO'S LETTERS 517 (Ronald Hamowy ed., Liberty Fund, Inc. 1995) (c. 1720).

Essentially, liberty was necessary for learning. When liberty was lacking, then so too was learning.

In a more general example, say people abruptly shunned beer (not likely, but suitable for demonstration purposes). If that were the case, then the current stock of beer would lose its goods-character. Additionally, all higher-order goods used specifically in the production of beer would also lose their goods-character. However, available capital could be transformed to fulfill some other human need and would still retain its goods-character. However, the goods-character for the capital that could not be transformed would be lost. This loss of capital will obviously result in a loss of value and a loss of wealth. The transformation of a "good" back to a "thing" can result not only from a change in desires but also because of legislation restricting those goods. (Although prohibition of alcohol did not result in a loss of goods-character for beer.) The passage of legislation restricting liberty leads to a specific investigation of the economics of liberty, or more specifically, the economic goods-character of liberty.

Just as in the previous example, a loss of liberty will ensure that all corresponding economic goods that required liberty to attain their character will suddenly return to a thing whose value will drop to zero. Those former economic goods are no longer produced because they will no longer have a calculable price. Therefore, the price of the remaining economic goods will likely begin to rise because the same amount of money is chasing a smaller pool of remaining economic goods. But if the supply of money also increases, imagine how quickly the price of remaining economic goods will rise. To complicate the issue further, imagine if a loss of liberty was due to some entity arbitrarily adding to the money supply. Not only will prices rise due to more money chasing fewer goods, but this will cause people to lose their willingness to hold money which will in turn increase the price of goods even more quickly. Now we begin to understand how valuable and critical liberty is to a people, and how important the link is between liberty and money.

Liberty is perhaps the most important complementary good. Nonetheless, we also established that, given enough time, liberty will yield to tyranny. Unfortunately, as we will examine in the next section, it is quite possible that liberty may be lost in a manner where few are able to recognize that it is disappearing and for what reason. In that case, it may take a long time before the cause is determined. In an attempt to prevent such a circumstance, we will examine how liberty creates its own demise by creating an abundance of wealth.

Section II: Liberty As Its Own Enemy

When liberty has been laid as a foundation of a society, such conditions generally result in a society that enjoys abundant wealth, but this does not address the distribution of such wealth. When the discussion strays towards some entity with the power of law that can determine how wealth should be distributed, we are no longer considering a society based on liberty, even though one may still argue that all people remain equal. However, then again, "[m]en are all equal in republican government; they are equal in despotic government; in the former, it is because they are everything; in the latter, it is because they are nothing."[208] Needless to say, we are considering here equality in a republican

---
[208] Montesquieu, The Spirit of the Laws 75 (Anne M. Cohler, Basia Carolyn Miller, & Harold Samuel Stone eds. & trans., Cambridge University Press 14th prtg. 2009) (1748).

government, where all have their rights (liberty to do or not do) and liberty equally secured, but the results of human action will obviously not be equal. We are not considering a government that attempts to achieve equal results by stepping on the people's rights in order to distribute the fruits of their activities equally.

When each person has the liberty to pursue those endeavors for which he or she is best suited, or for those that he or she finds most enjoyable, it is inevitable that these conditions will lead to a flourishing division of labor and a subsequent abundance of wealth. Adam Smith described the benefits of a division of labor with his oft-quoted phrase concerning an invisible hand. However, the quote is often misused, and presenting it within its proper context is necessary to ensure the correct understanding:

> But the annual revenue of every society is always precisely equal to the exchangeable value of the whole annual produce of its industry, or rather is precisely the same thing with that exchangeable value. As every individual, therefore, endeavours as much as he can both to employ his capital in the support of domestic industry, and so to direct that industry that its produce may be of the greatest value; every individual necessarily labours to render the annual revenue of the society as great as he can. He generally, indeed, neither intends to promote the public interest, nor knows how much he is promoting it. By preferring the support of domestic to that of foreign industry, he intends only his own security; and by directing that industry in such a manner as its produce may be of the greatest value, he intends only his own gain, and he is in this, as in many other cases, led by an **invisible hand** [emphasis added] to

promote an end which was no part of his intention. Nor is it always the worse for society that it was no part of it. By pursuing his own interest [maximization of satisfaction] he frequently promotes that of the society more effectually than when he really intends to promote it. I have never known much good done by those who affected to trade for the public good.[209] It is an affectation, indeed, not very common among merchants, and very few words need be employed in dissuading them from it.

What is the species of domestic industry which his capital can employ, and of which the produce is likely to be of the greatest value, every individual, it is evident, can, in his local situation, judge much better than any statesman or lawgiver can do for him. The statesman, who should attempt to direct private people in what manner they ought to employ their capitals, would not only load himself with a most unnecessary attention, but assume an authority which could safely be trusted, not only to no single person, but to no council or senate whatever, and which would nowhere be so dangerous as in the hands of a man who had folly and presumption enough to fancy himself fit to exercise it.[210]

---

209 Note here Smith's use of "public good" and compare his usage with the meaning of general welfare as expressed in this book. There is a substantial and significant difference between a government that secures rights and liberty as the means to promote the general happiness, and one that transgresses rights and liberty in order to "trade for the public good." The former generally results in material wealth while the latter will generally result in material poverty. The former is best understood as a market economy, and the latter is best understood as a collectivist economy. Ironically, the system that takes active measures to promote the public good, in a material sense, is the one that will ultimately result in the quite the opposite.
210 ADAM SMITH, THE WEALTH OF NATIONS 572-73 (Edwin Cannan ed., Bantam Books 2003) (1776).

The principle expressed by Adam Smith is an old one. It simply states that when men and women are left to their own pursuits and are able to keep what they produce, people will generally produce a quantity "X." On the other hand, when they are told what to produce and what portion of it will be taken, the quantity produced will inevitably be less than "X." In short, the best means to achieve the greatest wealth is by securing rights and liberty. "It is certain that despotism ruins men more by preventing them from producing than by taking the fruits of production away from them; it dries up the source of wealth and often respects acquired wealth. Freedom, on the contrary, begets a thousand times more goods than it destroys, and in the nations that know it, the resources of the people always grow more quickly than do taxes."[211]

Let's assume that a government is formed with an ultimate purpose that the people desire and accept. One such government that a majority of people would support is one whose purpose was to promote the general welfare by securing rights and liberty for all. If we apply that as the foundation for the end of government along with the invisible hand principle espoused by Adam Smith, then it's apparent that such a society would have flourishing trade and an abundance of wealth.[212] As we also

---

[211] ALEXIS DE TOCQUEVILLE, DEMOCRACY IN AMERICA 199 (Harvey C. Mansfield & Delba Winthrop eds. & trans., The University of Chicago Press, LTD. 2002) (1835).

[212] Even still, there will always be some who are incapable of production or simply choose not to produce. Additionally, there will always be some who are not as good at certain tasks as others. From a simple mathematical standpoint concerning an average, half are above and half are below. Even so, the society as a whole will have more wealth. Because of the division of labor and the principle of a comparative advantage, those of below average abilities will still have an opportunity to seek an occupation best suited to their abilities. Their ability of self-determination will result in more production of wealth than

noted, liberty will be a complementary economic good throughout nearly all of the orders of goods, regardless of whether the people realize it or not.

Paradoxically though, a content people, happily secure in their rights, enjoying their liberty, and producing goods and services as they see fit has laid the foundation of their downfall. Such conditions will inevitably produce substantial wealth, and all of that wealth invites those seeking to skim a portion of it in the hopes that taking a small piece of a large pie will go unnoticed.

> These great advantages of liberty have caused the abuse of liberty itself. Because moderate government has produced remarkable results, this moderation has been abandoned; because large taxes have been raised, one has wanted to raise excessive ones; and, disregarding the hand of liberty that gave this present, one has turned to servitude, which refuses everything.
>
> Liberty has produced excessive taxes, but the effect of these excessive taxes is to produce servitude in their turn, and the effect of servitude is to produce a decrease in taxes.[213]

---

any other method. The only argument would be if half the voting public (as out of the voting public half are above average ability and half are below) is too incompetent to determine what maximizes their own satisfactions. If that were the case, then I suppose a centrally planned economy would be the most practical to producing the most wealth. Observation and experience, however, do not show this to be the case.

213 MONTESQUIEU, THE SPIRIT OF THE LAWS 223 (Anne M. Cohler, Basia Carolyn Miller, & Harold Samuel Stone eds. & trans., Cambridge University Press 14th prtg. 2009) (1748).

Again, David Hume provides his thoughts on liberty yielding to tyranny because of the substantial benefits that ultimately arise from liberty itself.

> It is a violent method, and in most cases impracticable, to oblige the labourer to toil, in order to raise from the land more than what subsists himself and family. Furnish him with manufactures and commodities, and he will do it of himself; afterwards you will find it easy to seize some part of his superfluous labour, and employ it in the public service, without giving him his wonted return. Being accustomed to industry, he will think this less grievous, than if at once you obliged him to an augmentation of labour without any reward. The case is the same with regard to the other members of the state. **The greater is the stock of labour of all kinds, the greater quantity may be taken from the heap without making any sensible alteration of it** [emphasis added].[214]

Hume was making note of the principle of "marginal utility," although he expressed it using different language than what is used today. In the next Article, we will examine marginal utility in more detail.

Before closing this section, there is one other point to make. Besides liberty being its own enemy, the pace with which liberty yields will likely be slow. The reason is simple enough: big changes to something so valued are obvious to us while subtle changes pass by unnoticed. Because liberty is slowly lost in a

---

214 David Hume, Essays Moral, Political and Literary 268 (Henry Frowde reprt. 1904) (1741-42).

lengthy process, by the time all of the harmful effects are actually observed, not many people will have the ability to determine the root cause of its loss. This is especially the case, as we shall see, when it comes to something that is quite complex: money. It is similar to J.M. Keynes' quote: "Lenin was certainly right. There is no subtler, no surer means of overturning the existing basis of society than to debauch the currency. The process engages all the hidden forces of economic law on the side of destruction, and does it in a manner which not one man in a million is able to diagnose."[215]

Both Keynes and Lenin were correct. There is no subtler means of overthrowing the existing society than by slowly abolishing liberty through the destruction of its currency. It subjects the people to such arbitrary authority that few will be able to precisely identify the cause of their ruin. The process involves obscure economic forces, and it accomplishes this in a manner that few can perceive.

As we move to the next sections and articles, remember that an abundance of wealth is initially created when liberty flourishes, and that liberty is a complementary good throughout the order of goods. We will now examine in more detail the principle of marginal utility, and how some people exploit it to their own advantage.

ARTICLE IV: MAXIMIZATION OF SATISFACTION FROM ANOTHER ANGLE

In the practical art of war, the best thing of all is to take the enemy's country whole and intact; to shatter and destroy it is not so good.
– Sun Tzu[216]

215   JOHN MAYNARD KEYNES, THE ECONOMIC CONSEQUENCES OF THE PEACE 134 (Skyhorse Publishing reprt. 2007) (1919).
216   SUN TZU, THE ART OF WAR 15 (Dallas Galvin ed., Lionel Giles trans., Barnes & Noble Classics 2003) (c. 512 B.C.E.).

Sun Tzu's quote is merely pointing out the ideal goal in nearly all wars, at least from the aggressor's point of view. If a state is engaging in a war for the purposes of gaining more wealth, then it is counterproductive to conquer a territory after destroying most of its productive goods. Even worse would be conquering a territory devoid of all productive goods and requiring an application of capital to restart production. In that case, the aggressor would likely have been better off refraining from war altogether unless the prize was worth such an expense of capital. Either way, ideally, an aggressive war prosecuted to secure wealth would be to conquer a territory that has a significant amount of wealth without destroying any of it.

In the same manner, interested parties within a country will recognize the abundance of wealth created by a government based on liberty, and they will begin to strategize about how to obtain it.[217] All of that wealth will stir the passions of those who seek it, and the ideal method of attaining the wealth is to disturb society as little as possible in the process of attaining it. As Hume noted in the previous section, it also does not matter whether the people are actually secure in their liberty or not. What does matter is that the people *believe* they have liberty because the perception of having liberty is itself a vital complementary economic good.

Without that belief, there will be little wealth to be had. The challenge for those seeking control of such a government is to

---

217 "A nation has but two sorts of usurpation to fear; one from their neighbours, and another from their own magistrates: Nor is a foreign usurpation more formidable than a domestick, which is the most dangerous of the two, by being hardest to remove; and generally stealing upon the people by degrees, is fixed before it is scarce felt or apprehended...." 2 THOMAS GORDON & JOHN TRENCHARD, CATO'S LETTERS 551 (Ronald Hamowy ed., Liberty Fund, Inc. 1995) (c. 1720).

1913: From General To Specific Welfare

give the impression of liberty so that substantial wealth may be created, enough for it to be taken by those in positions of power within a government. Of course, if there were actual liberty, the wealth would not be subject to confiscation. As we shall examine, debasing the currency is a tactic that may successfully be employed to do exactly that, and it has been done often throughout the ages.

For the reader skeptical that the very fact of having an abundance of wealth would entice others to devise ways to take it, please reflect on the frequency of theft in contemporary society.

Upon observing others with wealth, one option to secure your own would be to apply your talents and produce it yourself. The other option would be to devise a plan to take wealth from others. The choice depends on the beliefs of the individuals or groups and what method will most maximize their satisfactions. Considering what we've discussed about human nature, we know some will choose the latter option.

Assuming that legislators, or any government employees, are not susceptible to passions is foolhardy. Undoubtedly some men and women inside government seek positions of power solely to gain special privileges and will pursue whatever measures will achieve this end. Ultimately, a legislator of this type who desires a position in Congress needs no more than 51 percent of the vote to win the election and will exploit the remaining 49 percent by relying on access to special privileges. This would've been more difficult to accomplish prior to 1913, but as we will examine in Part V, the monetary and fiscal structure post-1913 actually encourages this behavior.

Nonetheless, such legislators may increase their chances of success by avoiding any reference to the particular groups they will exploit in order to take their wealth. Instead, they would focus attention on all the groups they plan to help. It does little good to say they will help everyone (unless they intend to go down the path of general welfare by securing liberty and justice for all, but that will not be the intent for such legislators). Obviously, a legislator cannot give to everyone without taking from someone, and the latter begins to wonder who that will be. Instead, a savvy politician will appeal to as many groups as possible, recognizing that people are more inclined to find pleasure in being for something as opposed to being against anything. Being against something alienates those who support it. When you are for something, it is not nearly as apparent what you oppose, or from whom you plan to take resources to accomplish your goal.

Such a legislator knows to focus on the short term for achieving pleasure and, at the same time, pushing pain as far into the future as possible. Although this concept is becoming more prevalent in the United States with corporate and government pensions, it is actually not a new idea.[218] In fact, this strategy goes far back in history. Plato provides the following example:

---

218   I urge the reader to reflect on the seemingly short-term advantages of government pensions. For the government (assuming the obligations are not funded immediately but put off until a later date), wages for employees in the present can be much lower because a sizable portion of the compensation for the present labor will be paid at a later time. This reduction in wages results in less current expenditure for the current government, which appears to make for a favorable budget in the short-term. If the long-term is some distant date in the future, most of the current legislators and executive officers will be gone from their government positions. Their replacements will deal with a problem that was not of their making, and the knowledge of the unwritten conversations and handshake agreements will have been long forgotten.

1913: From General To Specific Welfare

So because what I say on any occasion is not designed to please, and because I aim not at what is most agreeable but at what is best [in the long- versus short-term], and will not employ those "niceties" which you advise, I shall have no defence to offer in a court of law. I can only repeat what I was saying to Polus; I shall be judged like a doctor brought before a jury of children with a cook as prosecutor. Imagine what sort of defence a man like that could make before such a court if he were accused in the following terms: "Children, this man here has done many bad things to you and hurts even the youngest of you – he cuts and burns you, he squeezes and strangles you until you are helpless, gives you horrible medicines and forces you to be hungry and thirsty. Now look at me – I put on parties for you, with lots of sweets and all kinds of goodies." What do you think the doctor would be able to say, caught up in this dreadful situation? If he told the truth: "I did all this, children, because I wanted to make you healthy", don't you think that a jury like that would make an uproar, and shout pretty loudly?[219]

Indeed, some things are constant throughout human history. If reason is not used to reflect on all the long-term consequences of actions, the passions will triumph in the short term, striving for pleasure every time regardless of any other concern.

The politically expedient legislator knows all this. All that is left is to apply his or her efforts to the situation to determine what means to pursue that will achieve the desired end: the end

---

219   PLATO, GORGIAS 128 (Walter Hamilton & Chris Emlyn-Jones trans., Penguin Books rev ed. 2004) (c. 380 B.C.E.).

being re-election while the means is transferring wealth from one to give to another. The principle of marginal utility supplies the means to achieve this desired end.

Marginal utility means that as we add an additional unit to our present total, the value of that addition is less than what a single unit of the previous total would have been. As an example, if we pay a set price for ten carrots, a single carrot will have a certain value based on our current total. If we add another carrot for a total of eleven, then each carrot individually will have less value than when we only had ten. This follows the same line of reasoning described by Menger and economic goods. If our needs or desires have not changed but the supply has risen, then the value of each individual unit will decrease. If we increased our quantity of carrots to a number so large that it eclipsed our possible desires, then carrots would cease to be economic goods.

In more practical terms, the following is how marginal utility is put in practice. For someone who has one million dollars, one hundred dollars affects him in a completely different manner than someone who has only ten dollars.[220] An astute legislator would exploit this advantage. If you take a small amount from a man who has a lot, it will be a small loss, perhaps even imperceptible. An individual who took no notice of the loss will not bear any ill will towards the taker, and someone who does notice the loss may shrug it off. If the loss is claimed to be used to reduce the suffering of the less fortunate, perhaps this alone will

---

220   Because currency is exchangeable for virtually anything, in a sense it seems immune to the principle of marginal utility. It seems that way because marginal utility is really concerned only with the value attributed to the fulfilling of a need through direct consumption versus in exchange for something to consume. When it comes to a thing that is readily exchangeable for nearly anything, each additional unit potentially represents something entirely different in the perception of the holder.

increase pleasure by reducing another's pain through sympathy. Regardless of whether someone notices or not, it is true that taking a small portion from a larger total is more tolerable than taking a large portion from a small total.

Now consider the individual who has little, and imagine how much it will mean to someone with only one hundred dollars to receive ten. Someone who has one million might not trouble himself to collect such a small sum of only ten dollars. For the individual who only has one hundred, another ten represents a ten percent gain. For the individual with one million, another ten dollars only represents a trifling .001 percent. The law of nature combined with the principles of mathematics shows the methods a legislator may employ to gather votes: put forth measures that take from those who have more and give to those who have less.

Securing rights and liberty inherently tends towards an increase in the wealth within a state, as we've explained. In fact, it creates so much wealth within a state that taking small amounts from the people may not be readily noticed. Even if noticed, the objections will be no more than minor grumblings. But if the small amounts taken are given to those in society who have the least, these amounts will have a significant impact.[221]

---

[221] As an aside, let us consider the general difference in wealth produced between a market economy and a collectivist economy. A market economy is defined here as a society where the capital is held by private individuals and where the regulations for the production and distribution of goods and services are determined by the men and women who either purchase or abstain from purchasing them. This is not meant to imply that there is no legislation making things such as fraud, theft, murder, etc. illegal. It is only meant that the people determine what is produced by either demanding more or less of a good or service. In a collective society, all of the capital is held by one entity (whether it be a political party, government, corporation, etc. or any combination thereof). This central body determines the production and distribution of goods and

Now that we understand how marginal utility can be manipulated in support of a political process, we can see how a scheming legislator will promise to do "something" for as many groups as possible, all the while avoiding any mention of who will by definition be excluded.[222] A skilled politician will put forth his proposals using emotion—enlivening the passions—and avoiding a discussion that relies on the faculties of reason. The promise of some provision offers pleasure, and the only requirement to receive that pleasure is a simple vote. When in office, the politician will work to remain there by putting the principle of marginal utility into practice, that is, take from those who have more and transfer that sum to those who have less. We will examine that

---

services. Therefore, there must be regulations that direct the efforts of those engaged in the production and distribution.

From our discussion, the former is the means to maximize the amount of wealth while the latter is the means to minimize it. In the former the disparity of wealth between those with the most and those with the least will be significantly larger than in the latter economic system. In theory, the latter will see equal distribution of wealth although practice typically shows that the ruling entity usually amasses more wealth than the rest. Nonetheless, logic would dictate that over time the wealth of the lower portion of society in the market economy will be more than the average citizen of the collectivist society.

As an example, say there is a group of 10 people. If I split 10 dollars equally, everyone receives 10%, or 1 dollar. Now imagine I have 100 dollars because each person was at liberty to use their talents as they saw fit, remembering the benefits of a division of labor and a comparative advantage. Take a case where say 50% went to the top person. That leaves the other 9 people with the remaining 50 dollars. I will leave the remainder of the exercise to the imagination of the reader. Suffice it to say, even though a pie may be divided unequally, it is possible to have a pie so large that the person who receives the least will still receive more than each person who receives an equal portion from a much smaller pie. Unfortunately, the passions of envy and jealousy are still powerful forces.

222   It should be obvious that granting special favors to one group denies those favors to all other groups. That is the difference between the spoken and unspoken; the spoken draws one's attention while the other does not.

aspect in more detail when exploring the topic of the Federal Reserve Act of 1913. For now, we will return to the topic of liberty's natural tendency to yield.

Article V: Special Knowledge

Special knowledge always has, and always will, provide a significant advantage to those who possess it over those who don't. The following quote by David Hume articulates the point precisely.

> The vulgar, who take things according to their first appearance, attribute the uncertainty of events to such an uncertainty in the causes as makes them often fail of their usual influence; though they meet with no impediment in their operation. But philosophers, observing that, almost in every part of nature, there is contained a vast variety of springs and principles, which are hid, by reason of their minuteness or remoteness, find, that it is at least possible the contrariety of events may not proceed from any contingency in the cause, but from the secret operation of contrary causes. This possibility is converted into certainty by farther observation, when they remark that, upon an exact scrutiny, a contrariety of effects always betrays a contrariety of causes, and proceeds from their mutual opposition. A peasant can give no better reason for the stopping of any clock or watch than to say that it does not commonly go right: But an artist easily perceives that the same force in the spring or pendulum has always the same influence on the wheels; but fails of its usual effects, perhaps by reason of a grain of dust, which puts a stop to the whole movement. From the observation of several parallel

instances, philosophers form a maxim that the connexion between all causes and effects is equally necessary, and that its seeming uncertainty in some instances proceeds from the secret opposition of contrary causes.[223]

When we focus on our self-evident law of nature, we know from experience that the very law that initially established liberty will be the exact same force that causes it to yield to tyranny. In fact, it is this law of nature that accounts for the adage commonly attributed to Mark Twain, referring to the repetitive nature of history: that history may not repeat, but it sure does rhyme.[224] What Twain was referring to is that we keep attempting the same strategy, or the use of means to achieve our end. Over time, the techniques or tactics may change based on the circumstances and technology of the time, but the general principle will remain the same—hence history repeating.

That principle addresses being able to apply knowledge to achieve a desired goal, or the ability to reason. When an individual possesses either the knowledge or the wisdom that others lack, then that person will understand what type of advantages he or she may secure if they are the only people who have attained this insight.

Knowledge common to all is special to none. If everyone knows that item "A" can be bought today for one unit and sold tomorrow for two, then who will be willing to sell today for one unit when they know that tomorrow they can sell for two?

---

[223] DAVID HUME, AN ENQUIRY CONCERNING HUMAN UNDERSTANDING 104-05 (Prometheus Books, 1988) (1748).
[224] JOSHUA MATZ & LAURENCE TRIBE, UNCERTAIN JUSTICE 257 (Henry Holt and Company, LLC 2014) (citing JOHN ROBERT COLOMBO, *A Said Poem*, in NEO POEMS 46 (Sono Nis Press 1970))..

Obviously, no one. However, suppose only a few individuals possess this information about the fluctuating price? They will certainly possess a distinct advantage over others. Shortly we will examine examples from past eras to emphasize how natural it is for some to possess special knowledge and how much power that knowledge affords the owner. However, before proceeding to those examples, let us explore why it is impossible to prevent special knowledge.

Although all people are born with equal rights in the context of a state of nature, no two are born with equal faculties. Not only that, but every person is also born with different desires and aversions. And people know that the authority to create law is a substantial source of power. Moreover, some may conclude that they can attain advantages by attempting to secure that power for themselves while prohibiting the same to others. Those with the special knowledge of the power of how to create law, who combine it with experience to determine how to acquire desired privileges, have succeeded in their goal of maximizing their satisfactions at the expense of the general welfare.

However, if we were to create a law whose purpose was to prohibit the application of such special knowledge, the law itself would provide an opportunity for exploitation by the very same people who crafted the law in the first place. The authors of the law that prohibited the application of special knowledge would likely know better than anyone else exactly how to apply special knowledge without "violating the law" they just created. This dilemma highlights the irony that confronted the Founders of the Constitution. For that matter, it is the same irony that has confronted all of those who have attempted to form a government whose goal was to secure rights and liberty to promote the general welfare. Regardless of what opinions one may have of Karl Marx, the following passage conveys his understanding of this dilemma.

> Free competition, the key-word of our present-day economists, is an impossibility. Monopoly at least intended to protect the consumer against counterfeit, even if it could not in fact do so. The abolition of monopoly, however, opens the door wide to counterfeit. You say that competition carries with it the remedy for counterfeit, since no one will buy bad articles. But that means that everyone has to be an expert in every article, which is impossible. . . . And the most important article – money – requires a monopoly most of all. Whenever the circulating medium has ceased to be a state monopoly it has invariably produced a trade crisis; and the English economists, Dr. Wade among them, do concede in this case the necessity for monopoly. But even monopoly is no protection against counterfeit money. One can take one's stand on either side of the question: the one is as difficult as the other. Monopoly produces free competition, and the latter, in turn, produces monopoly. Therefore, both must fall, and these difficulties must be resolved through the transcendence of the principle which gives rise to them.[225]

Marx not only touches on the topic of special knowledge, but he also articulates the larger theme of the tendency for liberty to yield to tyranny. Just as a powerful force may repel external

---

[225]   KARL MARX & FREDERICK ENGELS, *Communist Manifesto*, in ECONOMIC AND PHILOSOPHIC MANUSCRIPTS OF 1844 AND THE COMMUNIST MANIFESTO 199 (Martin Milligan trans., Prometheus Books 1988) (1847).

threats, a money monopoly will ensure there is no counterfeit from outside entities. However, similar to the difficulty of ensuring such a powerful force does not become an internal threat, how do outside entities ensure that the monopolist does not counterfeit by exploiting his or her special knowledge?

Whatever type of law is written in an attempt to limit an application of special knowledge, those with an advantage in some faculty will probably have less trouble in circumventing the newly created law than someone who does not possess the same faculties. So the creation of a law to prohibit the usage of special knowledge for special benefits more than likely will instead create a barrier to entry for those without special knowledge to compete.

Now let's continue with examples from past eras to illustrate that the application of special knowledge is not by any means a new phenomenon, and that such application can accrue vast power to the possessor of that special knowledge.

The first example comes from David Hume, as he explains a situation where one who understands the basics of cause and effect has the potential for significant power over one who does not.

> No Indian, it is evident, could have experience that water did not freeze in cold climates. This is placing nature in a situation quite unknown to him; and it is impossible for him to tell *à priori* what will result from it. It is making a new experiment, the consequence of which is always uncertain. One may sometimes conjecture from analogy what will follow; but still this is but conjecture. And it must be confessed, that, in the present case of freezing,

the event following contrary to the rules of analogy, and is such as a rational Indian would not look for. The operations of cold upon water are not gradual, according to the degrees of cold; but whenever it comes to the freezing point, the water passes in a moment, from the utmost liquidity to perfect hardness. Such an event, therefore, may be denominated *extraordinary*, and requires a pretty strong testimony, to render it credible to people in a warm climate: but still it is not *miraculous*, nor contrary to uniform experience of the course of nature in cases where all the circumstances are the same.[226]

Hume does not make an explicit reference to how powerful the application of special knowledge may be, but the case he presents does provide a situation ripe for manipulation. A deceptive and dishonest person, in possession of such knowledge, has the means necessary to take advantage of another's lack of knowledge, or ignorance. We can either say: "it is not the fault of one who possesses knowledge in relation to one who lacks it," or "it is the fault of the possessor, and steps must be taken to make the situation fair." The point here is not to assign blame to one party or the other, but to emphasize that special knowledge provides an advantage to those who possess it. Like nearly anything, something can be used for good or evil. Its use will depend on the beliefs of those who possess it. The one thing we can determine with certainty is that everyone will attempt to maximize his or her satisfaction by exploiting their special knowledge to their benefit, and it is their scruples that tell them how to proceed.

---

[226] DAVID HUME, ESSAYS MORAL, POLITICAL AND LITERARY 524 (Henry Frowde reprt. 1904) (1741-42).

Hume provides another example of how special knowledge can be applied to gain specific advantages in the following excerpt:

> It was a wise policy in that false prophet Alexander, who, though now forgotten, was once so famous, to lay the first scene of his impostures in Paphlagonia, where, as Lucian tells us, the people were extremely ignorant and stupid, and ready to swallow even the grossest delusion. People at a distance, who are weak enough to think the matter at all worth inquiry, have no opportunity of receiving better information. The stories come magnified to them by a hundred circumstances. Fools are industrious in propagating the imposture; while the wise and learned are contented, in general, to deride its absurdity, without informing themselves of the particular facts by which it may be distinctly refuted. And thus the impostor above mentioned was enabled to proceed, from his ignorant Paphlgonians, to the enlisting of votaries, even among the Grecian philosophers, and men of the most eminent rank and distinction in Rome: nay, could engage the attention of that sage emperor Marcus Aurelius, so far as to make him trust the success of a military expedition to his delusive prophecies.[227]

Interestingly, special knowledge has also been the basis for a phenomenon that is commonly labeled today as superstition. Thomas Gordon, in *Cato's Letters*, noted: ". . . [a]nd therefore we find, in many instances, that fools mislead and govern men of sense. In things where men know nothing, they are apt to think

---
227   *Id.* at 530-31.

that others know more than they; and so blindly trust to bold pretentions: And here is the great cause and first rise of sharpers and bubbles of all denominations, from demagogues and their followers, down to mountebanks and their mobs."[228]

John Trenchard, the other author of *Cato's Letters*, then continued, "[t]here are but two ways in nature to enslave a people, and to continue that slavery over them; the first is superstition, and the last is force: By the one we are persuaded that it is our duty to be undone; and the other undoes us whether we will or no."[229] Again, we return to the power of special knowledge.

When faced with a situation where a decision must be made without sufficient knowledge, one must ultimately ask the following question: am I willing to place my faith in the knowledge, experience, and wisdom of another? This question must be asked, because if we do not personally know but must rely on the claims of another, then we must in effect believe in him or her.

The application of special knowledge has been employed throughout history, and Hobbes provides a few examples.

> For such is the ignorance, and aptitude to error generally of all men, but especially of them that have not much knowledge of naturall causes, and of the nature, and interests of men; as by innumerable and easie tricks to be abused. What opinion of miraculous power, before it was known there was a Science of the course of the Stars, might a man have gained, that should have told the people, This hour, or day the Sun should be darkened? A Juggler by

---

[228] 1 THOMAS GORDON & JOHN TRENCHARD, CATO'S LETTERS 311 (Ronald Hamowy ed., Liberty Fund, Inc. 1995) (c. 1720).
[229] 2 THOMAS GORDON & JOHN TRENCHARD, CATO'S LETTERS 678 (Ronald Hamowy ed., Liberty Fund, Inc. 1995) (c. 1720).

the handling of his goblets, and other trinkets, if it were not now ordinarily practised, would be thought to do his wonders by the power at least of the Devil. A man that hath practised to speak by drawing in of his breath, (which kind of men in antient time were called *Ventriloqui,*) and so make the weaknesse of his voice seem to proceed, not from the weak impulsion of the organs of Speech, but from distance of place, is able to make very many men beleeve it is a voice from Heaven, whatsoever he please to tell them. And for a crafty man, that hath enquired into the secrets, and familiar confessions that one man ordinarily maketh to another of his actions and adventures past, to tell them him again is no hard matter; and yet there be many, that by such means as that, obtain the reputation of being Conjurers.[230]

Special knowledge may become more valuable, for example, in cases where it is the difference between harvesting crops at a particular time to sell at a favorable price or selling to just break even. Special knowledge becomes even more substantial when the situation migrates towards subjects such as military prowess, politics, money, or a combination of money with either of the other two. "As John Adams wrote to Thomas Jefferson in 1787, 'All the perplexities, confusions, and distress in America, arise, not from defects in their Constitution or Confederation, not from want of honor or virtue, so much as from downright ignorance of the nature of coin, credit, and circulation.'"[231]

When it comes to politics, or the sovereign entity with the

---

[230] THOMAS HOBBES, LEVIATHAN 291 (Barnes & Noble, Inc. 2004) (1651).
[231] RON PAUL, THE REVOLUTION 138 (Grand Central Publishing 2008).

authority to create law and money, the combination of the two has the potential to be the supreme power. If an individual possesses the special knowledge required to attain legislation that denotes legal tender as the paper that he or she creates, then that person has the ability to create whatever currency is necessary to buy the influence required to ensure that he will not lose that privilege. It's argued that the special knowledge concerning the combination of politics and the creation of money is the most powerful knowledge one may acquire. We leave that thought for the reader to reflect upon as we progress through the rest of our examination.

We will return to the topic of money and government again in due time. For now, let's continue with an examination of how instruments created by people to fulfill a need inevitably transform into an institution.

Article VI: From Instrument to Institution

All human constitutions are subject to corruption, and must perish, unless they are timely renewed, and reduced to their first principles. . . . – Algernon Sidney[232]

We keep returning to a fundamental law of nature: that people act to maximize their satisfaction. Part IV, Article V described another law of nature: that someone will always have some special knowledge that will give them an advantage over others. Armed with an understanding of these two laws, we are now able to move forward with an analysis of how they interact.

As was mentioned in Part I, Article I ("Science" of Human

---

[232] Algernon Sidney, Discourses Concerning Government 150 (Thomas G. West ed., Liberty Classics 1990) (1698).

Nature), we have used induction as a means to work backwards from the symptoms or effects to articulate the law of nature controlling those effects. With the general law clearly articulated, we are able to deduce its consequences. This article, dealing with instruments becoming institutions, combines these two laws of nature with other principles previously described. It is a precursor to understanding how the government of the United States followed the same path as any other instrument on its way to becoming an institution.

Carroll Quigley, author of *Tragedy and Hope* as well as *The Evolution of Civilizations*, does a superb job of describing how an instrument becomes an institution. He notes the same principles concerning economics and human action as described by Carl Menger. Again, he uses different language, but the principle is easily recognizable. Relative to our particular knowledge and experience, many things may appear new. However, in relation to the experiences and knowledge of eternity, nothing is "new." The following excerpt from *The Evolution of Civilizations* explains why this is:

> Since the levels of culture [from most to least concrete: military; political; economic; social; religious; and intellectual] arise from men's efforts to satisfy their human needs, we can say that every level has a purpose. Assuming the sixfold division we have made, we can speak of six basic human needs [which is the basis for value]: (1) the need for group security [provide for the common defense], (2) the need to organize interpersonal power relationships [Constitution – to some extent], (3) the need for material wealth [general welfare through means of liberty], (4) the

need for companionship, (5) the need for psychological certainty, and (6) the need for understanding. To satisfy these needs, there come into existence on each level social organizations seeking to achieve these. These organizations, consisting largely of personal relationships, we shall call "instruments" as long as they achieve the purpose of the level with relative effectiveness. But every such social instrument tends to become an "institution." This means that it takes on a life and purposes of its own distinct from the purpose of the level [due to maximization of satisfaction by each individual]; in consequence, the purpose of that level is achieved with decreasing effectiveness. In fact, it can be stated as a rule of history that "all social instruments tend to become institutions [as one would expect based on the law that all humans acts to maximize their satisfaction]." The meaning of this rule will appear as we discuss its causes.

An instrument is a social organization that is fulfilling effectively the purpose for which it arose. An institution is an instrument that has taken on activities and purposes of its own, separate and different from the purposes for which it was intended. As a consequence, an institution achieves its original purposes with decreasing effectiveness. Every instrument consists of people organized in relationships to one another. As the instrument becomes an institution, these relations become ends in themselves to the detriment of the ends of the whole organization. When people want their society to be defended, they create an organization called an army. This army consists of many persons with different duties. Each person takes as his purpose the fulfilling of his duties, but this soon leaves no one in the organization with the purpose of the organization as his primary purpose. The purpose of the organization – in this case, to defend society - becomes no more than a secondary aim for everyone in the organization. Defense becomes secondary to discipline, keeping authority in channels, feeding and paying the troops, providing supplies or intelligences, and keeping visiting congressmen, or the people as a whole, happy about the army, the personal comforts of the soldiers, and so on. Moreover, as a second reason why every instrument becomes an institution, everyone in such an organization is only human and has human weakness and ambitions, or at least has the human proclivity to see things from an egocentric point of view. Thus, in every organization, persons begin to seek their own advancements or to act for their own advantages: seeking promotions, decorations, increases in pay, better or easier assignments; these begin to absorb more and more of the time and energies of the members of the organization.[233]

This excerpt does an excellent job in summarizing the interaction of many of the key principles we're discussing. First, it makes note that people have desires that require satisfaction. When we take action to fulfill them, we fulfill them in a manner that will provide us with a maximization of satisfaction. Of course, as Aristotle pointed out, a limited reasoning ability may

---

[233] CARROLL QUIGLEY, THE EVOLUTION OF CIVILIZATIONS 101-02 (Liberty Fund, Inc. reprt. 1979).

result in a realization that the actions we took did not actually maximize our satisfactions. Still, at the time, based on our current beliefs, needs, desires, and understanding, we took actions that we believed would bring the most satisfaction.

To meet our desires, we form organizations. Quigley refers to these organizations as instruments. When the purpose is fresh in our mind, it is relatively easy to remain focused on it. However, as time marches on and regardless of the attempted diligence to remember, the original purpose begins to be lost.[234]

As an example, consider the different labels given to the various programs used in production businesses just over the last 50 years. Whatever the name, whether Total Quality Management, Lean Six Sigma, Theory of Constraints, etc., the principle is the same. The business was established to create a good, which hopefully would be demanded by enough consumers to produce a sufficient return on the capital invested, but which is no longer occurring. The task is to determine what means are being employed that no longer contribute toward fulfilling the end. In other words, inefficiency and waste must be eliminated.

There may be different causes for losing sight of the end, and one may simply be that no one remembers the original purpose.

---

[234] Thomas Hobbes, in *Leviathan*, notes the importance of keeping the end in mind. The following passage relates to religion and government, but the principle is certainly similar. He says, "[f]ourthly, seeing people cannot be taught this, nor when 'tis taught, remember it, nor after one generation past, so much as know in whom the Sovereign Power is placed, without setting a part from their ordinary labour, some certain times, in which they may attend those that are appointed to instruct them; It is necessary that some such times be determined, wherein they may assemble together, and (after prayers and praises given to God, the Sovereign of Sovereigns) hear those their Duties told them, and the Postive Lawes, such as generally concern them all, read and expounded, and be put in mind of the Authority that maketh them Lawes." THOMAS HOBBES, LEVIATHAN 220-21 (Barnes & Noble, Inc. 2004) (1651).

When this has occurred, the instrument has already become an institution, as the members of the business are already more concerned with their own personal advantages than accomplishing the original end. Even more to the point, when the end is forgotten, the probability of achieving it becomes quite low. This often happens in business. Now reflect on the number of people who would agree to the end of our government. We established that the end is the general welfare, and the general means consist of securing rights and liberty through a constitutional structure that protects against internal threats, a common defense from external threats, establishing justice, and domestic tranquility, while the specific means are laid out in Article I, Section 8. If few understand the end of our government, then it should not be surprising to see that we fail to achieve the end. Remembering the purpose of an instrument may not be sufficient to prevent it from turning into an institution, but forgetting the purpose is sufficient for the transformation.

Before examining the process of a governmental instrument transforming to an institution, we will briefly review that process for a non-governmental instrument. In a market economy, where the customers determine the rules by either purchasing or abstaining from a good or service, an instrument is either directly or indirectly designed to satisfy the desires of consumers. When the goods or services are produced in a manner that satisfies a desire and the demand is greater than the supply, then the good or service has become an economic good and hence has a calculable price. If the owner of the instrument fails to deliver a desirable good and recover costs, then he will no longer be in business.

True, the business may survive for a time, though many

working for that business may have forgotten what the end of the instrument was. Alternatively, the owner and employees may have remained aware of the purpose, but the consumer may have had a change of desire that went unnoticed by the owner. Regardless of the situation, the business must adapt to the situation and either eliminate the waste to return to a state that achieves the original end, or refine the end in order to satisfy the changing needs of the customer. If the business owner is unable to do so, then the return on, and likely the return of, his capital will be lost.

Let's now turn our attention to how government institutions transform from an instrument to an institution. The last sentence of Quigley's passage sums up the principle nicely: "[t]hus, in every organization, persons begin to seek their own advancements or to act for their own advantages: seeking promotions, decorations, increases in pay, better or easier assignments; these begin to absorb more and more of the time and energies of the members of the organization."[235] As mentioned, the process is generally slow and subtle.

For anyone who has ever been a part of a large institution, especially a bureaucracy, reflect on your own experiences. How often do you recall yourself or others doing actions where no one could declare with certainty what was the purpose of their activities? How often have you observed an obsolete system or program continue when the original creators who developed the instrument were no longer there? Even though the executors of a system are unaware of its purpose, the obsolete system continues on through sheer bureaucratic inertia. Without passing on the

---

[235] CARROLL QUIGLEY, THE EVOLUTION OF CIVILIZATIONS 102 (Liberty Fund, Inc. reprt. 1979).

purpose to their successors, the original creators are in danger of perpetuating a tool that no longer accomplishes its intended end.

Additionally, once a program has been in existence, it is not necessarily an easy task to abolish it. People who have worked on the program develop an emotional attachment to it. This relation makes it difficult to dismantle what they helped to produce and perpetuate. Moreover, change from the status quo to something new takes more effort than continuing on with the present practice. For these two reasons, an instrument that has lost its ability to achieve its end is difficult to reform. The institution continues to absorb resources but no longer serves a useful purpose of satisfying the original need. And more troublesome, this may continue much longer in a governmental institution than in a business.

The reason a governmental instrument turned institution may survive longer than a private one is due to the fact that a governmental institution has no pricing mechanism, per se. Yes, it has a budget, which is comprised of income (funding from taxpayers) and expenses. These may be combined to give some semblance of profit. I say "semblance of profit" because profit generally considers the difference between expenses and revenue, where the revenue was generated due to sales of the good or service provided. A government entity may provide a good or service, but its costs are borne by the taxpayer and not the entity.

So a governmental institution is not capable of producing a profit; it is only able to spend what was allocated and nothing more. There is little incentive to not spend the allocated budget, regardless of whether or not the end was achieved.

To continue the comparison of governmental and private

instruments turned institutions, private institutions receive timely feedback of the satisfaction of consumer desires in the form of price, which is a key ingredient to revenue that in turn is a critical component to a private company's bottom line. If a leader of a private institution attempts to promote or otherwise increase compensation for employees on a basis other than their ability to achieve the entity's end, then the results will be detrimental to the entity's bottom line and compromise its ability to remain solvent.

The leader of a private institution is subject to the immediate demands of the consumer whose desires the entity attempts to satisfy. There is obviously a limit to how much waste a private institution can afford before it is in jeopardy of going under.

When one reflects on a governmental institution, the principle is the same, but as noted, the timeliness of the feedback is substantially different. The individual is the ultimate consumer of the service. However, a governmental institution is different in that the government has a monopoly on the use of force to ensure compliance with the law. The customer has no choice in the form of either purchasing or abstaining from purchasing in the same manner as one does in a market. The government has the power to tax and fund institutions despite the people's displeasure with the results. Because of this, leaders of governmental institutions are not as receptive to feedback as a leader of a private institution. The result is that efforts not directed toward accomplishing the end, or waste, will continue unnoticed much longer in a governmental institution than in a private one.

ARTICLE VII: SUMMARY

The title of Part IV, Liberty Yields While Tyranny Reigns,

encapsulates the law that all men and women act to maximize their satisfactions. The instant the ink was dry on the ratification of the U.S. Constitution, some people inevitably began to strategize how to exploit the new system to best serve their particular interests.

Wise men from Plato to Franklin have understood this dilemma. Plato felt the solution was to establish academies to instruct the state's leaders to be philosopher kings. That would prove to be a temporary solution because such an academy would be subject to the same law of nature that all individuals act to maximize their satisfactions, and then move from being an instrument to becoming an institution. On the other hand, Franklin was confident that an educated and enlightened citizenry was necessary to ensure a continuation of the United States republic. Jefferson believed that pitting ambition against ambition would be a necessary safeguard to prevent the destruction of the government from within. Both options have merit, but we have shown in Part IV that eventually human nature would ensure that any instrument will turn to an institution, and that liberty would yield while tyranny reigned.

We explained this in our examination of reason in Part IV, Articles I and II discussing how reason would remain as a deterrent to the nature of individuals and our susceptibility to passions and emotions. Because of people's nature to maximize their satisfaction, there is a tendency to focus on the specific advantages that may be gained for themselves or their particular group. Not only is there a tendency towards the particular group, but there is also a tendency towards the short term versus the long term. In addition, there is a tendency to focus on the seen versus the unseen.[236] Reason has the ability to temper and potentially prevent these just-mentioned passions. However, reason alone is useless if men and women have neither the understanding of reason's power nor the will to use it. The first two articles of Part IV explained this never-ending back and forth between the two.

Part IV, Article III focused on the value of liberty, specifically from an economic aspect as a complementary good throughout the hierarchy of the production of goods. We mentioned that liberty is not necessary for the production of goods or services. However, it is a necessary element when considering the methods capable of facilitating a society's maximum productive capacity. Because conditions of liberty create such productive powers, liberty leads to substantial wealth. Substantial wealth invites opportunists who will scheme to confiscate wealth if there is no pushback from those who had their wealth confiscated.

Finally, Part IV ended with the principle of special knowledge, and how those who are so inclined are able to use such special knowledge to acquire substantial advantages. This advantage, combined with the previously noted tendencies and principles, will ultimately turn any instrument into an institution. When this institution is one that has the power of creating and enforcing law, then the revolution in human affairs has completed one more cycle. The question then, based on history, is not if, but when. This brings us to Part V.

Because we have already examined the why and how, here in Part V is where we will examine what transformed the United States government from general to specific welfare. The "what" consists of the 16th and 17th Amendments plus the Federal

---

[236] *See* M. FREDERIC BASTIAT, ESSAYS ON POLITICAL ECONOMY 49-118 (G. P. Putnams & Sons 3rd ed. reprt. 1874).

Reserve Act of 1913. The objective of Part V does not include an analysis of the motives, claims, and tactics surrounding these three events, although such an examination would likely be quite illuminating. That is not to say that some specifics in this area are not mentioned during the analysis—they are. But the focus here is only on the effects of the "what," not on the "how" these three events came to be.

PART V:

UNITED STATES CONSTITUTION – POST-1913

Few men at fir[s]t [s]ee the danger of little changes in fundamentals; and tho[s]e who de[s]ign them, u[s]usally act with [s]o much craft, as be[s]ides the giving [s]pecious rea[s]ons, they take great care that the true rea[s]on [s]hall not appear. Every de[s]ign therefore of changing the con[s]titution ought to be mo[s]t warily ob[s]erved, and timely oppo[s]ed – John Lord Somers, circa 1681[237]

. . . [t]hat whilst the foundation and principle of a government remains good, the superstructure may be changed according to occasions, without any prejudice to it. – Algernon Sidney[238]

In Part III, United States Constitution—Pre-1913, we examined the significant aspects and effects of the Preamble, enumerated powers, the Necessary and Proper Clause, taxes, purpose of the Senate (specifically concerning the means of electing state Senators), and the monetary aspects of the Constitution.

---

237   JOHN LORD SOMERS, THE SECURITY OF ENGLI[S]HMEN'S LIVES: OR THE TRUST, POWER AND DUTY OF GRAND JURIES OF ENGLAND 78 (Kessinger Publishing reprt. n.d.) (1681).
238   ALGERNON SIDNEY, DISCOURSES CONCERNING GOVERNMENT 175 (Thomas G. West ed., Liberty Classics 1990) (1698).

In this section, we will examine the 16th Amendment, 17th Amendment, and the Federal Reserve Act of 1913 (FRA). If we ask the question of whether an Act of Congress can nullify parts of the Constitution, the answer is definitely NO, as the only means of amending the Constitution is through the amendment process as defined in the Constitution, Article V.

Nonetheless, the Amendments *and* the FRA certainly did have a profound impact on federal governance. The focus in Part V will be on the effects each Amendment and the FRA had on the Preamble, the enumerated powers, taxes, the Senate, and the Constitution's monetary aspects.

Although it's intriguing to examine the motives of those behind the 16th and 17th Amendments and the FRA, that is beyond the scope of our discussion. As previously mentioned, in Part V the purpose is to analyze the three critical components of the "what."

As noted in the opening quotation to Part V, it is often the seemingly insignificant modifications to the law that result in the most substantial changes. A critical aspect in reforming an institution is identifying the root cause, which may have long since passed and thus be difficult to identify. However, when we examine the changes of 1913, it is apparent how the balance of human nature in our government was knocked askew. Once unbalanced, it is only natural that the benefits migrate from the less powerful to the more powerful. As Hume noted, "[b]ut a republican and free government would be an obvious absurdity, if the particular checks and controls, provided by the constitution, had really no influence, and made it not the interest, even of bad men, to act for the public good."[239] Moreover, the relevance

---

[239] DAVID HUME, ESSAYS MORAL, POLITICAL AND LITERARY 14 (Henry Frowde reprt. 1904) (1741-42).

of the second passage by Sidney at the beginning of Part V concerns how these events of 1913 acted to alter the foundation of our federal government. Sidney notes that one may tinker with the superstructure while the foundation and principle remain solid. However, if the foundation or principle has been changed from an end of general welfare to specific welfare, it matters little how one changes the superstructure—the machine has been re-engineered to produce special favors. On that thought, let us begin by examining three vital changes that occurred in 1913, beginning with the 16th Amendment.

Article I: Taxes and the 16th Amendment

The 16th Amendment[240] is brief, yet its effects are wide-ranging. As applied today, the 16th Amendment is the source of the power that allows the central government to determine what portion of a person's income—gained through labor, capital, or land—may be taken. Moreover, that portion may be taken without apportionment according to representatives in the House of Representatives.

The ratification of the 16th Amendment over one hundred years ago did not happen on a whim; it was a lengthy process that was decades in the making. In Part III, Article III, we examined the important relationship between liberty and the apportionment of direct taxes. Because this link is so vital, we will risk being repetitive in addressing some of the circumstances, as well as Supreme Court cases from the late 1800s that influenced

---

240   "The Congress shall have power to lay and collect taxes on incomes, from whatever source derived, without apportionment among the several States, and without regard to any census or enumeration." U.S. Const. amend. XVI.

the eventual ratification. The background is important because it provides context to our understanding of the Amendment. Significant change seldom happens in one fell swoop. Instead, significant change comes about in a gradual, evolutionary process that in this case, culminated in the ratification of the 16th Amendment.

It is reminiscent of the old adage of a camel poking his nose under the tent. A camel need not get his entire body into the tent all at once; he does so little by little, seemingly unobtrusively at first, until he's crowded himself inside and it's the devil trying to get him back out. This adage is simply an illustration that describes the most effective way to institute change toward a desired result, which is to do so slowly and incrementally.

That is not to say that a change to the status quo cannot be accomplished in a rapid manner. Revolution is the term used to describe rapid change in governmental affairs, and it often leads to social upheaval. However, the end state may not be the one imagined by the advocates of change. Therefore, a planned change for a specific, desired result is much more likely through a gradual process than with a sudden and drastic one.

The point is not to prove that advocates of the 16th Amendment intended to bring about our current understanding and application of it back in 1913. Instead, the point is that this Amendment served as the proverbial nose of the camel under the tent. Once a direct tax no longer needed to be apportioned, it was inevitable that such a substantial source of revenue for the central government would be transformed over time to our current system, as promulgated in the tax laws.

In order to explain the significant change that occurred over the last 100 years, the remainder of this Article is composed of two sections: a review of the events leading up to the Amendment, followed by a review of the effects. Let us now examine some of the circumstances leading up to ratification.

SECTION I: LEAD UP TO THE 16TH AMENDMENT

Perhaps the most significant event that led to the 16th Amendment was the case of *Pollock v. Farmers' Loan Trust Co.*, 157 U.S. 429 (1895). In *Pollock*, the plaintiff claimed that the tax laid upon income from property was a direct tax. Because the tax was not apportioned, the tax was therefore invalid.[241] The Court held that such a tax on income was a direct tax, and the tax was invalid because it was not apportioned.[242] Chief Justice Fuller delivered the opinion of the court, and his opinion provides a trenchant explanation of the powerful and delicate balance between direct taxation and apportionment in relation to liberty. Similarly, it should be obvious what the effects will be when the link between representation and taxation is effectively severed. If liberty requires apportionment of direct taxes, then a lack of apportionment of direct taxes may lead to a lack of liberty. For this reason, substantial portions of Justice Fuller's opinion are included because he provided such a convincing explanation of the importance of apportioned direct taxes.

Because liberty is freedom from arbitrary authority, our liberty in a monetary sense is secure if we are able to decide how much we will provide for the support of the general government. Of course in a republican form of government, we don't personally create legislation. Instead, a representative creates the laws on our behalf. By linking direct taxes with apportionment,

---

241   *Pollock*, 157 U.S. at 555.
242   *Id.* at 583.

that is the most practical means to ensure that we consent to the amount of tax we are willing to pay. Another way to describe the link between direct taxes and apportionment is "taxation with representation," a twist on the oft-repeated slogan of protest from the events leading to the founding of the United States. We see this same principle expressed throughout the opinion of Chief Justice Fuller.

The first item of interest in Chief Justice Fuller's opinion was his observation that there had never been any dispute as to whether the central government ever lacked any power of taxation, with the exception of the power to tax exports from a state.[243] On the contrary, the people accepted that the general government had plenary powers of taxation. The only question concerned the class upon which a particular tax fell, either as a direct or indirect tax. As Chief Justice Fuller noted,

> Thus, in the matter of taxation, the Constitution recognizes the two great classes of direct and indirect taxes, and lays down two rules by which their imposition must be governed, namely: The rule of apportionment as to direct taxes, and the rule of uniformity as to duties, imposts and excises. . . .
>
> And this view was expressed by Mr. Chief Justice Chase in *The License Tax Cases*, 5 Wall. 462, 471, when he said: "It is true that the power of Congress to tax is a very extensive power. It is given in the Constitution, with only one exception and only two qualifications. Congress cannot tax exports, and it must impose direct taxes by the rule of

---

243   *Id.* at 613.

apportionment, and indirect taxes by the rule of uniformity. Thus limited, and thus only it reaches every subject, and may be exercised at discretion."

And although there have been from time to time intimations that there might be some tax which was not a direct tax nor included under the words "duties, imposts and excises," such a tax for more than one hundred years of national existence has as yet remained undiscovered, notwithstanding the stress of particular circumstances has invited thorough investigation into sources of revenue.[244]

Chief Justice Fuller noted that the issue of what constitutes direct and indirect taxes is an argument that goes back to the days soon after the ratification of the Constitution. In fact, *Hylton v. United States*, 3 Dall. 171 (1796) was a case dealing with this very issue. As a means to understand the general issue in *Hylton*, the Act in question provided that a tax shall be laid upon carriages used for the conveyance of people.[245] The Court declared the Act to be constitutional because the tax was an indirect tax and thus did not need to be apportioned.[246] More importantly, the case is evidence that the subject of direct and indirect taxes went back to the early days of our republic.

Returning to *Pollock*, Chief Justice Fuller went on to list instances where the United States actually had laid direct taxes that were apportioned to the states, respectively. "By the act of July 14, 1798, when a war with France was supposed to be impending, a direct tax of two millions of dollars was apportioned

---

244	*Id.* at 557.
245	*Hylton*, 3 Dall. at 172.
246	*Id.* at 175.

to the States respectively...."[247] Chief Justice Fuller provided that the United States laid direct taxes apportioned to the states in 1813, 1815, and 1861 followed by multiple acts laying direct taxes between 1861 and 1870.[248] "These acts [those between 1861 and 1870] grew out of the war of the rebellion, and were, to use the language of Mr. Justice Miller, 'part of the system of taxing incomes, earnings, and profits adopted during the late war and abandoned as soon after that war was ended as it could be done safely.'"[249] At least according to Chief Justice Fuller and Justice Miller, the series of direct taxes laid between 1861 and 1870 were necessary due to the large debts incurred during the "war of the rebellion."[250]

In Chief Justice Fuller's opinion we see it explained that direct taxes were not unknown to the states and to their citizens. In fact, the United States had levied a substantial number of direct taxes beginning shortly after ratification of the Constitution. Instead, the issue in *Pollock* was levying direct taxes without apportionment, and it was this issue that would have significant effects on the balance of powers within the Constitution, which would of course affect the liberty of every individual. On that note, let us return to Chief Justice Fuller's opinion in *Pollock*.

Concerning the supposed use of direct taxes only during emergencies (although by no means expressed in the Constitution), Chief Justice Fuller provided:

> That the original expectation was that the power of direct taxation would be exercised only in extraordinary

---

247   *Pollock,* 157 U.S. at 572.
248   *Id.* at 573.
249   *Id.*
250   *Pollock,* 157 U.S. at 573.

exigencies, and down to August 1894, this expectation has been realized. The act of that date was passed in a time of profound peace, and if we assume that no special exigency called for unusual legislation, and that resort to this mode of taxation is to become an ordinary and usual means of supply, that fact furnishes an additional reason for circumspection and care in disposing of the case.[251]

Not only were there no exigent circumstances such as war, but there were also surpluses in the years leading up to 1894. According to James Bryce in *The American Commonwealth*, "[t]he Report of the Secretary of the Treasury for 1887 states the surplus in the treasury on 1st December of that year at $55,000,000, and estimates the surplus for the financial year ending 30th June 1888 under the law then in force at $140,000,000. For twenty-two years there have been surpluses, the smallest of $2,344,000 in 1874, the largest of $145,543,000 in 1882."[252]

Bryce commented further on the state of revenue of the central government in the mid 1880s. "The present state of things is evidently exceptional. America is the only country in the world whose difficulty is not to raise money but to spend it."[253] While discussing the formation of a party known as the Prohibitionists, he noted that ". . . the Federal government raises a large revenue by its high import duty on wines, spirits, and malt liquors, and also levies an internal excise. As this revenue is no longer needed for the expenses of the national government [certainly a strange

---

251   *Id.* at 574.
252   1 JAMES BRYCE, THE AMERICAN COMMONWEALTH 178 n.1 (Neil H. Alford et al. eds., Leslie B. Adams, Jr. The Legal Classics Library spec. ed. reprt. 1987) (1888).
253   *Id.* at 178 (footnote omitted).

concept based on the fiscal condition of the federal government today], it has been proposed to distribute it among the States, or apply it to some new and useful purpose, or to reduce both customs duties and the excise."[254] It would certainly seem, based on the comments from Chief Justice Fuller and Bryce, that there was no fiscal emergency making it necessary to institute a direct tax in 1894.

But like many things concerning human nature, there is rarely a lack of those who seek to use the force of law for a particular advantage. To emphasize what Chief Justice Fuller noted, there was no emergency that required the institution of a direct tax,[255] and according to Bryce, there was a general government surplus from the years 1866 to 1888. Chief Justice Fuller provided in his opinion that one of the contentions of the complainant was the following: "[t]hat the law in question, in imposing a tax on the income or rents of real estate, imposes a tax upon the real estate itself; and in imposing a tax on the interest or other income of bonds or other personal property held for the purposes of income or ordinarily yielding income, imposes a tax upon the personal estate itself; that such tax is a direct tax, and void because imposed without regard to the rule of apportionment; and that by reason thereof the whole law is invalidated."[256] So, despite no emergency or lack of revenue, the general government had passed into law a direct tax on certain incomes. If the traditional reasons, such as an emergency as expressed in *The Federalist*,[257]

---

254   2 JAMES BRYCE, THE AMERICAN COMMONWEALTH 13 (Neil H. Alford et al. eds., Leslie B. Adams, Jr. The Legal Classics Library spec. ed. reprt. 1987) (1888).
255   *Pollock*, 157 U.S. at 574.
256   *Pollock*, 157 U.S. at 555.
257   THE FEDERALIST No. 36, at 193 (Alexander Hamilton) (George Stade ed., Barnes & Noble, Inc. 2006).

1913: From General To Specific Welfare

were not the impetus for a direct income tax, what other potential causes could there be? One belief system, expressed by Karl Marx and carried on by the Labor Party in the United States, embraced an income tax as one of their tenets, and a slight digression is needed here to examine those beliefs.

In 1848 Karl Marx published his work, the *Manifesto of the Communist Party*. How much Marx influenced the Labor Party—who in turn promoted the tax act of 1894, which laid the groundwork for the composition of the 16th Amendment—is a topic for a separate examination. Because our point is not to examine who specifically desired the non-apportioned income tax, we won't dwell on the matter. The more important point is to examine the effects of the 16th Amendment, especially how it resulted in a transformation from general to specific welfare. For now, let us return to the means described by Marx to bring about the communist revolution.

> The communist revolution is the most radical rupture with traditional property relations; no wonder that its development involves the most radical rupture with traditional ideas.
>
> But let us have done with the bourgeois objections to communism.
>
> We have seen above that the first step in the revolution by the working class is to raise the proletariat to the position of ruling class, to win the battle of democracy.
>
> The proletariat will use its political supremacy to wrest, by

United States Constitution – Post-1913

degrees, all capital from the bourgeoisie, to centralize all instruments of production in the hands of the state, i.e., of the proletariat organized as the ruling class, and to increase the total of productive forces as rapidly as possible.

Of course, in the beginning this cannot be effected except by means of despotic inroads on the rights of property and on the conditions of bourgeois production; by means of measures, therefore, which appear economically insufficient and untenable, but which in the course of the movement, outstrip themselves, necessitate further inroads upon the old social order, and are unavoidable as a means of entirely revolutionizing the mode of production.

These measures will of course be different in different countries.

Nevertheless, in the most advanced countries the following will be pretty generally applicable:

1. Abolition of property in land and application of all rents of land to public purposes.
2. *A heavy progressive or graduated income tax* [emphasis added].
3. Abolition of all right of inheritance.
4. Confiscation of the property of all emigrants and rebels.
5. Centralization of credit in the hands of the state, by means of a national bank with state capital and an exclusive monopoly.
6. Centralization of the means of communication and transportation in the hands of the state.

7. Extension of factories and instruments of production owned by the state; the bringing into cultivation of wastelands, and the improvement of the soil generally in accordance with a common plan.

8. Equal liability of all to labor. Establishment of industrial armies, especially for agriculture.

9. Combination of agriculture with manufacturing industries; gradual abolition of the distinction between town and country, by a more equable distribution of the population over the country.

10. Free education for all children in public schools. Abolition of children's factory labor in its present form. Combination of education with industrial production, etc.[258]

Obviously Marx's philosophic, economic, and governmental system was vastly different from that espoused in the Constitution. Nonetheless, one important aspect of the Constitution's system was that it did not prohibit someone with Marxist beliefs from advocating their platform, though there are elements of the Constitution that would make implementation of Marx's beliefs impossible. To cover only a few, the Constitution was a document with only enumerated powers. Therefore, from the perspective of the central government, many of his means would need far-reaching Amendments to the Constitution. His advocacy for the abolishment of private land and the confiscation of all emigrant property would have been difficult to reconcile with the rest of the Constitution, even if codified in any specific

---

[258] KARL MARX & FREDERICK ENGELS, *Communist Manifesto*, in ECONOMIC AND PHILOSOPHIC MANUSCRIPTS OF 1844 AND THE COMMUNIST MANIFESTO 230-31 (Martin Milligan trans., Prometheus Books 1988) (1847).

amendment. Even still, in 1913, the 16th Amendment was ratified and became a part of the Constitution despite the fact that its effects still did not reconcile with the rest of the Constitution. Let us now continue with the lead up to it by including the platform and desires of the Labor party in the late 1880s and early 1890s.

The Labor Party superseded the Greenback Party, which held a Nominating Convention in 1876. The Greenback Party also put forward candidates in 1880 and 1884. As Bryce noted:

> The Labour party has of late years practically superseded the Greenbackers, and seems to have now drawn itself such adherents as that party retained. . . . Speaking generally, the reforms advocated by the leaders of the Labour party include the "nationalization of the land," the imposition of a progressive income tax, the taking over of railroads and telegraphs by the National government, the prevention of the immigration of Chinese and of any other foreign labourers who may come under contract, the restriction of all so-called monopolies, the forfeiture (where legally possible) of railroad land grants, the increase of the currency, the free issue of inconvertible paper, and above all, the statutory restriction of hours of labour.[259]

While there are general similarities between Marx's pronouncements and the tenets of the Labor Party, the specific similarity concerning income taxes is nearly an exact match. Though the Labor Party was not the only group seeking an income tax,

---

259 JAMES BRYCE, THE AMERICAN COMMONWEALTH 11-12 (Neil H. Alford et al. eds., Leslie B. Adams, Jr. The Legal Classics Library spec. ed. reprt. 1987) (1888).

they were obviously one group who did advocate such a tax during a period where there was neither an emergency nor a significant revenue shortfall. Something so transformational to the foundation of government does not happen by chance; it happens through purposeful and relentless effort. The point for now is to simply make note of a couple of the groups who staunchly advocated the principle of the 16th Amendment. With that, let us return to Chief Justice Fuller's insightful opinion on direct taxation.

> The men who framed and adopted that instrument had just emerged from the struggle for independence whose rallying cry had been that 'taxation and representation go together.' The mother country had taught the colonists, in the contests waged to establish that taxes could not be imposed by the sovereign except as they were granted by the representatives of the realm, that self-taxation constituted the main security against oppression. As Burke declared, in his speech on Conciliation with America, the defenders of the excellence of the English constitution 'took infinite pains to inculcate, as a fundamental principle, that, in all monarchies, the people must, in effect, themselves, mediately or immediately, possess the power of granting their own money, or no shadow of liberty could subsist.' The principle was that the consent of those who were expected to pay it was essential to the validity of any tax.
>
> ... they [the States] were careful to see to it that taxation and representation should go together, so that the sovereignty reserved should not be impaired, and that when

Congress, and especially the House of Representatives, where it was specifically provided that all revenue bills must originate, voted a tax upon property, it should be with the consciousness, and under the responsibility, that in so doing the *tax so voted would proportionately fall upon the immediate constituents of those who imposed it* [emphasis added].[260]

Chief Justice Fuller then succinctly addressed the first question to be considered.

The first question to be considered is whether a tax on the rents or income of real estate is a direct tax within the meaning of the Constitution. Ordinarily, all taxes paid primarily by persons who can shift the burden upon someone else, or who are under no legal compulsion to pay them, are considered indirect taxes; but a tax upon property holders in respect of their estates, whether real or personal, or of the income yielded by such estates, and the payment of which cannot be avoided, are direct taxes.[261]

Chief Justice Fuller added:

Nevertheless, it may be admitted that, this definition of direct taxes is *prima facie* correct, and to be applied in the consideration of the question before us, yet that the Constitution may bear a different meaning, and that such different meaning must be recognized. But in arriving at

---

260   *Pollock*, 157 U.S. at 556.
261   *Id.* at 558.

1913: From General To Specific Welfare

any conclusion upon this point, we are at liberty to refer to the historical circumstances attending the framing and adoption of the Constitution as well as the entire frame and scheme of the instrument, and the consequences naturally attendant upon the one construction or the other.

We inquire, therefore, what, at the time of the Constitution was framed and adopted, were recognized as direct taxes? What did those who framed and adopted it understand the terms to designate and include?

We must remember that the fifty-five members of the constitutional convention were men of great sagacity, fully conversant with governmental problems, deeply conscious of the nature of their task, and profoundly convinced that they were laying the foundations of a vast empire. . . .

The Federalist demonstrates the value attached by Hamilton, Madison, and Jay to historical experience, and shows that they had made a careful study of many forms of government. Many of the framers were particularly versed in the literature of the period, Franklin, Wilson, and Hamilton, for example. Turgot had published in 1764 his work on taxation, and in 1766 his essay on "The Formation and Distribution of Wealth," while Adam Smith's "Wealth of Nations" was published in 1776. Franklin in 1766 had said upon his examination before the House of Commons that: 'An external tax is a duty laid on commodities imported; that duty is added to the first cost and other charges on the commodity, and, when it is offered to sale makes a part of the price. If the people do not like it at that price, they refuse it; they are not obliged to pay it. But an internal tax is forced from the people without their consent, if not laid by their own representatives. The stamp act says, we shall have no commerce, make no exchange of property with each other, neither purchase nor grant, nor recover debts; we shall neither marry nor make our wills, unless we pay such and such sums; and thus it is intended to extort our money from us or ruin us by the consequences of refusing to pay."[262]

Chief Justice Fuller proceeded to give more historical examples to further explain and clarify the meaning of direct taxes and indirect taxes, including the critical link between taxation and representation on the one hand, and apportionment, direct taxes, and liberty on the other.

Perhaps former Secretary of the Treasury, Albert Gallatin, best summarized the concepts when he said in his *Sketch of the Finances of the United States*, published in 1796:

> The most generally received opinion, however, is that, by direct taxes in the Constitution, those are meant which are raised on the capital or revenue of the people; by indirect, such as are raised on their expense. As that opinion is, in itself, rational and confirmable to the decision which has taken place on the subject of the carriage tax [Hylton], and as it appears important, for the sake of preventing future controversies, which may be not more fatal to the revenue than to the tranquility of the Union, that

---

[262]   Id. at 558-59.

a fixed interpretation should be generally adopted, it will not be improper to corroborate it by quoting the author from whom the idea seems to have been borrowed. The remarkable coincidence of the clause of the Constitution with this passage in using the word "capitation" as a generic expression, including the different species of direct taxes, an acceptation of the word peculiar, it is believed, to Dr. Smith, leaves little doubt that the framers of the one had the other in view at the time, and that they, as well as he, by direct taxes, meant those paid directly from, and falling immediate on, the revenue, and, by indirect, those which are paid indirectly out of the revenue by falling immediately upon the expense.[263]

With regards to the first question arising from the contention of the claimant, Chief Justice Fuller summarized the opinion with the following:

Nothing can be clearer than that what the Constitution intended to guard against was the exercise by the general government of the power of directly taxing persons and property within any State through a majority made up from the other States. It is true that the effect of requiring direct taxes to be apportioned among the States in proportion to their population is necessarily that the amount of taxes on the individual taxpayer in a State having the taxable subject-matter to a larger extent in proportion to its population than another State has, would be less than in such other State, but this inequality must be held to have

---
263   *Id.* at 569-70.

been contemplated, and was manifestly designed to operate to restrain the exercise of the power of direct taxation to extraordinary emergencies, and to prevent an attack upon accumulated property by mere force of numbers.

It is not doubted that property owners ought to contribute in just measure to the expenses of the government. As to the States and their municipalities, this is reached largely through the imposition of direct taxes. As to the Federal government, it is attained in part through excises and indirect taxes upon luxuries and consumption generally, to which direct taxation may be added to the extent the rule of apportionment allows. And through one mode or the other, the entire wealth of the country, real and personal, may be made, as it should be, to contribute to the common defence and general welfare.

But the acceptance of the rule of apportionment was one of the compromises which made the adoption of the Constitution possible, and secured the creation of that dual form of government, so elastic and so strong, which has thus far survived in unabated vigor. If, by calling a tax indirect when it is essentially direct, the rule of protection could be frittered away, one of the great landmarks defining the boundary between the Nation and the States of which it is composed, would have disappeared, and with it one of the bulwarks of private rights and private property.

We are of the opinion that the law in question, so far as it levies a tax on rents or income of real estate, is in violation of the Constitution, and is invalid.[264]

Despite the fact that the Supreme Court noted the significance of the link between direct taxes and apportionment, the 16th Amendment was ratified. "The Congress shall have power to lay and collect taxes on incomes, from whatever source derived, without apportionment among the several States, and without regard to any census or enumeration."[265] With a clear understanding of liberty's reliance on apportionment of direct taxes, the 16th Amendment should make anyone who holds liberty dear shudder in disbelief.

The general government always had the power to lay and collect such a tax. However, because a direct tax was considered so onerous, and because such a tax was so pivotal to liberty, it had previously required apportionment. Based on what Secretary Gallatin believed to be a word whose meaning Adam Smith had created, an income tax—from whatever source derived and which had been clearly understood to be a direct tax—was suddenly excluded from the requirement of apportionment. In light of the importance placed on apportionment of direct taxes, of which income had certainly been considered a part, it should be obvious that severing the requirement of income from apportionment would have significant ramifications to the balance of power among the general government, the states (discounting for now the 17th Amendment of the same year), and the people. When combined with the Federal Reserve Act, the balance of power became even more skewed, but for now we will focus on the effects of the 16th Amendment.

---

264 *Id.* at 582-83.
265 U.S. Const. amend. XVI.

Section II: Effects of the 16th Amendment

In this section, we will only concentrate on two key aspects of today's effects:

1) Over the last 40 years, the federal income tax has provided approximately 45 percent of the revenue of the federal government, which as the Court held in *Pollock* in 1895, would have required apportionment if not for the 16th Amendment.[266] For this large proportion of governmental revenue that is non-apportioned, the link between taxation and representation has effectively been severed; and

2) A contemporary application of the 16th Amendment allows for taxes to be used to grant special privileges and/or favors versus only ". . . to pay the Debts and provide for the common Defence and general Welfare of the United States. . . ."[267] Along with severing taxation and representation, the 16th Amendment significantly altered the balance of power between the governed and governors. When the power between the governed and the governors is not in balance, then the governed have lost their liberty, which begins the process of instituting tyranny. If securing rights and liberty requires linking a representative's power to levy and collect direct taxes with apportionment, then allowing a direct tax to be levied by representatives from the several States without any requirement to face election from the citizens upon whom they levy a direct tax has severed a significant safeguard to secure rights and liberty. Let us now turn our examination to the first effect.

---

266 *Fiscal Year 2017 Budget of the U.S. Government: Historical Tables*, Table 2.2-Percentage Composition of Receipts by Source: 1934-2021, Office of Management and Budget, *available at* https://www.whitehouse.gov/sites/default/files/omb/budget/fy2017/assets/hist.pdf (last visited Nov. 28, 2016).

267 U.S. Const. art. I, § 8, cl. 1.

1913: From General To Specific Welfare

As defined by Adam Smith, Chief Justice Fuller, and Benjamin Franklin, direct taxes encompass things that would provide vast sources of revenue. However, the access to this vast revenue was intended to be painful upon those who paid it through apportionment, who then passed that pain to their representatives by not re-electing them. In the context of people seeking to maximize their satisfactions, it is not difficult to imagine legislators seeking to make the access to the revenue less painful to themselves in an effort to make generating revenue easier. For this reason, combined with the fact that direct taxes are so onerous due to their unavoidability, the founders of the Constitution required their apportionment. When this prohibitive requirement is lifted, is there any wonder that the percentage of direct taxes in the form of income has risen to approximately 45 percent of all governmental revenue?[268] To expect anything else would be akin to transforming a law of nature—an impossibility. Any reasonable person would expect that when the restrictions placed on the means to such a vast source of wealth—in this case, income—are erased, human nature dictates that the level of tax on that income will rise.

Additionally, the amount of wealth that a government is able to generate with indirect taxes is limited since a tax beyond a certain limit will result in less revenue.[269] The Founders understood this principle, which is why indirect taxes were not subject

---

268   *Fiscal Year 2017 Budget of the U.S. Government: Historical Tables*, Table 2.2-Percentage Composition of Receipts by Source: 1934-2021, OFFICE OF MANAGEMENT AND BUDGET, *available at* https://www.whitehouse.gov/sites/default/files/omb/budget/fy2017/assets/hist.pdf (last visited Nov. 28, 2016).

269   *See* ADAM SMITH, THE WEALTH OF NATIONS 1121 (Edwin Cannan ed., Bantam Books 2003) (1776) (noting that "[w]hen the diminution of revenue is the effect of the diminution of consumption, there can be but one remedy, and that is the lowering of the tax").

to apportionment. It was within the power and will of the individual to simply abstain from purchasing that particular item and subsequently avoid the collateral indirect tax.

As stated previously, the conditions of liberty will naturally promote a significant increase in aggregate wealth. Substantial wealth draws those with a particular interest who want a part of it. Remembering the methods people employ to maximize their satisfactions, it's not surprising to see a government, comprised of men and women, employ slow and incremental steps to eventually attain the power to tax incomes directly without apportionment among the states. Once the power has been attained, there is no easy remedy to undo the tax. The established mechanism for redress (election of new representatives because the previous batch were responsible for the large, apportioned direct taxes) is broken. There is little to stop the continuing increase in direct taxes until there is no wealth left to tax. When circumstances reach that point, then the institution undergoes reform, peacefully or otherwise. In summary, one effect of the 16th Amendment is that approximately 45 percent of all federal government revenue is attained through what are non-apportioned direct taxes. Once this amendment was ratified, such an outcome was easily predicted.

Let's move on to the second effect previously noted: the contemporary application of the 16th Amendment that allows for taxes to be used to grant special privileges and favors versus only ". . . to pay the Debts and provide for the common Defence and general Welfare of the United States. . . ."[270]

Of course any tax has an upper limit. It is similar to the adage of killing the goose that laid the golden egg. If in an effort

---

270   U.S. CONST. art. I, § 8, cl. 1.

1913: From General To Specific Welfare

to achieve the maximum revenue possible, the government exceeds a specific limit, then instead of maximizing the revenue the result may very well be a total loss of all revenue from that source. This principle is easier to see when applied to an indirect tax than a direct tax. When an indirect tax makes the purchase price too high, the consumer has the liberty of refraining from purchasing. That is not necessarily the case with a direct tax, even more so when it is a non-apportioned direct tax. Therefore, a more in-depth examination is necessary of the income tax, which was and is commonly understood to be a direct tax.

When direct taxes were apportioned, the remedy to express displeasure with a high tax was through electing different representatives every two years in the House. This process required time to rectify a perceived grievance, but it was a straightforward process to express displeasure and used to abolish the tax. Today, however, the option of expressing displeasure via electing a different representative is basically pointless because income taxes are not apportioned

Even still, there is obviously a limit to how high a government may levy a direct tax. Rebellions and insurrections in our own history have occurred because of onerous taxation with no other option for redress.[271] As mentioned, this is generally not the case with indirect taxes that are set beyond what the citizens are willing to pay. Instead, a significantly high indirect tax oftentimes results in less revenue as people abstain from exchanging it.

Based upon the just-mentioned considerations, it is likely that a government may prefer to levy a higher direct tax than an indirect tax. The individual has essentially no lawful means to

---

271   The Whiskey Rebellion and the War of Independence against King George are two examples.

avoid the tax and no means to change it. If people exert force as a means to resist what is considered an onerous direct tax, then the ramifications to the people and the government become much more severe.[272] Now consider the distinction between apportioned and non-apportioned direct taxes. With a non-apportioned direct tax, it effectively removes the ability to change or eliminate an onerous tax. If we compare the three methods of taxation—indirect taxes; direct and apportioned taxes; and direct non-apportioned taxes—we can say that a non-apportioned direct tax is the means that allows a government to levy the highest tax of the three.

An understanding of this principle allows us to see how taxation takes on a completely different purpose than the purpose stipulated in the Constitution: ". . . to pay the Debts and provide for the common Defence and general Welfare of the United States. . . ."[273] By having the power to levy a tax that nearly all the people must pay, the government can set a level of taxation above that necessary for the required revenue. Once the level has been set, then special interests can influence cooperative politicians to carve away deductions while still generating the required revenue (discounting the current practice of running large deficits, which is more of a function of the monetary system than of fiscal conditions).

Interestingly, this practice of diverting tax revenue for special interests is at least as old as the late 1700s, and Adam Smith provides his reflections on the same practice. The only difference

---

272   An understanding of this principle by the Founding Fathers is evidenced in the requirement for direct taxes to be apportioned coupled with all bills for generating revenue originating in the House whose members faced election every two years. Obviously, the ratification of the 16th Amendment severed this balance.
273   U.S. CONST. art. I, § 8, cl. 1.

is that he uses the term "mercantile," which is rarely used today, whereas today we use similar words or phrases such as lobbying or special interests. As Smith wrote, "[t]he saying of Dr. Swift, that in the arithmetic of the customs two and two, instead of making four, make sometimes only one, holds perfectly true with regard to such heavy duties, which never could have been imposed, had not the mercantile system taught us, in many cases, to employ taxation as an instrument not of revenue, but of monopoly."[274]

Machiavelli, circa 1532 in *The Prince*, noted a similar principle concerning the relationship between taxes and exemptions. Machiavelli discussed a prince being thrifty so that he may be able to accomplish necessary functions without having to resort to raising taxes. He noted that people generally dislike being made to pay taxes, or alternatively prefer exemptions. Machiavelli's observation is certainly true today, and we provide this explanation to underscore the point.[275]

The instant that a deduction is instituted in the tax structure, the purpose of taxes has subtly, yet significantly changed. The purpose is no longer to pay debts but to instead provide favors to particular groups. The taxpayer may conclude that a deduction means the tax was never paid. However, that is not the case when viewed from a different perspective.

The following analogy shows the principle in play. If there were an indirect tax levied on the sale of corn and some of the tax was given to the growers of cotton (simply because someone successfully lobbied for such a transfer), then it would be

---

[274] ADAM SMITH, THE WEALTH OF NATIONS 1117-18 (Edwin Cannan ed., Bantam Books 2003) (1776) (citation omitted).
[275] NICCOLÒ MACHIAVELLI, THE PRINCE 49 (David Wootton ed. & trans., Hackett Publishing Company, Inc. 1995) (1532).

obvious that Article I, Section 8, Clause 1 of the Constitution prohibits such use of the tax.[276] In this example, the payment of tax money is not satisfying a debt and it is certainly not preventing external and internal threats to liberty. With the use of taxes in this manner, it would actually be establishing a usurpation of authority since Congress has no such power to grant this subsidy. Therefore, it certainly could not be providing for the general welfare, but rather, a specific welfare.

The same principle applies in the case of deductions. However, due to the nature of indirect actions, it is not readily apparent.[277] If we are provided with purchasing power (which is what granting an exemption to the taxes paid is), is the difference of any distinction to the recipient? Does it matter whether he receives a payment or is excluded from a payment when the end result is exactly the same from the standpoint of purchasing power? The answer is of course, no.

In the case of an income tax set at a particular rate with multiple exemptions, the taxpayers without the exemptions are providing purchasing power to those with the exemptions. This purchasing power does not pay a debt, and it certainly does not

---

[276] To see this principle clearly, one must discount the current understanding of the term "welfare," which has been masterfully transformed over the centuries by people seeking to maximize their satisfactions who also possess an understanding of human nature (one must admit that the transformation of the word "welfare" from 1788 to today is testament to John Locke's insights on the abuse of words). Instead one must substitute maximizing one's satisfaction, or happiness, in place of welfare. When combined with "general," it gives the impression of a sense of general happiness springing from the fact that each individual is at liberty to pursue actions to maximize their personal satisfactions. Taking from one to give a gift to another is special welfare for only one half of the two; securing the rights and subsequent liberty for both is providing welfare for both, or general welfare.

[277] *See* M. FREDERIC BASTIAT, ESSAYS ON POLITICAL ECONOMY 49-118 (G. P. Putnams & Sons 3rd ed. reprt. 1874) (explaining the seen versus unseen).

provide for the common defense or the general welfare. With regards to preventing internal threats to liberty, it actually accomplishes the opposite. Worse still, it is no longer merely a threat, but has evolved instead into an action that will destroy liberty. And even worse, it accomplishes this in a manner whose effects are indirect and nearly unseen.[278]

Because of the 16th Amendment, today we find ourselves in a situation where purchasing power in the form of tax exemptions is given to a plethora of certain special individuals or groups. Because the Constitution requires that taxes are only to be used to pay a debt, provide for the general defense, or provide for the general welfare, no one can honestly claim that such actions are in accordance with the Constitution.

Contemporary debate focuses on who should be granted the most purchasing power, whether it be in the form of who should pay more or who should be granted deductions. Rarely is the concept of re-instituting apportionment for direct taxes discussed. If the income tax were apportioned, do we believe that the situation of citizens of one state voting to take the money from those of another would continue for any appreciable amount of time, let alone 100 years?

---

[278] The use of credit cards and debit cards is a good example of how indirect and nearly unseen effects are tolerated while the same direct and seen effects are avoided. Today many people use debit cards and credit cards to make many of their everyday purchases. Often times the card company provides certain advantages to the user depending on how much money is spent or how often the card is used. The card company charges the merchant a fee for processing the card versus charging the purchaser. The merchant may simply raise the prices of his goods to compensate for the fee for using the card. (The merchant could simply add the fee to the purchase price when paid for with a card, but often times the merchant does not). Ultimately, the person who does not use the credit card pays a higher price than he normally would if no one used a credit/debit card.

Since 1913, people have invoked all of the tactics described above to maximize their satisfactions. Rarely is granting purchasing power to special groups viewed from the perspective of eradicating liberty. Instead, taxes remain non-apportioned, and the debate focuses on shifting tax burdens to those who have more than their fair share, despite the fact that eminent thinkers such as Adam Smith have noted that there is no such thing as fair or equal taxes. "Every tax, it must be observed once and for all, which falls finally upon one only of the three sorts of revenue above mentioned [rent, profit, or wages], is necessarily unequal, in so far as it does not affect the other two."[279]

Rhetoric is used to invoke an individual's passions. Advocates for revenue often claim it is needed for defense, the children, or the old. Remembering the power of an appeal to passions, especially sympathy, oftentimes the claims encompass all of the people whose downtrodden conditions are no fault of their own—the old, the very young, the mentally or physically handicapped.[280] When skillfully framed, a person who seeks to maximize his own interests sets the precedent for various methods of taxation by drawing attention to examples that invoke sympathy. Once the precedent has been set and the practice becomes routine, then slight shifts can be implemented to attain the original goal of diverting tax revenue for special interests, whatever those may be. These tactics are the same ones described resulting from the law of nature that all seek to maximize their own satisfactions. It's no surprise that with the ratification of the 16th Amendment, we find today that the collection of income taxes

---

[279] ADAM SMITH, THE WEALTH OF NATIONS 1043 (Edwin Cannan ed., Bantam Books 2003) (1776).
[280] See Part IV, Article II.

requires pages upon pages of complicated rules specifying who may claim certain deductions. Although the Constitution was written specifically to secure the blessings of liberty by progressing beyond a state of nature, the 16th Amendment has gone a long way towards returning us to a state of nature. No person's property is secure (in this case the fruits of their labor in the form of purchasing power from their income). Instead, there is no apportionment based upon our Congressional representatives, and seemingly the best that each of us can hope for is to secure special favors in the form of deductions and exemptions from the income tax. Our society has made one complete revolution. The Constitution began with using the law to secure our liberty, which in turn would lead to the ultimate end of any society: its general welfare. We have regressed to the point where law is now used as the source of tyranny with seemingly little opportunity for rectifying the situation. We have returned to a state of nature where it is every person for himself. Everyone uses the law as his or her means to secure special privileges for themselves or their group.

These oblique methods of taxation are in their own way a threat to liberty. However, such a threat pales in comparison to the roundabout methods of granting purchasing power as a result of our revised monetary system that began with the Federal Reserve Act of 1913, which is the next topic of discussion.

ARTICLE II: THE FEDERAL RESERVE ACT AND THE UNITED STATES MONETARY SYSTEM

And I sincerely believe with you that banking establishments are more dangerous than standing armies, and that the principle of spending money to be paid by posterity, under the name of funding, is but swindling futurity on a large scale. - Thomas Jefferson[281]

We will not speculate as to which of the three events under examination are most responsible for the transformation from general to specific welfare. But key to understanding that subject is making sense of the Federal Reserve System (FRS), which was the result of the Federal Reserve Act (FRA). The foundation of the FRS is the Federal Reserve Note (FRN). FRNs are more properly labeled currency but are commonly called money, which is what we will call FRNs to align with contemporary usage. Because FRNs are a purely manmade thing, they can be as labyrinthine or as straightforward as people make them.

After our previous examination of maximizing satisfactions, special knowledge, and the substantial power one may have by controlling the creation of more FRNs, it should not be surprising that the topic of money, and those things related to it, are difficult to understand. A topic this complex provides opportunities for special knowledge, which leads to opportunities for special privileges. On the other hand, when issues are explained in a manner that most people understand, then the opportunity for special privileges is minimized. In fact, a principle that was acknowledged and used in drafting the Constitution was to ensure the language was understandable by most, if not all. For if the language was to be unintelligible to its source of sovereign power (the people), who would believe that the people would remain the power behind the government?

So it follows that the topic of the FRS and its influence on

---

[281] THE POLITICAL WRITINGS OF THOMAS JEFFERSON 53 (Edward Dumbauld ed., The Bobbs-Merrill Company, Inc. 1955) (citing Jefferson's letter to John Taylor, Monticello, May 28, 1816).

the U.S. monetary system must be examined in a manner that is easily understood, and there are two options to accomplish that task. The first option would be to trace all the various legislation, executive orders, regulations, and codes that govern our monetary system from 1789 until the present day.[282] However, these laws are generally written in language specific to money and banking. With an advanced market economy and its accompanying advanced division of labor, relying on this option would be especially challenging to those who do not have specialized knowledge in money and banking specifics, or even a general understanding, for that matter.

Instead, we'll focus on the other option, which is key to understanding the effects of the FRS on our monetary system. This approach will explain the effects of the system as they occur *today*, in a manner that those outside of money and banking may understand. Ultimately, today's monetary structure is one of interests that receive special privileges and favors from those in a position to make law, create money, or both. The structure of the FRS, the notes used by the FRS, and the method used to create more of these notes are seemingly inscrutable and obscure.

So in this Article we will explain those three topics: the structure of the FRS, its notes, and the process of creating more of them via fractional reserve lending. These topics are explained primarily through the United States Code. By referring directly to the code, these three topics become surprisingly clear and easy to understand.

---

282 For two references that use that type of method, *see generally* EDWIN VIERA, Jr., PIECES OF EIGHT: THE MONETARY POWERS AND DISABILITIES OF THE UNITED STATES CONSTITUTION (RR Donnelly & Sons, Inc. 2d rev. spec. ed. 2011); MILTON FRIEDMAN & ANNA JACOBSON SCHWARTZ, A MONETARY HISTORY OF THE UNITED STATES, 1867-1960 (Princeton University Press 9th prtg. 1993) (1963).

Before going any further, it is necessary to explain one important aspect of the current monetary system as compared to the one in 1792: the ability to create new money now resides with the Federal reserve agents; on the other hand, during the origins of the United States it rested with the people as a whole, where Congress provided for "free coinage."[283] If we were to read some of the congressional debates concerning monetary powers that took place from 1789 until the present day, it is difficult to determine whether our reaction would be to laugh or cry.[284]

The power to create money is without a doubt a center of gravity. With a monetary system such as the one defined in the Coinage Act of 1792, the power to create money was left to the efforts of individuals acting in a market economy. Mining for gold or silver was subject to the price of the factors of production, those being labor, land, and capital. Interest rates were the result of individuals' time preferences along with a premium for uncertainty.[285] When the prices of the factors of production exceeded the price at which the good (in this case gold or silver) can be sold, then production would cease and the mines closed. The power of creating money was left in the hands of individuals based on their desire to increase holdings of money, which would lead to an increase in the purchasing power of money

---

[283] 1 EDWIN VIERA, Jr., PIECES OF EIGHT: THE MONETARY POWERS AND DISABILITIES OF THE UNITED STATES CONSTITUTION 191 (RR Donnelly & Sons, Inc. 2d rev. spec. ed. 2011).

[284] See generally id. at 461-70; 476-503; 529-53; 564-90.

[285] A person's time preference is simply a measure of how much a person prefers to consume in the present as compared to various times in the future. A strong desire to consume in the present results in a person being willing to pay a lender that much more in the future in order to access the lender's money in the present. On the other hand, where a person has a weak demand to consume in the present, such person will only borrow money for consumption when the rate of return is sufficiently low.

and a subsequent relative reduction in the prices of the goods and services that money will purchase. Nonetheless, the power to create paper currency is too enticing, and the structure of 1792 was eventually transformed to the current system where the Board of Governors of the FRS has the sole authority to issue new FRNs.[286]

Not only do individuals have a need for money, but governments also have a need as well. When we consider the government's need for money—vast amounts of it—and add to that the natural law we've examined, then that combination stokes the temptation of ethically compromised politicians willing to subvert the Constitution for personal gain. For individuals or groups seeking to secure special privileges, such politicians are a natural attraction. History shows too many instances of financiers aligning with such politicians.[287] The susceptible politicians grant the financiers the privilege to create paper money that will be used in some manner resembling legal tender. In return, the financiers pledge to provide funding for those same politicians. With regards to the people, it matters little whether a private entity, governmental entity, or some other similar form creates the paper currency. In the end, liberty is sacrificed to the special privileges of the entity creating the paper and those entities that receive the new paper first.

With history as a guide, it is probable that if not for the FRA, some other similar act would have occurred with similar results. Nonetheless, we will use the FRA as a significant causal event

---

286 12 U.S.C. § 411 (2012).
287 *See* CHARLES MACKAY, EXTRAORDINARY POPULAR DELUSIONS & THE MADNESS OF CROWDS 1-91 (Three Rivers Press reprt. 1980) (1841) (describing the details of John Law's and the South Sea Company's plans for financing government debt).

that led to today's system. Because human nature is such that all people will act to maximize their satisfaction, it was inevitable that we would devolve to the present monetary system. In that same vein, it is inevitable that we will eventually migrate beyond that to a financial state similar to that of 1789.

Before continuing to the structure of the FRS, we must explain fractional reserve lending. Fractional reserve lending is not something we find explicitly labeled as such in the FRA. Instead, the term "reserve ratios" is used, which is a basis for "reserve lending." This is another way to state that loans may be made from existing deposits with only a fraction of the deposit held as a reserve, should the depositor attempt to claim it. Thus, fractional reserve lending, or more properly only a fractional reserve for deposits, plays a significant role in our present monetary system, especially because this practice plays a crucial role in the transformation from general to specific welfare. It is doomed to fail at some point unless the thing being lent can be created at will at virtually no cost. As it stands today, the Federal Reserve Notes are the fractional reserves, and they are obligations of the Treasury.[288] There is virtually no limitation on how many may be created, although reaching the U.S. Government debt limit does to an extent create a limit. Even still, legislation has until now *always* been passed to increase the debt limit.

The significant problem for fractional reserve lending is, and always has been, a "run on the bank." However, in the case of the monetary system as it currently stands (although this was not the case in 1913), the issue of a lack of reserves can seemingly be averted. A central bank, or a lender of last resort, has so far

---

[288]   12 U.S.C. § 411 (2012) (providing that FRNs shall be obligations of the United States).

1913: From General To Specific Welfare

been able to obtain sufficient FRNs and provide them to their member banks to prevent such a run.[289]

One other point to emphasize is that regardless of one's opinion on other matters, we must acknowledge the foresight, persistence, and powers of persuasion of the individuals who created a central bank in 1913. A central bank, regardless of the initial intentions and selling points, is too much power to remain unabused. Human nature is such that eventually any useful instrument will be transformed into an institution. Despite this fact and the experiences of the people with the first two central banks, the advocates for a central bank were successful, which is impressive from that standpoint alone. The salient point is not how it was done, but the fact that the end was actually achieved, for a third time no less.[290] Now let us examine the structure of the FRS.

SECTION I: STRUCTURE OF THE FEDERAL RESERVE SYSTEM

Because the banking industry, which by its nature has a close association with money, wields such power, it deserves additional explanation before exploring the structure of the FRS. When an economy has advanced to the point where most if not all transactions involve money, then one half of each transaction deals with money. If one person or group has the power to create more money, then that entity controls its supply, or one half of the two factors that determine price (the other determining factor for

---

289   See Part V, Article II, Section III.
290   *See* 1 EDWIN VIERA, Jr., PIECES OF EIGHT: THE MONETARY POWERS AND DISABILITIES OF THE UNITED STATES CONSTITUTION 260 (RR Donnelly & Sons, Inc. 2d rev. spec. ed. 2011) (noting the first bank was incorporated in 1791 and the second in 1816).

price being demand). Before continuing on with the structure of the FRS, let us digress slightly to further investigate this important concept of setting the price of money, more specifically the manner in which control of the supply of money will result in the ability to set the price.

As described by Jesús Huerta de Soto and Murray Rothbard,[291] it is an individual's preference for present goods versus future goods that determines the pure interest rate.[292] Each individual's time preference taken together in aggregate comprises the pure interest rate, which manifests itself in the market interest rate, which takes into account numerous factors. The most appropriate label for these other factors that comprise the market rate of interest is uncertainty. In times of increased economic

---

291   See MURRAY ROTHBARD, MAN, ECONOMY, AND THE STATE: A TREATISE ON ECONOMIC PRINCIPLES WITH POWER AND MARKET 376 (Ludwig von Mises Institute 2nd ed. 2009) (defining the pure rate as "the going rate of time discount, the ratio of the price of present goods to that of future goods"); JESÚS HUERTA DE SOTO, MONEY, BANK CREDIT, AND ECONOMIC CYCLES 285 (Melinda A. Stroup trans., Ludwig von Mises Institute 2006) (defining "market price" as the price of present goods in relation to future goods versus using the term "pure interest rate").

292   The evidence is in the common adage that I will give you two hamburgers tomorrow for one hamburger today. We have already discussed the importance that needs and desires have, and how the satisfaction of needs or desires with goods and/or services is a key to giving them value. If I possess one unit of something that will satisfy one of my needs, then only something more dear will convince me to part with the opportunity to satisfy that need in the present. If we are only concerned with similar, or homogenous units, then to forego one unit today I will require some number more than one in the future. That is the basic principle expressed by the two authors noted previously concerning time preference and how each of us will prefer some good in the present compared to the same good in the future. Just for extra emphasis, this should not be misconstrued to mean that one would never observe someone giving to another a gift. Of course if one is fond of another, for example, one may very well give him or her the hamburger today for seemingly nothing in the future. However, that is taking numerous other considerations into account, and it is focusing on perhaps the seen (concrete) versus the abstract (unseen).

uncertainty, the rate of interest is higher than it would be with lower uncertainty.

However, we can't declare that an individual's time preference creates the pure interest rate, while on the other hand declare that the pure interest rate determines the time preference. That would be circular logic at its best. One key point to remember is that people react based in part on their perceptions of their surroundings. Although individual preference determines the pure interest rate and the subsequent market interest rate, the current market rate of interest could be, and likely is, a factor in setting the individual's time preference, which of course determines the pure interest rate in the future.

Therefore, if one entity has the power to set the interest rate (or price of money) by increasing the supply of money, then that same entity will likely affect the demand for money in the future as well. In this manner, that entity may control the price of money and subsequently the price of every good and service exchanged. That is quite an impressive power, one that can surely be used or abused. Additionally, it will undoubtedly attract those who are more inclined to use such a power for their own advantage versus those who place a higher value on liberty for all. But before we get too far ahead of ourselves, let us now return to the structure of the banking system.

The Federal Reserve System's structure is fairly easy to understand. All that is required is a careful reading of the United States Code, Title 12—more specifically, 12 U.S.C. §§ 221-63 (2012), which explains the nature and structure of the system. On that note, let us begin with an explanation of the basic structure of the FRS. We will start with what is effectively the preamble of the Federal Reserve Act, which was enacted in 1913, followed by excerpts from the United States Code.

The short title of the legislation is the Federal Reserve Act.²⁹³ Much like the Preamble to the Constitution, the Act begins by stating its purpose. "An Act To provide for the establishment of Federal reserve banks, to furnish an elastic currency, to afford means of rediscounting commercial paper, to establish a more effective supervision of banking in the United States, and for other purposes."²⁹⁴

Consider the purpose "to furnish an elastic currency" in comparison to the Constitution's reference to the dollar²⁹⁵ and the Coinage Act of 1792 where the dollar is defined as 371 ¼ grams of fine silver.²⁹⁶ Perhaps the original intent of the FRA was not to covertly tax the people's wealth. Nonetheless, the contemporary application of an elastic currency (monetary policy) does exactly that, not to mention the effects of an elastic currency when combined with a "capital gains" tax (fiscal policy).²⁹⁷ With

---
293   12 U.S.C. § 226 (2012).
294   Federal Reserve Act, Dec. 23, 1913, ch. 6, 38 Stat. 251.
295   *See* U.S. CONST. art. I, § 9, cl. 1; U.S. CONST. amend. VII.
296   Coinage Act of 1792, ch. 16, § 9, 1 Stat. 246 (repealed 1982), *available at* http://memory.loc.gov/cgi-bin/ampage?collId=llsl&fileName=001/llsl001.db&recNum=369.
297   The first topic of this footnote is the government taking purchasing power unsuspectingly. The federal government secures additional purchasing power through the creation of its obligations that circulate as modern day "currency." The purchasing power is newly created without any reasonable expectation of redeeming the obligation in anything other than more obligations, which will be created in the same manner. What separates the government creating purchasing power with newly created paper from a counterfeiter is that the former is legal while the latter is not. Even still, both entities gain what they are seeking with their actions: purchasing power. The next topic is the subject of "capital gains." The phrase is in quotes since one may not necessarily gain any actual capital; the price may have simply increased due to the number of newly created units of currency. As an example, assume there is an ounce of gold that was originally purchased for 100 FRNs. This ounce will undoubtedly increase in price due to the continued debasement of the currency through more issuance of FRNs by the government. When one sells that same ounce

such an explicit purpose, we must then understand the benefits of an elastic currency and to whom the benefits accrue. If the benefits are to the people of the United States, why was an elastic currency not included as an enumerated power? Were those who drafted and ratified the Constitution not aware of an elastic currency, its benefits, and its effects?

From the previous excerpts concerning past experiments with paper and elastic currency, our Founders were well aware of both, and thoroughly rejected them.[298] Seeing that the advantages of an elastic currency, which in fact has meant the creation of additional currency, accrue to the entities who receive the new currency first (in this case the government and the members of the FRS), it is inconceivable that such a monetary system would be the means to the end of *general* welfare.[299] Instead,

---

say 10 years later for a nominal 150 FRNs, one is required to pay a capital gains tax on the difference in price between 100 and 150 FRNs. The physical ounce of gold did not materially change at all, yet the government is able to effectively gain a portion of the ounce's purchasing power through taxing what is labeled a capital gain. In fact, the government is taxing the result of a depreciation of the currency that they create with the stroke of a pen and then stamp with legal tender status. I leave the deduction to the reader as to whether such a monetary and fiscal system results in general or specific welfare and whether it secures or subverts the liberty of the citizens.

298 The usage of gold and silver as the basis for a monetary system actually does provide an elastic money supply. Both metals are subject to the forces of the market. A high demand for money increases its purchasing power, which results in an opportunity to profitably extract more from the earth. It is less reasonable to expect a destruction of existing gold and silver although it is not entirely impossible – just unrealistic. The point is that both gold and silver as well as FRNs are elastic although certainly to different degrees. The more significant distinction is who has the authority to create more of them: in the former it is the people and the government (for the government could certainly mine for gold and silver); in the latter it is only the government.

299 See generally JOHN MAYNARD KEYNES, A TRACT ON MONETARY REFORM 1-51 (BN Publishing reprt. 2008) (describing how increases in the supply of money affect different groups in different ways).

such measures would provide for the specific welfare of the government and the FRS. The Founders correctly opted to specify the dollar as a fixed and defined weight of silver. Market forces, by people purchasing or abstaining from purchasing a monetary unit, were left to determine the appropriate supply.

The explicit purpose "to afford means of rediscounting commercial paper" seems to imply that prior to this Act, there were no means of rediscounting commercial paper.[300] That was certainly not the case, as short of a prohibition barring other individuals or groups from rediscounting commercial paper, individual time preferences and the working of a market economy will always provide the means of rediscounting commercial paper. Of course, the market price for rediscounting such paper will be subject to individual time preferences. A more truthful purpose would be, "to afford means of rediscounting commercial paper at a rate more favorable to the desires of government and members of the FRS."

The Federal Reserve Act of 1913 solidified the foundation for our current banking industry and monetary system. Today, it is composed of 12 Federal reserve districts, and each district will have only one Federal reserve city.[301] "A Federal reserve bank shall include in its title the name of the city in which it is situated, as 'Federal Reserve Bank of Chicago[,]'"[302] as an example.

If there is a national banking association within that district, then it is required to subscribe to be a member of the FRS.[303]

---

[300] Where "discounting" is providing the present value of a security in the form of money in exchange for the commercial paper (or in other words, providing money in exchange for some type of security), and where "rediscounting" is simply doing the same with a security that has already been discounted once. A security could be rediscounted any number of times.
[301] 12 U.S.C. § 223 (2012).
[302] 12 U.S.C. § 225 (2012).
[303] 12 U.S.C. § 222 (2012).

Every national banking association within each Federal reserve district shall be required to subscribe to the capital stock of the Federal reserve bank for that district in a sum equal to six per centum of the paid-up capital stock and surplus of such bank, one-sixth of the subscription to be payable on call of the Board of Governors of the Federal Reserve System, one-sixth within three months and one-sixth within six months thereafter, and the remainder of the subscription, or any part thereof, shall be subject to call when deemed necessary by the Board, said payments to be in gold or gold certificates.[304]

Each Federal reserve bank is governed by a board of directors. The board of directors is composed of three classes: A, B, and C. Each class is composed of three directors for a total of nine directors.[305] The language from the United States Code is quoted because what is expressed is of significance. We have already examined the importance of representation and how the representative ultimately acts on behalf of those who selected or elected him or her. The United States Code specifies whom the directors are theoretically supposed to represent. However, despite what the Code provides concerning whom the directors are supposed to represent, each of the directors is selected or elected by the member banks of the Federal reserve district or the Federal Reserve Board of Governors. This situation raises the question of how the directors are expected to represent the public when the public has little input for the directors' appointments.

---

304   12 U.S.C. § 282(2012).
305   12 U.S.C. § 302 (2012).

Class A shall consist of three members, without discrimination on the basis of race, creed, color, sex, or national origin, who shall be chosen by and be representative of the stockholding banks.

Class B shall consist of three members, who shall represent the public and shall be elected without discrimination on the basis of race, creed, color, sex, or national origin, and with due but not exclusive consideration to the interests of agriculture, commerce, industry, services, labor, and consumers.

Class C shall consist of three members who shall be designated by the Board of Governors of the Federal Reserve System. They shall be elected to represent the public, without discrimination on the basis of race, creed, color, sex, or national origin, and with due but not exclusive consideration to the interests of agriculture, commerce, industry, services, labor, and consumers.[306]

Discounting the impossibility of simultaneously representing the interests of consumers and labor, who have nearly opposite interests, the preceding section seems to indicate that six of the nine members represent the public. However, when we consider the source and manner that each member is selected, we can see that these directors represent those who selected or elected them. The public is represented in name only.

---

[306] 12 U.S.C. § 302 (2012).

Directors of class A and class B shall be chosen in the following manner: The Board of Governors of the Federal Reserve System shall classify the member banks of the district into three general groups or divisions designating each group by number. Each group shall consist as nearly as may be of banks of similar capitalization. Each member bank shall be permitted to nominate to the chairman of the board of directors of the Federal reserve bank of the district one candidate for director of class A and one candidate for director of class B.[307]

Both class A and B directors are chosen by the same entities, the member banks. Whomever the class A and B directors are supposed to represent is immaterial if those directors expect to remain in the position beyond the initial term. Human nature being what it is, if the directors are not pursuing the interests of those whom they represent, then the member banks will likely choose someone who will.

Turning to the class C directors, these are chosen by the Board of Governors of the Federal Reserve System. They too are supposed to represent the public, but the improbability of this actually occurring has been expressed already due to the method of selection. "Class C directors shall be appointed by the Board of Governors of the Federal Reserve System. They shall have been for at least two years residents of the district for which they are appointed, one of whom shall be designated by said board as chairman of the board of directors of the Federal reserve bank and as 'Federal reserve agent.'"[308]

---

307   12 U.S.C. § 304 (2012).
308   12 U.S.C. § 305 (2012).

In summary, Class A members are chosen by banks and represent the member banks. Class B members are chosen by banks and are theoretically required to represent the public. Class C are chosen by the Board of Governors of the Federal Reserve System and are also theoretically required to represent the public. Even though none of the members are selected or elected by the public, despite this, six of the nine are supposed to represent the public.

Presiding over the structure of the 12 Federal reserve banks and their respective 12 Federal reserve districts is the Board of Governors of the Federal Reserve System (BoG). The Board of Governors is the portion of the system that makes the FRS a quasi-governmental institution since the Board is ". . . to be appointed by the President, by and with the advice and consent of the Senate. . . ."[309] It is currently composed of seven members. The duties of the Board of Governors are enumerated in 12 U.S.C. § 248. The more significant powers include, but are not limited to: 1) "[p]ermitting or requiring rediscounting of paper at specified rate"; 2) "[s]uspending reserve requirements"; and 3) "[s]upervising and regulating issue and retirement of notes[.]"[310]

The first power deals effectively with setting the market rate of interest, or the price of money due to the nature of the FRS. The second power deals with the amount of credit, which effectively acts as an additional stock of money, that member banks of the FRS are potentially able to create. The third power deals again with the power to regulate the supply of notes, which again effectively means the power to affect the total supply of money.

The Board of Governors also comprises 7 of the 12 members

---

309   12 U.S.C. § 241 (2012).
310   12 U.S.C. § 248(b), (c), (d) (2012).

of the Federal Open Market Committee (FOMC). The other five members of the FOMC are selected by the various boards of the Federal reserve banks. The purpose and duties of the FOMC and the BoG are the following: "[t]he Board of Governors of the Federal Reserve System and the Federal Open Market Committee shall maintain long run growth of the monetary and credit aggregates commensurate with the economy's long run potential to increase production, so as to promote effectively the goals of maximum employment, stable prices, and moderate long-term interest rates."[311] We will return to what is effectively the mission statement of the FRS, and continue the examination of the Board and the FOMC. At that point we will examine the means provided to accomplish the mission statement. For now, it is necessary to make a short detour from the FRS's structure to review some economic principles that will help us better understand the mission of the FRS.

SUBSECTION A: KEYNES' REFLECTIONS

At this point a review of the work by Mr. John M. Keynes is quite helpful because his ideas and principles are reflected in portions of the United States Code, specifically the purpose of the board and committee cited above. If Keynes' work was so important it was included in the mission of the FOMC and BoG, then it is certainly worthwhile to understand Mr. Keynes' beliefs.

The following analysis is taken from Keynes' books, *A Tract on Monetary Reform* and *The General Theory of Employment, Interest, and Money*. In the second book, Keynes notes that in a monetary economy, changes in future expectations not only change the direction of employment, but they change the

---

311   12 U.S.C. § 225a (2012).

quantity of employment as well. "A monetary economy, we shall find, is essentially one in which changing views about the future are capable of influencing the quantity of employment and not merely its direction."[312]

There is nothing groundbreaking with the observation that changing views about the future affect the direction of employment. Obviously, if workers expect that future pay in a particular line of work will increase, then they potentially may pursue that line of work. However, Keynes' more noteworthy observation concerns the aspect of influencing the quantity of employment. In this case, changing views about the future of a monetary economy may indirectly create an increase in workers who previously did not work at what they perceived to be a lower wage but who are now willing to work at what is believed to be a higher wage. This effect was Keynes' most significant observation: changes in nominal wages had a significantly different influence on employment than changes in real wages. This difference is key to Keynes' theory and to the mission of the BoG and the FOMC.

Let's pause to define the difference between a nominal and a real wage. A nominal wage is one based on how much you get paid, and a real wage is based on how much you can buy with what you were paid. Keynes used the term money-wage to represent what today we commonly label as labor's nominal price, and used wage-good to represent what we label today as the real wage.[313] The difference between money-wage (nominal

---

312 JOHN M. KEYNES, THE GENERAL THEORY OF EMPLOYMENT, INTEREST, AND MONEY 3 (Classic House Books reprt. 2008).
313 See id. at 9. Adam Smith in *The Wealth of Nations* summarizes the same notion but used real and nominal versus "wage-money" and "wage-goods," respectively. "In this popular sense, therefore, labour, like commodities, may be said to have a real and a nominal price. Its real price may be said to consist in the quantity of the necessaries and conveniences of life which are

wage) and wage-goods (real wage) is the heart of his theory, and because people often think of wages in money versus goods, a further explanation of wage-goods (real wage) is warranted.

As stated, the real wage is what a unit of labor will purchase in goods excluding money as a medium of exchange. Say for example, there are three items: an apple, money (measured in one ounce), and a unit of labor. One apple exchanges for one ounce, which exchanges for one unit of labor. Say there is a large increase in the number of ounces. Discounting all the other factors, we could expect the one unit of labor to now require more ounces in exchange. In other words, the money-wage (nominal wage) of labor will rise. Assuming that the relation between apples and labor has not changed, one unit of labor will still purchase one apple even though the entire relationship between apples, money, and labor has been altered by a change in the supply of money. In this sense, the nominal, or money-wage, is one way to measure the price of labor while another way is through the real wage, or what one unit of labor will purchase excluding money in that particular case. The point to understand is that the money-wage is the nominal price of labor and the wage-goods is the real price of labor.

Keynes noted that the classical economists' theories were based on an assumption that people not only understood the difference between real and nominal prices, but also that they could practically apply the distinction on a routine basis in their daily lives. The case considered by the classical economists was actually a special case of money-wages, and Keynes was articulating a *general* theory concerning real-wages. "I shall argue that

---

given for it; its nominal price, in the quantity of money." ADAM SMITH, THE WEALTH OF NATIONS 48 (Edwin Cannan ed., Bantam Books 2003) (1776).

the postulates of the classical theory are applicable to a special case only and not to the general case, the situation which it assumes being a limiting point of the possible positions of equilibrium. Moreover, the characteristics of the special case assumed by the classical theory happen not to be those of the economic society in which we actually live, with the result that its teaching is misleading and disastrous if we attempt to apply it to the facts of experience."[314]

Keynes further elaborates on this point by explaining that the classical economists have all along assumed that labor was using money-wages as their measuring stick. He also believed that there are some people who choose to remain voluntarily unemployed, based on the current nominal price for labor. Of those who remain voluntarily unemployed, he believes there is a tacit, or perhaps overt, agreement that prevents a lowering of the money-wage.

> For admittedly, more labour would, as a rule, be forthcoming at the existing money-wage if it were demanded. The classical school reconcile this phenomenon with their second postulate by arguing that, while the demand for labour at the existing money-wage may be satisfied before everyone willing to work at this wage is employed, this situation is due to an open or tacit agreement amongst workers not to work for less, and that if labour as a whole would agree to a reduction of money-wages more employment would be forthcoming.

---

[314] JOHN M. KEYNES, THE GENERAL THEORY OF EMPLOYMENT, INTEREST, AND MONEY 5 (Classic House Books reprt. 2008).

1913: From General To Specific Welfare

If this is the case, such unemployment, though apparently involuntary, is not strictly so, and ought to be included under the above category of 'voluntary' unemployment due to the effect of collective bargaining, etc.

This calls for two observations, the first of which relates to the actual attitude of workers towards real-wages and money-wages respectively and is not theoretically fundamental, but the second of which is fundamental."[315]

In other words, Keynes is simply acknowledging that labor follows the laws of supply and demand in the same manner as all other goods and services. When there are fluctuations in capital, labor, land, consumer goods or services, or the medium used to trade them, the real price of labor will rise or fall in relation to the others. Depending on the circumstances of the situation, the price of labor may need to fall in order to reach the price where surplus supply is cleared. Fortunately or unfortunately, depending on our view of the economy, the real price of labor tends to fall more slowly due to what Keynes attributed to a tacit, or perhaps overt, agreement among laborers not to work for less in nominal terms.

If it is possible to raise nominal prices of other goods and services, it will effectively lower the wage-goods (real) price of labor. This happens in a seemingly magical manner. The real-wage will be temporarily lowered, and unemployment will be lowered due to an increase in demand for labor at the new, reduced real-wage.

For a contemporary example of what Keynes is explaining,

---
315   *Id.* at 8-9.

this same principle can be seen by the way consumer goods are packaged. Sellers of packaged consumer goods realize that raising prices of goods has a detrimental impact on the demand. Sellers would like to sell at a higher price to generate a greater income, but the current price is what the market will bear. The sellers realize the same principle observed by Keynes. If the money price is raised, people easily identify the increase. If the money price remains the same but the quantity (by weight or volume) is reduced, then effectively the real price has been increased. The consumer is paying the same but receives less. The critical aspect for the seller is that a large number of the buyers do not notice the increase in the real price as many are only focused on the nominal price.

To elaborate further, let's assume that there is only one geographical area, or market, where people may purchase in one of two categories: meats or fruits. Assume that the money taken in exchange at the market is legal tender, which only one entity may create. And assume that all meats and fruits are for sale for 10 monetary units. Suppose that the entity that creates the legal tender desires to lower the price of fruits. The entity could achieve his goal through one of two methods: lowering the nominal price or the real price.

Lowering the nominal price is a fairly evident process. Instead of selling for 10 units, the entity now sells fruits for 9 units. Lowering the real price is accomplished in a more involved manner, using these following steps: the entity could create more money and give it to certain groups. However, in order to ensure the real price of fruits is reduced in relation to meat, the owner would need to stipulate that the new money may only be used to purchase meat. Using this approach, inevitably the price of meats would rise in relation to fruits; the nominal price of fruits would remain the same; and the real price of fruits (in relation to meats) would decrease.

If the entity uses the second option, then two points need further explanation. First, it makes no sense to give the newly created money to everyone. If that was the case, all that would likely happen is that the nominal-price level of the two categories would both rise. It is not possible to predict if the prices of the two categories will rise by the same amount, but it is reasonable to expect that the prices of both will rise. Secondly, to ensure that the real price of fruits is reduced, the entity must stipulate that the new money given to certain groups may only be used to purchase meat. Without this stipulation, the result may be the opposite of the intended goal. Nonetheless, by creating new money with this stipulation, the entity could achieve a reduced real price of fruits.

The following is another excerpt from Keynes where he explains this process:

> Let us assume, for the moment, that labour is not prepared to work for a lower money-wage and that a reduction in the existing level of money-wages would lead, through strikes or otherwise, to a withdrawal from the labour market of labour which is now employed. Does it follow from this that the existing level of real wages accurately measure the marginal disutility of labour? Not necessarily. For, although a reduction in the existing money-wage would lead to a withdrawal of labour, it does not follow that a fall in the value of the existing money-wage in terms of wage-goods would do so, if it were due to a rise in the price of

the latter. In other words, it may be the case that within a certain range the demand of labour is for a minimum money-wage and not for a minimum real-wage. The classical school have tacitly assumed that this would involve no significant change in their theory. But this is not so. . . .

Now ordinary experience tells us, beyond doubt, that a situation where labour stipulates (within limits) for a money-wage rather than a real wage, so far from being a mere possibility, is the normal case. Whilst workers will usually resist a reduction of money-wages, it is not their practice to withdraw their labour whenever there is a rise in the price of wage-goods. It is sometimes said that it would be illogical for labour to resist a reduction of money-wages but not to resist a reduction of real wages. For reasons given below (p.14), this might not be so illogical as it appears at first; and, as we shall see later, fortunately so. But, whether logical or illogical, experience shows that this is how labour in fact behaves.[316]

Keynes also explains the means that may be used to achieve the end he has expressed: the creation of money and its subsequent influence on interest rates. Before examining his explanation of interest rates as a tool to achieve his proposed end, we must make yet another brief detour to explain the importance and effects of some entity (such as the government) setting an artificial price that is either above or below the price set by the market.

Say the market price for a particular car is 1,000 units, but

---

316   Id. at 9-10.

the government fixes the price at 900 units. The artificial price fixed by the government is below the market price, and an artificial maximum price will result in more demand from those who would otherwise be unable to purchase the car. The artificial maximum price will result in shortages of cars due to the government fixing the price. Conversely, if the government fixed a minimum price of 1,200 units, then there would be a surplus of cars due to less demand at that more expensive price. In one case cars are overvalued with a resulting surplus, and in the other case are undervalued and in a shortage.

Returning to Keynes' idea of using money and interest rates to move the real price of labor, he noted that every individual has a purpose for holding savings in the form of cash. One significant reason is due to cash's quality of being perhaps the most liquid form of money. Keynes details a few reasons why people may hold cash, but ultimately it is a result of individuals' beliefs that they feel cash is best suited to achieve whatever end they have in mind.[317]

Keynes also noted that if a person receives additions to his income without any change to his desire to consume or to hold savings in the form of cash, then that "surplus" money must go somewhere.[318] Based on Keynes' theory, when the surplus is channeled into investments, or capital, it results in a lowering of the rate of interest.[319] Therefore, when some entity creates an additional supply of money, there will be a surplus that drives up the price of capital, which will relatively lower the real price

---

317   JOHN MAYNARD KEYNES, A TRACT ON MONETARY REFORM 75 (BN Publishing reprt. 2008).
318   Id. at 75-76.
319   JOHN M. KEYNES, THE GENERAL THEORY OF EMPLOYMENT, INTEREST, AND MONEY 323 (Classic House Books reprt. 2008).

of wages (quite similar to the example of meats and fruits). The lower real price of wages will result in lower unemployment.

When the money supply has been expanded, in the long run the prices of land, labor, capital, and the goods and/or services they provide will shift towards a new equilibrium. However, it is in the short run where Keynes' theory has the more observable effects. In the long run, of course, conditions will seek equilibrium. However, it is the short run where policy makers may influence change with focused action. "*In the long run* we are all dead. Economists set themselves too easy, too useless a task if in tempestuous seasons they can only tell us that when the storm is long past the ocean is flat again."[320] Keynes simply articulated a theory about what may be done, which history has demonstrated is possible in the short run. Even still, interventions in the short run to seemingly solve present problems will inevitably create long run problems that otherwise would have never been created—a paradox indeed.

These practices are simply fixing the price of money using the same principles concerning overvaluing and undervaluing. The difference is that for Keynes' processes to achieve their end, a large portion of wage earners must not realize what has been overvalued and undervalued in relation to the market price. Realistically though, some small portion of society will have special knowledge of what is happening. In the circumstances described by Keynes, the intention is that it is difficult to determine that real wages have been decreased in relation to land and capital. Even still, the effects of price fixing will eventually appear; the only question is when.

---

320   JOHN MAYNARD KEYNES, A TRACT ON MONETARY REFORM 80 (BN Publishing reprt. 2008).

Keynes did note that this process of expanding the money supply to lower interest rates and increase employment has some disadvantages. Prior to Keynes' reflections on his general theory, he wrote the following:

> Lenin is said to have declared that the best way to destroy the Capitalist System was to debauch the currency. By a continuing process of inflation, governments can confiscate, secretly and unobserved, an important part of the wealth of their citizens. By this method they not only confiscate, but they confiscate *arbitrarily;* and, while the process impoverishes many, it actually enriches some. The sight of this arbitrary rearrangment of riches strikes not only at security, but at confidence in the equity of the existing distribution of wealth. . . . As the inflation proceeds and the real value of the currency fluctuates wildly from month to month, all permanent relations between debtors and creditors, which form the ultimate foundation of capitalism, become so utterly disordered as to be almost meaningless; and the process of wealth-getting degenerates into a gamble and a lottery.[321]

Keynes also explained these disadvantages, or advantages depending on who is receiving the money first, quite eloquently in his book, *A Tract on Monetary Reform*.[322] Despite the ramifications of his theory concerning money, interest, and employment,

---

321 JOHN MAYNARD KEYNES, THE ECONOMIC CONSEQUENCES OF THE PEACE 134 (Skyhorse Publishing reprt. 2007) (1919).
322 *See* JOHN MAYNARD KEYNES, A TRACT ON MONETARY REFORM 5-32 (BN Publishing reprt. 2008) (describing the effects of changes in the value of money on the investing class, the business class, and the earning class).

his theory is the foundation for the purpose of the BoG and the FOMC. To continue with the means he proposed to achieve the end, the following excerpts traced his thoughts concerning the use of money to affect the interest rate.

> The justification for a moderately high rate of interest has been found hitherto in the necessity of providing a sufficient inducement to save. But we have shown that the extent of effective saving is necessarily determined by the scale of investment and that the scale of investment is promoted by a low rate of interest, provided that we do not attempt to stimulate it in this way beyond the point which corresponds to full employment. Thus it is to our best advantage to reduce the rate of interest to that point relatively to the schedule of the marginal efficiency of capital at which there is full employment.[323]

In the particular case of his general theory, he acknowledged that his theory would require expansive powers of some entity, whether it be a government or a central bank. "The central controls necessary to ensure full employment will, of course, involve a large extension of the traditional functions of government."[324] In some of his other writings, he was certainly aware of human nature, and humanity's propensity to maximize their satisfactions.[325] However, in his general theory, he did not pay much

---

323   JOHN M. KEYNES, THE GENERAL THEORY OF EMPLOYMENT, INTEREST, AND MONEY 323 (Classic House Books reprt. 2008).
324   *Id.* at 328.
325   *See generally* JOHN MAYNARD KEYNES, A TRACT ON MONETARY REFORM 41 (BN Publishing reprt. 2008) (noting how people in government have often resorted to printing money as a means of taxation when the government could survive by no other means); JOHN MAYNARD KEYNES, THE

respect to the fundamental law of nature. Furthermore, in this section of his general theory, he did not acknowledge Lord Acton's observation that there is a tendency for absolute power to corrupt absolutely, nor did he acknowledge Washington's quip that few have the virtue to outlast the highest bidder. Instead, he explained the benefits of granting such power over money to a government without much mention of the potential for abuse.

> Whilst, therefore, the enlargement of the functions of government, involved in the task of adjusting to one another the propensit[y] to consume and the inducement to invest, would seem to a nineteenth-century publicist or to a contemporary American financier to be a terrific encroachment on individualism, I defend it, on the contrary, both as the only practicable means of avoiding the destruction of existing economic forms in their entirety and as the condition of the successful function of individual initiative.[326]

The point of explaining Keynes' reflections on his general theory was only to provide context to the structure and purpose of the FRS. Keynes did not devote much of his general theory to its compatibility with the U.S. Constitution. Nonetheless, his reflections are important in order to understand the expressed purpose of the BoG and FOMC, or what is essentially the mission of the FRS.

What Keynes detailed is how an entity may achieve conditions

ECONOMIC CONSEQUENCES OF THE PEACE 134 (Skyhorse Publishing reprt. 2007) (1919) (noting how people in government may confiscate a citizen's wealth in a stealthy manner through inflation).

326   JOHN M. KEYNES, THE GENERAL THEORY OF EMPLOYMENT, INTEREST, AND MONEY 328-29 (Classic House Books reprt. 2008).

of full employment, stable prices, and low interest rates, which are all dependent upon the definitions affixed to each concept. This happens by increasing the supply of money, which will likely lower the price of money (interest rates) in relation to what the interest rate would have been without the addition of new money. This will hopefully raise the nominal price of capital and land, which will lower the real price of labor.

Voilà! Full employment, stable prices, and low interest rates!

The tradeoff is that a group of 12 people set the price of money at some place other than where the market would have set the price. Furthermore, those groups who have access to the new money first receive substantial advantages compared to those who receive the new money last.

Section I (continued): Structure of the Federal Reserve System

Now with a more comprehensive understanding of the purpose of the Board of Directors and the Federal Open Market Committee as detailed by Keynes, we may now return to the specified means available to the BoG and FOMC according to the United States Code.

> (b) No Federal Reserve bank shall engage or decline to engage in open-market operations under sections 348a and 353 to 359 of this title except in accordance with the direction of and regulations adopted by the Committee. The Committee shall consider, adopt, and transmit to the several Federal Reserve banks, regulations relating to the open-market transactions of such banks.

1913: From General To Specific Welfare

(c) The time, character, and volume of all purchases and sales of paper described in sections 348a and 353 to 359 of this title as eligible for open-market operations shall be governed with a view to accommodating commerce and business and with regard to their bearing upon the general credit of the country.[327]

This excerpt of the Code specifies that the Board and Committee shall determine the regulations governing open-market operations, and the banks comprising the FRS are obligated to comply. "Open-market operations" is another phrase for buying and selling securities on the market (or perhaps intervention in the market, depending on one's perspective).

Continuing on with the specific means to achieve the purpose, 12 U.S.C. § 353 provides for the "[p]urchase and sale of cable transfers, acceptances and bills."[328] "Any Federal reserve bank may, under rules and regulations prescribed by the Board of Governors of the Federal Reserve System, purchase and sell in the open market, at home or abroad, either from or to domestic or foreign banks, firms, corporations, or individuals, cable transfers and bankers' acceptances and bills of exchange of the kinds and maturities by this chapter made eligible for rediscount, with or without the indorsement of a member bank."[329] One point to keep in mind is that one individual engaging in such actions is subject to the market price. However, when one entity with the resources and power such as the FRS engages in this and the following means, that entity essentially may become the "market." In fact, if the practice continues long enough and is pervasive

---

327 12 U.S.C. § 263 (2012).
328 12 U.S.C. § 353 (2012).
329 Id.

enough, what would normally be considered a fixed price either above or below the market price will become the market price.

12 U.S.C. § 354 provides additional means and authority to intervene and essentially fix, or at a minimum, move, the price of gold. However, the means are more subtle than simply stating, for example, that one ounce of gold is 100 FRNs. § 354 provides: "[e]very Federal reserve bank shall have power to deal in gold coin and bullion at home or abroad, to make loans thereon, exchange Federal reserve notes for gold, gold coin, or gold certificates, and to contract for loans of gold coin or bullion, giving therefore, when necessary, acceptable security, including the hypothecation of United States bond or other securities which Federal reserve banks are authorized to hold."[330]

Two other sections are significant with regards to the additional authority the United States Code provides to fix interest rates, or the price of money: "§ 355. Purchase and sale of obligations of National, State, and municipal governments; open market operations; purchases and sales from or to United States; maximum aggregate amount of obligations acquired directly from or loaned directly to United States[;]"[331] and "§ 357. Establishment of rates of discount."[332] In the case of § 357, it is vital to Keynes' general theory as it sets the discount rate (effectively the same thing as an interest rate) between Federal reserve banks and their member banks. "Every Federal reserve bank shall have power to establish from time to time, subject to review and determination of the Board of Governors of the Federal Reserve System, rates of discount to be charged by the Federal reserve bank for each class of paper, which shall be fixed

---
330 12 U.S.C. § 354 (2012).
331 12 U.S.C. § 355 (2012).
332 12 U.S.C. § 357 (2012).

1913: From General To Specific Welfare

with a view of accommodating commerce and business, but each such bank shall establish such rates every fourteen days, or oftener if deemed necessary by the Board."[333]

We've gone over some of the specific means that put Keynes' observations and subsequent theory into practice. We see the authority to set a price for money, or interest rates, but how do these authorities allow the FRS to increase the supply of money? The answer lies in another fundamental aspect of the FRS: Federal reserve notes (FRNs), our next subject to examine.

SECTION II: FEDERAL RESERVE NOTES (FRNs)

FRNs impact the lives of every individual in the United States, and abroad for that matter. Federal reserve notes' status as legal tender is the underpinning that gives them such significance, and because they are so significant, a further examination of them is warranted.

In Part III, Article V, bills of credit were explained. There can be little doubt that FRNs are actually bills of credit, which the Constitution prohibited both the state and federal governments from issuing.[334] Also, as previously noted, FRNs are more properly called currency. Nonetheless, for ease of understanding, we will refer to FRNs as money because that is how people today refer to them. To briefly summarize the issue of whether FRNs are bills of credit, the United States Code provides that FRNs are obligations of the United States;[335] they circulate as a medium

---

333   12 U.S.C. § 357 (2012).
334   Nonetheless, the Supreme Court in *Veazie Bank v. Fenno*, 75 U.S. 533, 548 (1869) provided in dictum that Congress has the authority to emit bills of credit based on the "uniform practice of the government and by repeated decisions . . ." although the Court did not cite to the previous decisions. *Id.* at 548.
335   12 U.S.C. § 411 (2012).

of exchange; they are legal tender for taxes, customs, and other public dues;[336] and they contain no stipulation as to duration. That is the exact substance and function of bills of credit that the Founders intended to prohibit for the reasons that we discussed. Nonetheless, in *Veazie Bank v. Fenno*, 75 U.S. 533, 548 (1869), the Supreme Court held that Congress has the constitutional authority to issue bills of credit. "It cannot be doubted that under the Constitution the power to provide a circulation of coin is given to Congress, and it is settled by the uniform practice of the government and by repeated decisions that Congress may constitutionally authorize the emission of bills of credit."[337] Obviously, Madison and Justice Story, among others, had a drastically different understanding of what secures the rights and liberty of the individual and what does not, but today the opinion of the Supreme Court is the one that counts, not theirs.

So what exactly is a Federal Reserve Note?

> Federal reserve notes, to be issued at the discretion of the Board of Governors of the Federal Reserve System for the purpose of making advances to Federal banks through the Federal reserve agents [a particular member of the class C directors] as hereinafter set forth and for no other purpose, are authorized. The said notes shall be obligations of the United States and shall be receivable by all national and member banks and Federal reserve banks and for all taxes, customs, and other public dues. They shall be redeemed in lawful money on demand at the Treasury Department of the United States, in the city of Washington, District of Columbia, or at any Federal Reserve bank.[338]

---

336   *Id.*
337   *Veazie Bank v. Fenno*, 75 U.S. 533, 548 (1869).
338   12 U.S.C. § 411 (2012).

One interesting and significant point to note from the United States Code's definition of a FRN is that FRNs shall be "redeemed in lawful money" at either the Treasury or any Federal Reserve bank. On the other hand, the Treasury's website provides that FRNs are not redeemable at all and are backed by nothing.[339] If the Supreme Court were to hold that the Treasury's declaration is law, then FRNs are irredeemable, and thus there is no limit to how many may be created so long as there is sufficient collateral.[340] As we shall see in the following explanation, even if the Supreme Court were to find that the Treasury's declaration does not override the statute, FRNs are effectively irredeemable regardless. For the sake of argument, however, we will assume that the Court would find that the statute prevails, and thus, FRNs are redeemable. This of course raises the question: if FRNs are redeemable in "lawful money," what is lawful money?

After thorough research of relevant material, the only definition that may be found is the following, which is likely a holdover from the early 1900s:[341] "[t]he term 'lawful money of the United States,' as used in section 16 [of the Federal Reserve Act of 1913] in prescribing what may be used by a Federal Reserve bank to reduce its liability for outstanding reserve notes, may be defined

---

339   *Legal Tender Status*, U.S. DEP'T OF THE TREASURY, https://www.treasury.gov/resource-center/faqs/Currency/Pages/legal-tender.aspx (last visited Nov. 17, 2016); *see also* Christopher M. Bruner, *The Changing Face of Money*, 30 Rev. Banking & Fin. L. 383, 395-96 (2010).
340   12 U.S.C. § 412 (2012).
341   *See generally* Edwin Vieira, Jr., *The Forgotten Role of the Constitution in Monetary Law*, 2 Tex. Rev. L. & Pol. 77, 80-82 (1997) (arguing that FRNs themselves are not lawful money, and that the statutory requirement requiring redeemability in lawful money is a holdover from an earlier period when FRNs where redeemable in gold by bearer on demand).

as legal tender and includes silver certificates."[342] Therefore, a FRN is an obligation of the Treasury, and the Treasury is obligated to redeem the notes in legal tender, which FRNs certainly are. It makes no sense to exchange one obligation for another of the same type. What about exchanging the paper obligations for coins minted by the Treasury, which are also legal tender?

On that point, the Secretary of the Treasury is authorized to mint and issue various types of coins with various denominations that are considered legal tender.[343] The composition of the coins includes but is not limited to the following: copper, nickel, zinc, gold, silver, and platinum.[344] For coins that include gold, silver, and platinum the Secretary is authorized to "... sell the coins minted under this subsection [(i)] to the public at a price equal to the market value of the bullion at the time of sale, plus the cost of minting, marketing, and distributing such coins (including labor, materials, dies, use of machinery, and promotional and overhead expenses)."[345] Based on the types of coins that the Secretary is authorized to mint and issue, one may break them into two categories:

1) Where the Secretary is authorized only to sell the coins at market price in addition to other costs, i.e., not for redemption, but only for sale; and

---

342 Digest of Rulings of the Board of Governors of the Federal Reserve System from 1914 to October 1, 1937, Including Digests of Opinions of the Attorney General of the United States and Reported Court Decisions Construing the Federal Reserve Act, Together with Textual Changes made in the Federal Reserve Act by Amendments Enacted Prior to October 1, 1937. Compiled under the Direction of the Board of Governors of the Federal Reserve System in the Office of its General Counsel, § 16.301.
343 31 U.S.C. § 5103 (2012).
344 31 U.S.C. § 5112(a),(b),(e) (2012).
345 31 U.S.C. § 5112(i)(2)(A) (2012).

2) Where the Secretary is authorized to use coins for redeeming FRNs based on nominal value.

The coins made of gold, silver, and platinum fall under the first category, while the other coins fall under the second.

The face value given to the gold, silver, and platinum coins is a classic example of price fixing on two counts, one for the initial sale and the other for circulation upon sale. Take as an example 12 U.S.C. § 5112(a)(11): "The Secretary of the Treasury may mint and issue only the following coins: . . . (11) A $50 dollar gold coin that is of an appropriate size and thickness, as determined by the Secretary, weighs 1 ounce, and contains 99.99 percent pure gold."[346] The coin is one ounce of .999 fine gold, which the current price for one ounce of gold is $1,260.[347] The current sales price at the Mint for a one-ounce gold coin is $1,560,[348] a markup of approximately 23.8%. Therefore, the initial sales price for the coin is well above the market price for the bullion itself. This may be considered what some have labeled *seignorage* or *agio*. However, that is not the point here. Instead, the point is that the price is set well above the market price of the bullion, which makes the coin overvalued. The seller (in this case the Treasury) normally would find they are unable to sell the item at that fixed price, and the result is excess in supply.

Furthermore, the face value of fifty dollars—if one were to use the coins to pay taxes to the government—is well undervalued. Therefore, one could hardly expect that they would be used for tax payments. Who would give a coin worth $1,600 on the

---

346   31 U.S.C. § 5112(a)(11) (2012).
347   Kitco, http://www.kitco.com (Dec. 18, 2017, 2:35 PM).
348   *American Eagle One Ounce Gold Proof Coin*, United States Mint, https://catalog.usmint.gov/american-eagle-2017-one-ounce-gold-proof-coin-17EB.html?cgid=gold-coins#start=1 (Dec. 18, 2017, 2:42 PM).

market, to the government for a $50 tax payment? In light of how the market has adapted to the fixed prices of the government (prices are denominated in FRNs versus any sort of measurement in weight, such as ounces or grams), the user of the coin in the market would also find the coin to be well undervalued, with the exception of taking the coin to a dealer in precious metals or coins. In short, for gold, silver, and platinum coins, they are legal tender, but they may not be redeemed in exchange for FRNs (the reason is based upon specific authority in the United States Code). Instead, they may only be purchased from the Treasury at a price well above the market price of the bullion. The coins subsequently may be used to pay taxes at their face value, making them well undervalued, and nearly guaranteeing no one will use them for that purpose.

Concerning the other group of coins in the second category, they are composed of nickel, copper, and zinc, and they are given a face value well above the market value of the content of the coins. For the purposes of redeeming paper FRNs, these coins are the other form of legal tender for which FRNs may be redeemed at the Treasury (besides exchanging one piece of paper for another). The issue is that these coins are overvalued based upon their content and their face value.[349] For example, a dime has a nominal value of 10 cents, but the actual metal content of the dime is worth less than 10 cents. For all practical purposes, redeeming FRNs for pennies, nickels, dimes, quarters, half

---

349   This is normally the case. However, if prices of the base metals were to rise sufficiently (generally through extensive issue of FRNs), one could find that the market value of the coin could actually be higher than the nominal value stamped on its face. This situation could effectively create the same issue as when the United States was on the previous gold standard: there would be more claims being printed (in the form of FRNs) than there were coins that could be redeemed. Essentially, there would be a modern day bank run on such coins.

dollars, and dollar coins would be similar to redeeming FRNs in exchange for other FRNs. Before continuing with an explanation of FRNs, let us review our discussion of them so far.

FRNs are obligations of the United States that are advanced to the FRS and are redeemable in lawful money. Lawful money is anything that is legal tender. However, some types of legal tender may only be sold at the current market price plus various other costs as listed in the United States Code. Therefore, the only lawful money for which FRNs may be exchanged, besides exchanging one FRN for another, are coins that are well overvalued. Thus, from a monetary perspective, it would not be worth our efforts to redeem FRNs for something of equal or lesser value. The legal tender for which it would be monetarily advantageous to exchange FRNs is not authorized because legal tender coins made of gold and silver may only be sold at a price well above the market value of the bullion.

In light of this analysis, regardless of whether the Supreme Court would find that the FRNs are redeemable in accordance with the statute or not, there is seemingly no restraint on the amount of paper claims that may be created because there is nothing authorized for which the paper claims may be exchanged that are anything but lesser value. There is the potential for a problem depending on how many claims are issued, where the market value could actually be above the nominal value if a sufficient number of FRNs were issued. Nonetheless, the Congress could simply change the law and alter the content of the coin to place the nominal value back above the market value, thus preventing a potential "run on FRNs."

The authority granted to the Secretary of the Treasury to procure gold and silver is interesting when viewed in the context of the FRS and the process of issuing FRNs:

(a)(1) With the approval of the President, the Secretary of the Treasury may –

(A) buy and sell gold in the way, in amounts, at rates, and on conditions the Secretary considers most advantageous to the public interest; and

(B) buy the gold with any direct obligations of the United States Government or United States coins and currency authorized by law, or with amounts in the Treasury not otherwise appropriated.[350]

With this authority, the Secretary may use FRNs to purchase bullion at the current market price. The bullion may then be coined and sold at a price that covers what the Secretary determines to be the cost of coining. In the case of the $50 gold coin, the Secretary may use FRNs to purchase one ounce of bullion at say $1,600, sell at $2,000, and stamp the coin with a face value of $50. There is seemingly no limit to the amount of bullion the Secretary may purchase, no limit to the amount that may be sold, and consequently no limit to where the Treasury may attempt to move the price of gold and silver.

Additionally, the Secretary is also granted authority to buy obligations of the United States. With an understanding that FRNs are an obligation of the United States, it must be admitted that using FRNs to purchase other obligations doesn't make sense. Essentially, the Secretary is authorized to purchase obligations with obligations. As an analogy, let us assume we still had the monetary system as defined in the Constitution with a dollar being 371 ¼ grains of fine silver. If this were the case, then the Secretary would be authorized to buy silver bullion with silver

---

[350] 31 U.S.C. § 5116 (2012).

bullion. The net effect of such a transaction would be a loss in the sense that one would receive the same thing that was given, minus the expense of conducting the transaction. Granted, when debt instruments are involved and the interest rates are lower now than when the original obligations were issued, then one may save money by issuing obligations with a lower rate to repurchase those with a higher rate. Nonetheless, although the short-run issue of redeeming the initial obligation may be forestalled, ultimately the debt must be repaid. That is the fundamental problem of pyramiding claims on top of claims that are on top of other claims. At some point, those people holding claims must be able to exchange them for the actual things they desire, or they must recognize that their claims are no longer valid.

With that explanation as a foundation, the following excerpt from the United States Code details the authority granted to the Secretary of the Treasury concerning dealing in obligations of the United States:

(a) The President may direct the Secretary of the Treasury to make an agreement with the Federal reserve banks and the Board of Governors of the Federal Reserve System when the President decides that the foreign commerce of the United States is affected adversely because-
(1) the value of coins and currency of a foreign country compared to the present standard value of gold is depreciating;
(2) action is necessary to regulate and maintain the parity of United States coins and currency;
(3) an economic emergency requires an expansion of credit; or

(4) an expansion of credit is necessary so that the United States Government and the governments of other countries can stabilize the value of coins and currencies of a country.

(b) Under an agreement under subsection (a) of this section, the Board shall permit the banks (and the Board is authorized to permit the banks notwithstanding another law) to agree that the banks will-
(1) conduct through each entire specified period open market operations in obligations of the United States Government or corporations in which the Government is the majority stockholder; and
(2) buy directly and hold an additional $3,000,000,000 of obligations of the Government for each agreed period, unless the Secretary consents to the sale of the obligations before the end of the period.[351]

The Secretary also has at his discretion a stabilization fund for stabilizing exchange rates and arrangements.

(a)(1) The Department of the Treasury has a stabilization fund. The fund is available to carry out this section, section 18 of the Bretton Woods Agreement Act (22 U.S.C. 286e-3), and section 3 of the Special Drawing Rights Act (22 U.S.C. 286o), and for investing in obligations of the United States Government those amounts in the fund the Secretary of the Treasury, with the approval of the President, decides are not required at the time to carry out

---

351   31 U.S.C. § 5301 (2012).

this section. Proceeds of sales and investments, earnings, and interest shall be paid into the fund and are available to carry out this section. However, the fund is not available to pay administrative expenses.

(2) Subject to approval by the President, the fund is under the exclusive control of the Secretary, and may not be used in a way that direct control and custody pass from the President and the Secretary. Decisions of the Secretary are final and may not be reviewed by another officer or employee of the Government.[352]

22 U.S.C. § 286e-3 authorizes the transfer of funds from the International Monetary Fund to the stabilization fund as previously specified in 31 U.S.C. § 5302.

Any purchases of currencies or gold by the United States from the International Monetary Fund may be transferred to and administered by the fund established by section 5302 of Title 31, for use in accordance with the provisions of that section. The Secretary of the Treasury is authorized to utilize the resources of that fund for the purpose of any repayments in connection with such transactions.[353]

The excerpts detailing the monetary authorities of the Secretary of the Treasury, along with those of the BoG and the FOMC, explain the means granted to the respective entities to achieve the purpose of the BoG and the FOMC. Again, this purpose was outlined by Keynes: to buy and sell securities in order

---

352   31 U.S.C. § 5302 (2012).
353   22 U.S.C. § 286e-3 (2012).

to set a target interest rate, which in theory seeks to keep unemployment low and prices stable—keeping in mind the substantial advantages that accrue to the people who get access to the new credit first. We also examined the structure of the FRS and the characteristics of FRNs. The next task is to examine the code concerning the FRS and FRNs such that we may fully comprehend the workings of the United States' monetary system.

Synthesis of Federal Reserve System and Federal Reserve Notes

The Federal Reserve System consists of a Board of Governors, which is composed of seven members nominated by the President. The BoG, along with five other members (chosen by the Federal reserve banks), comprises the Federal Open Market Committee. The FOMC sets the discount rate that the Federal reserve banks use when providing loans to their member banks. The rate set by the FOMC may be above or below the rate otherwise determined by the market. The purpose of the FOMC is to ". . . maintain long run growth of the monetary and credit aggregates commensurate with the economy's long run potential to increase production, so as to promote effectively the goals of maximum employment, stable prices, and moderate long-term interest rates."[354]

In order to accomplish this goal, the FRS uses means described by Keynes. The FOMC seeks to increase the price of capital in relation to the price of labor. When there is "slack in the productive capacity," the FOMC seeks to lower interest rates, hoping that the new money and credit will flow to investments in capital, thus increasing the price of capital, lowering real wages, and subsequently increasing employment. The BoG and the FOMC

---

354   12 U.S.C. § 225a (2012).

use assets that they acquired through its previous operations. If the BoG and FOMC desire to increase money and credit, they purchase assets while selling FRNs. If they desire to decrease money and credit, they sell assets while purchasing FRNs.

The FRNs are issued by the United States and advanced to the Federal reserve agent that has made the request. FRNs are statutorily obligations of the United States redeemable in lawful money, but effectively they are redeemable in nothing but themselves. The Federal reserve bank is charged for the cost of creating the notes and must pay interest for those notes (as set by the Board) above what is secured by gold certificates.[355] Additionally, the FRNs become a lien against the respective Federal reserve bank per the United States Code cited below:

> The Board of Governors of the Federal Reserve System shall have the right, acting through the Federal Reserve agent, to grant in whole or in part, or to reject entirely the application of any Federal Reserve bank for Federal Reserve notes; but to the extent that such application may be granted the Board of Governors of the Federal Reserve System shall, through its local Federal Reserve agent, supply Federal Reserve notes to the banks so applying, and such bank shall be charged with the amount of the notes issued to it and shall pay such rate of interest as may be established by the Board of Governors of the Federal Reserve system on only that amount of such notes which equals the total amount of its outstanding Federal Reserve notes less the amount of gold certificates held by the Federal Reserve agent as collateral security. Federal Reserve notes issued

---

355   12 U.S.C. § 414 (2012).

to any such bank shall, upon delivery, together with such notes of such Federal Reserve bank as may be issued under subchapter XIII of this chapter upon security of United States 2 per centum Government bonds, become a first and paramount lien on all the assets of such bank.[356]

A Federal reserve bank may request FRNs, pay for the cost of making them with a portion of the notes received, and may request additional notes to pay the interest charged on previous issues. Moreover, the FRS uses the FRNs to purchase bills, notes, and bonds sold by the Treasury. In effect, the United States self-finances by issuing notes to the FRS that the government itself created. Then the FRS subsequently uses the FRNs to purchase the debt of the United States. In theory, there is a limitation on the number of FRNs that may be issued as they are redeemable in lawful money, at least per statute despite the Treasury's claim to the contrary. But in reality, the limitation is rendered moot because they may only be redeemed for something of equal or lesser value.

As noted by Keynes and others, the expansion of money and credit is most beneficial to those who receive the new money and credit first. In the case of the current monetary system, this is the Federal reserve banks and the United States Government. It should be obvious that the current monetary system negates any notion of the government being dependent on the people.

However, the process just described is simply the first step in the creation of money and credit. The second step involves fractional reserve lending among the Federal reserve banks and their members. With that in mind, we will next examine how the

---

356   *Id.* (footnote omitted).

banks create additional money and credit once the FRNs have been issued.

SECTION III: CREATION OF "CREDIT" (OR MONEY), AND EXPANSIONS OF THE SUPPLY

Due to the relation of the FRS with the central government, combined with the nature of Federal Reserve Notes, the increase in the supply of what effectively acts like money is twofold. The first expansion occurs when the federal government issues an increase of FRNs to the Federal reserve agent at the associated Federal reserve bank. The second expansion occurs through the extension of credit by the FRS itself. The latter involves the practice of fractional reserve lending. We will begin our examination of the expansion of money with the first process followed by the second.

The process begins with a Federal reserve agent making a request for FRNs to the Board of Governors of the Federal Reserve. The United States Bureau of Printing and Engraving actually creates the physical FRNs, and as described, the FRNs become an obligation of the United States as well as a first lien on the respective Federal reserve bank that received the notes. This is the first step in the creation of FRNs—of what we use as money. From this point, where the FRNs are held by a Federal reserve bank, there are different paths the FRNs may take. We will only examine one of the paths so that we may understand how the FRS expands the supply of credit, which functions at least for a short period of time just like money. Therefore, we will use as an example what may happen under the authority granted by 31 U.S.C. § 5301, where a Federal reserve bank may "buy directly and hold an additional $3,000,000,000 of obligations of the Government for each agreed period, unless the Secretary consents to the sale of the obligations before the end of the period."[357]

Let's assume that a Federal reserve bank uses the FRNs that were recently issued to it to purchase Treasury debt directly from the government. Incidentally, this practice would be monetizing the debt, which is interesting considering the issue surrounding whether or not the FRS is "printing money."[358] Nonetheless, from this process, the government has now monetized its own debt.[359] The government now has the money, which it can use to purchase goods and services. When the providers of these goods and services obtain FRNs, they may either spend them or save

---

357   31 U.S.C. § 5301.
358   Based on the United States Code, only the United States Treasury has the authority to print FRNs. If the FRS were actually printing FRNs, they would be in violation of the code. Nonetheless, as we shall see, when the FRS creates credit, it often times acts exactly as if the FRS were printing money.
359   It is beyond the scope here to detail all of the court rulings and arguments in Congress that cover the debate of whether a central bank's notes are bills of credit. In short, the argument proceeds as follows: FRNs are not the government's bills of credit because the FRS is not a part of the government; therefore, the bills are not the government's bills of credit. However, if that point is conceded, it raises another constitutional issue: the FRS's notes have a role in the United States' borrowing process, and the result is that the government is borrowing on something other than solely its own credit, which the Constitution explicitly grants the power to the Congress "[t]o borrow Money on the credit of the United States...." U.S. CONST. art. I, § 8, cl. 2. If the FRS is not a part of the government, then the United States would be borrowing on the credit of the FRS versus on the credit of the United States - no matter how small the degree. *See generally* 1 EDWIN VIERA, Jr., PIECES OF EIGHT: THE MONETARY POWERS AND DISABILITIES OF THE UNITED STATES CONSTITUTION 411-30 (RR Donnelly & Sons, Inc. 2d rev. spec. ed. 2011) (summarizing the issues of the first argument); *see generally* 2 EDWIN VIERA, Jr., PIECES OF EIGHT: THE MONETARY POWERS AND DISABILITIES OF THE UNITED STATES CONSTITUTION 1536-38 (RR Donnelly & Sons, Inc. 2d rev. spec. ed. 2011) (summarizing the issues of the second argument).

them. If they save them, they may deposit them in a bank, and this is when the process of fractional reserve lending (more appropriately labeled fractional reserve deposits) begins.

The following quote from *Modern Money Mechanics,* a book produced by the Federal Reserve Bank of Chicago, sheds light on the creation of money and credit through fractional reserve lending.

> The actual process of money creation takes place primarily in banks. As noted earlier, checkable liabilities [depositor's checking accounts] of banks are money. These liabilities are customer's accounts. They increase when customers deposit currency and checks and when the proceeds of loans made by the banks are credited to borrower's account.
>
> In the absence of legal reserve requirements, banks can build up deposits by increasing loans and investments so long as they keep enough currency on hand to redeem whatever amounts the holders of deposits want to convert into currency. This unique attribute of the banking business was discovered many centuries ago.
>
> It started with goldsmiths. As early bankers, they initially provided safekeeping services, making a profit from vault storage fees for gold and coins deposited with them. People would redeem their "deposit receipts" whenever they needed gold or coins to purchase something, and physically take the gold or coins to the seller who, in turn, would deposit them for safekeeping, often with the same

banker. Everyone soon found that it was a lot easier simply to use the deposit receipts directly as a means of payment. These receipts, which became known as notes, were acceptable as money since whoever held them could go to the banker and exchange them for metallic money.

Then, bankers discovered that they could make loans merely by giving their promises to pay, or bank notes, to borrowers. In this way, banks began to create money. More notes could be issued than the gold and coin on hand because only a portion of the notes outstanding would be presented for payment at any one time. Enough metallic money had to be kept on hand, of course, to redeem whatever volume of notes was presented for payment.

Transaction deposits are the modern counterpart of bank notes. It was a small step from printing notes to making book entries crediting deposits of borrowers, which the borrowers in turn could "spend" by writing checks, thereby "printing" their own money.[360]

Returning to the specifics of fractional reserve lending, we'll use the example of a producer depositing his money in a bank, where the basis for the following examples is taken from *Modern Money Mechanics*.[361] The bank now has an account to document this transaction similar to the one below:

---

360   FEDERAL RESERVE BANK OF CHICAGO, MODERN MONEY MECHANICS: A WORKBOOK ON BANK RESERVES AND DEPOSIT EXPANSION 3 (reprt. 1994) (c. 1992) (footnote omitted).
361   *Id.* at 7-10.

1913: From General To Specific Welfare

BANK A

Asset	Liability
1,000 units	IOU for 1,000 units to depositor

The bank has its books balanced with an asset of 1,000 units and a checking account for the depositor, which is the bank's liability, as at any moment the depositor may demand redemption. In that case, the liability would decrease by the same amount as the asset side, and once again the bank would have a balanced statement.

The next step involves the reserves that must be kept by the bank, which is determined by the Board of Governors. Currently, the reserve ratios are set between zero and ten percent.[362] Obviously, with a reserve of zero there is in theory no limit to the amount of additional credit or money that a bank would be able to create. For the purposes of a demonstration, we will use a reserve ratio of ten percent. Therefore, based on the preceding chart, the bank is only required by the Board of Governors, which is granted such authority by the United States Code, to maintain 100 units on reserve. It has an excess of 900 units that it may loan out to another person.[363] At this point, an updated statement would look like the following:

---

[362] *Reserve Requirements*, BOARD OF GOVERNORS OF THE FEDERAL RESERVE SYSTEM, https://www.federalreserve.gov/monetarypolicy/reservereq.htm (last update Oct. 27, 2016).

[363] The reader may still be asking how it can loan out 900 units when there is a potential for the original depositor to demand all of his or her deposit. It would normally be a problem in that it would effectively be a run on the bank if enough depositors all demanded their money. However, as mentioned previously, that is where a lender of last resort such as the FRS, who may receive FRNs issued by the central government, stands ready at all times to supply the missing reserves. Additionally, a bank would typically have equity of its own that it may use to stem the tide in the short-term.

BANK A[364]

Asset	Liability
1,000 units	IOU for 1,000 units to depositor

Excess Reserves
900

A bank with 900 units in reserves has the potential, from its perspective at least, to put this money to further use to include generating interest by loaning it to a borrower. The next step in the process of fractional reserve lending is when the bank loans the excess reserves to another borrower. After this step, the bank's balance sheet concerning these transactions would look like the following:

BANK A

Asset	Liability
1,000 units from depositor	IOU from bank to depositor for 1,000 units (checking acct)
IOU from borrower to bank for 900 units	IOU from bank to borrowe for 900 units (checking acct)

Instead of continuing through multiple transactions, the total amount of deposit expansion possible from the initial 1,000 units, with a reserve ratio of ten percent, is 9,000 units. For quick reference, the total amount of expansion may be represented by $[((1/\text{reserve ratio})*(\text{initial deposit}))-\text{initial deposit}]$.[364] In the

---

364   *Id.* at 8.

case of the example, 1,000 units with a reserve ratio of ten percent are capable of expanding to an additional 9,000 units.

This short example demonstrates the principle that banks use to create credit, which acts very similarly to money. Notice that there was actually no increase in physical deposits. There was only an increase in credit, which acts just like money as long as confidence in the bank exists.

The process of fractional reserve lending used by member banks, combined with the structure of the FRS, is the heart of the monetary system of the United States.[365] With an understanding of the principle of fractional reserve lending and its associated expansion of credit, there are three issues of significance that must also be explored:

1) the pyramiding of credit upon the initial deposit;

2) the inability to satisfy all obligations to repay the principal with interest unless there is an addition of FRNs; and

3) a likely cascading of defaults.

Beginning with the first issue and the example just described, we must remember there are only 1,000 physical units, or FRNs in the case of the FRS. Money, or in this case FRNs or currency, is what is required when redemption is demanded. All of the IOUs pyramided atop the initial deposit are only claims to that initial deposit, and there will likely be many more claims than

---

[365] From a macro perspective, it reaches much further than just the United States. Based on the US Code, the United States is a member of numerous global banking corporations operating throughout the world, and the Federal Reserve System operates as a depository institution for these other corporations. The FRS is a depository institution for the following entities detailed in 22 U.S.C. § 282-86: International Finance Corporation; Inter-American Development Bank; Inter-American Investment Corporation; Asian Development Bank; and the International Monetary Fund and Bank for Reconstruction and Development.

deposits with fractional reserve lending. The IOUs may be sold to another party to raise money or FRNs, but they will generally be sold at a discount since IOUs entail a difference between the present and future values, or in other words: a factor accounting for time. Conversely, money or FRNs do not possess this aspect since money or FRNs are the underlying thing. Nonetheless, all of the depositors cannot have their deposits back at the same time when a bank engages in fractional reserve lending. That would be the quintessential and disastrous run on the bank. In the case of the FRS, the central bank acts as a lender of last resort to protect its member banks from just such a situation. Nonetheless, runs on a bank are inherent in the process of fractional reserve lending.

The second issue concerns the impossibility of repayment of principal and interest without an expansion of the stock of money. Based on our example of Bank A, it is impossible to repay the principle and interest at the same time, assuming there are only 1,000 units in existence. As an example, we will assume that the expansion of deposits described previously terminated after one transaction. We will assume the borrower never spent the 900 units, exchanged his labor to acquire the interest payments (either from the bank or the initial depositor), and then repaid the principal with the interest. The bank has in its possession the original 1,000 units. However, who has claim to those units is different than when the units were deposited. A small portion of that sum is theoretically the property of the bank. That creates an issue since the original depositor is still owed his 1,000 units, there are only 1,000 units on hand at the bank, and the bank appears to now have a claim of its own on a small portion of that 1,000-unit sum because of the interest accrued to

1913: From General To Specific Welfare

the bank. Moreover, it is irrelevant whether the borrower spent the money and then reacquired it to repay the loan, or whether the borrower never spent the money and simply repaid it. The point remains that in a debt-based system such as ours, without an expansion of the supply of money, it is not possible to repay loans made with positive interest.[366]

Furthermore, we have already examined the process of an addition to the stock of money when money is a commodity, and we have determined that the person who receives newly added money first benefits more than any other (Part V, Article II, Section I). The difference between FRNs and a commodity is that the authority to create more FRNs rests with one board composed of seven members.[367] The authority to create more of a commodity rests with the desires of people to hold more units of the commodity and with the producers of the commodity. The former inherently lends itself to a significant consolidation of power while the latter tends more towards a diffusion of power, notwithstanding an individual's propensity to strive for power as a means to maximize his satisfactions. The current FRS is one of the most consolidated power structures one could devise, and in its current form is vastly more concentrated than a monetary system based on silver and gold, which remains the system described in the Constitution.

---

366   There is no reason why loans could not be made with negative interest rates if that is what the market determined the appropriate rate to be based on the prevailing conditions. However, probably due to the same principle observed by Keynes concerning nominal and real prices, humans are predisposed to have difficulty grasping the fact that one may receive more by receiving less; said another way, one may receive less units with greater purchasing power per unit such that the total number of units may buy more than what a greater number bought previously. Granted, this aspect of money may be confusing. In fact, this aspect is a substantial factor that plays a significant role in Keynes' general theory.

367   12 U.S.C. § 414.

The last issue to examine concerning fractional reserve lending is that cascading defaults are built into the system. An easy way to examine this aspect of fractional reserve lending is by comparing it to a system where there is no fractional reserve lending.

For example, let's assume that every loan made to a bank is made in a manner where the lender understands that every one of his units will be provided as a loan by the bank to some borrower. There is no need for a reserve because it was in fact a loan. When a bank then finds a borrower for the funds loaned to the bank, and then the borrower fails to repay the loan, the effects end with the bank and the lender to the bank, who in theory assessed and accepted the risk of default and charged the appropriate interest rate. They do not cascade from one lender to the next lender, and so on.

Contrast this example with the previous example that used Bank A. Assume that the process has progressed to the point where credit has expanded through multiple transactions. Also, for the sake of example, assume that ten different entities were involved in the expansion of deposits. When any one of those entities fails to repay the loans, it affects every other member in the chain of deposit expansion. Granted, the bank should have a reserve of equity that could be used to cover the losses. In addition, the FRS has the Federal Reserve Banks as a lender of last resort to prevent such an issue.[368] Nonetheless, the practice of

---

368   In reality, this situation is precisely what occurred during the recent subprime issue of 2007-2008. The issue was a run on the bank when money was demanded, but there was not enough to be had. The disadvantage to preventing a run on the bank is a surge in the stock of money, or FRNs as the case may be. More money will result in an increase in prices, assuming other conditions remain the same. It is my contention that the issue from 2007-2008 is far from completion. Instead, it was more than likely forestalled to some point in the

fractional reserve lending opens itself up to the potential for cascading defaults throughout the banking system.

These three aspects of fractional reserve lending are certainly significant, and they also have the potential to result in situations that are detrimental to those who stand to lose portions of what they thought was their wealth. Despite these detrimental effects, fractional reserve lending is a foundational premise of the United States' current monetary system. When combined with the FRS and FRNs, it is another tool that may be used to accomplish the vague goals of the BoG and the FOMC provided in the United States Code and as described by Keynes.

This closes our examination of the monetary system as it stands today, and we can see that it is drastically different from the Coinage Act of 1792. The initial creation of what is understood to be money is now the sole authority of the Board of Governors, who grant the FRNs to the Federal reserve banks. The FRS is a creation of the government, and FRNs are used to purchase the government's debt. The benefits accrue to those who receive the new money first. The disadvantages accrue to those who receive the money last. With this understanding, it should come as no surprise that large disparities between wealth will develop. How could they not?

Nonetheless, we are now armed with a basic understanding of our current monetary system and can pinpoint the exact cause of this disparity of wealth: the FRA of 1913 and its consequences. Because of the FRA of 1913, which began the chain of events

---

future. The structure of the system ensures that there eventually will be one of two outcomes despite the best efforts to walk a fine line described by Keynes and given as a charge to the Federal Open Market Committee: substantial defaults, a substantial increase in prices (whether the rise is in asset prices or prices of consumption goods), or perhaps both situations at different time periods.

that led to today, we now have a monetary system that provides for the specific welfare versus the general welfare. When combined with the 16th Amendment, the opportunity for specific welfare is even more pronounced. Having examined two of the events of 1913, we will now turn to an examination of the third: the 17th Amendment.

Article III: 17th Amendment

Part III, Article IV explained the significance of the Senate and the states' legislators sent to represent the states in the United States Congress. A significant aspect of the Senate was to act as a balance of power between the passion of the people represented in the House and the ambition of the President, who is charged as the executor of the laws.

With the ratification of the 17th Amendment, the Senate effectively lost a critical aspect of its ability to act as a balance between the central government and the people. Additionally, the 17th Amendment decreased the influence of reason in deliberations concerning legislation and subsequently allowed the influence of passions to rise without sufficient opposition.

In our republican system of governance, people elect someone to act on their behalf. This representative is expected to act in accordance with the duties prescribed in the Constitution, and it is also generally understood that the representatives will act in the interests of those they are representing. Prior to 1913 the states' legislatures chose two senators to act on behalf of the state. However, in 1913 the 17th Amendment altered that condition. Instead of state legislatures choosing their representative, the people of the states chose the two senators from their state to represent them in the United States Congress: "The Senate of the United States shall be composed of two Senators from each State, elected by the people thereof, for six years; and each Senator shall have one vote."[369]

If the purpose was to have two separate branches of the legislature to check ambition against ambition, then this principle implies competing interests. When the states' interests are eliminated, the only interest left is that of the people. Although this surely sounds like an advantageous reason to have only one branch of a legislature, it is not when one considers all of the disadvantages of a single branch.

Once again, the one thing that remains new in this world is the history we do not know. Perhaps, if the people of 1913 had referred to arguments in *Discourses Concerning Government* or *The Federalist* at the time of ratification, the 17th Amendment may not have been ratified. Therefore, in order to examine the effect of the 17th Amendment on the ability of the Senate to act as a balance between the people and the executive, we will review James Madison's reflections concerning the "... inconveniences which a republic must suffer from the want of such an institution [senate]."[370] Then we will review Algernon Sidney's thoughts on the subject in *Discourses Concerning Government* and a brief return to Madison. We rely on quotes from Mr. Madison and Mr. Sidney because it is illuminating to hear the principles expressed so clearly over 200 and 300 years ago, respectively, which are just as true today as they were then.

Before examining Sidney's reflections, we must point out Madison's certainty concerning the importance of the state legislatures choosing the senators.

---

369   U.S. CONST. amend. XVII.
370   THE FEDERALIST NO. 62, at 344 (James Madison) (George Stade ed., Barnes & Noble, Inc. 2006).

It is equally unnecessary to dilate on the appointment of senators by the state legislatures. Among the various modes which might have been devised for constituting this branch of the government, that which has been proposed by the convention is probably the most congenial with the public opinion. It is recommended by the double advantage of favouring a select appointment, and of giving to the state governments such an agency in the formation of the federal government, as must secure the authority of the former, and may form a convenient link between the two systems.[371]

Noteworthy is Madison's use of the word authority. The meaning of authority is derived from the word author. An author is one who owns the actions done or the words spoken, while the actor is simply one who acts or speaks on behalf of the owner or author.[372] Subsequently, the actor acts only by authority of the author. ". . . so the Right of doing any Action, is called AUTHORITY. So that by Authority, is always understood a Right of doing any act: and *done by Authority*, done by Commission, or Licence from him whose right it is."[373] In the case of the means of electing a senator, whether the author is the people, whose representation is already provided through the House, or whether the author is a state legislature, which is the closest body able to represent the state itself, makes all the difference. The former seeks the interest peculiar to the individuals they represent while the latter seeks the interest of the state. With the ratification of the 17th Amendment, the states lost the means to their

---

371   Id. at 342.
372   THOMAS HOBBES, LEVIATHAN 99 (Barnes & Noble, Inc. 2004) (1651).
373   Id. at 100.

representation in the United States Congress because they no longer have the means to select the senators. The states' authority was essentially eliminated, and their basis for countering the power of the executive was severely mitigated, if not eliminated completely.[374]

Sidney provides his reflections on what one may expect when the nobility, or the Senate in our case, has been effectively eliminated. The quote is somewhat lengthy, but it is certainly worthwhile. That is not to say that the 17th Amendment is the sole cause of the similar conditions today. Instead, the point to note is that effectively the nobility has been eradicated, and the aftereffects today reflect those that Sidney noted from a historical perspective.

> They [Sidney's ancestors] knew that the kings of several nations had been kept within the limits of the law, by the virtue and power of a great and brave nobility; and that no other way of supporting a mix'd monarchy had ever been known in the world, than by putting the balance into the hands of those who had the greatest interest in nations, and who by birth and estate enjoy'd greater advantages than kings could confer upon them for rewards of betraying their country. . . . It was not to be imagined that through the weakness of some, and malice of others, those dignities should by degrees be turned into empty titles, and become the rewards of the greatest crimes, and the

---

[374] During ratification debates, many of the Anti-Federalists expressed concern that the central government would swallow the state governments. Of course, today the state governments still exists, but as shown, their authority has essentially been eliminated. The Anti-Federalists understood human nature and what would inevitably result, but it took over 100 years after ratification for that stroke to occur.

vilest services; or that the noblest of their descendants for want of them, should be brought under the name of commoners, and deprived of all privileges except such as were common to them with their grooms. Such a stupendous change being in process of time insensibly introduced, the foundations of that government which they had established, were removed, and the superstructure overthrown. The balance by which it subsisted was broken; and 'tis as impossible to restore it, as for most of those who at this day go under the name of noblemen, to perform the duties required from the ancient nobility of England. . . . By this means all things have been brought into the hands of the king and the commoners, and there is nothing left to cement them, and to maintain the union. The perpetual jarrings we hear every day; the division of the nation into such factions as threaten us with ruin, and all the disorders that we see or fear, are the effects of this rupture. These things are not to be imputed to our original constitutions, but to those who have subverted them: And if they who by corrupting, changing, enervating and annihilating the nobility, which was the principal support of the ancient regular monarchy, have driven those who are truly noblemen into the same interest and name with the commons, and by that means increased a party which never was, and I think never can be united to the court, they are to answer for the consequences; and if they perish, their destruction is from themselves.

The inconveniences therefore proceed not from the institution, but from the innovation. The law was plain, but it has been industriously rendered perplex: They who were to have upheld it are overthrown. That which might have been easily performed when the people was armed, and had a great, strong, virtuous and powerful nobility to lead them, is made difficult, now they are disarmed, and that nobility abolished. Our ancestors may evidently appear, not only to have intended well, but to have taken a right course to accomplish what they intended. This had effect as long as the cause continued; and the only fault that can be ascribed to that which they established is, that it has not proved to be perpetual; which is no more than may be justly said of the best human constitutions that ever have been in the world.[375]

Returning to Madison, he also notes what will likely happen when the state legislatures no longer elect the senators, or what is the same thing, when the Senate is transformed such that it is no longer able to perform one of its vital functions. Because Mr. Madison's prose is so clear and easy to understand to this day, I will quote significant portions of three of the four inconveniences he noted. Mr. Madison's first inconvenience is the following:

First. It is a misfortune incident to republican governments, . . . that those who administer it may forget their obligations to their constituents, and prove unfaithful to their important trust. In this point of view, a senate, as a second branch of the legislative assembly, distinct from, and dividing the power with, a first, must be in all cases a

---

375 ALGERNON SIDNEY, DISCOURSES CONCERNING GOVERNMENT 526-27 (Thomas G. West ed., Liberty Classics 1990) (1698).

salutary check on the government. It doubles the security to the people, by requiring the concurrence of two distinct bodies in schemes of usurpation or perfidy, where the ambition or corruption of one would otherwise be sufficient. This is a precaution founded on such clear principles, and now so well understood in the United States, that it would be more than superfluous to enlarge on it. I will barely remark, that, as the improbability of sinister combinations will be in proportion to the dissimilarity in the genius of the two bodies, it must be politic to distinguish them from each other by every circumstance which will consist with a due harmony in all proper measures, and with the genuine principles of republican government.[376]

Of special note is Mr. Madison's reference to the proportionality of sinister combinations and similarity between the two bodies. His understanding is that the more the two bodies resemble each other, the more likely there will be sinister combinations. Perhaps the most striking and significant difference prior to the 17th Amendment was whom the senators represented. Subsequent to 1913, the senators represented the same constituents as the representatives in the House. If Mr. Madison's opinion is true, then the 17th Amendment made the two bodies more similar.

Take for example the contemporary use of wedge issues to divide the public. A wedge issue inherently relies on passion and emotion, which is a natural fit when the entire Congress has become a House of Commons/Representatives. As previously

---

[376] THE FEDERALIST NO. 62, at 344 (James Madison) (George Stade ed., Barnes & Noble, Inc. 2006).

mentioned, where the people are concerned, passions and emotions generally have a significant advantage over reason. The Senate was supposed to be an appeal to reason, invoking the two salutary results that reason may have, according to Aristotle (see Part IV, Article I). After 1913 and the 17th Amendment, that feature was substantially reduced, if not eliminated.

Instead, now each wedge issue can be successfully employed to "turn out the vote" by various groups with various motives. A group advancing a particular wedge issue may simply be using one issue to mask another that the group would rather not have discussed. It results in senators, whose primary interest is that of the people, to be continuously conscious of public opinion. If a wedge issue has been successfully employed in a particular election, then being on the side of the minority may lose the election.

More importantly, there is now no august body such as the Senate as it existed prior to 1913, which theoretically was the body of the Congress whom the people could rely on to use reason in their decision-making process. By using reason, the Senate would provide a double security to the people. Because the senators were elected by members of a legislature who were ostensibly well versed in the faculty of reason, senators would be afforded the opportunity to refrain from appeals to passion and emotion. In this manner, the Senate could return to the Preamble's end of general welfare, the general means of the Preamble, and the specific means located in the body of the Constitution.

With a Senate elected by the legislature, the idea is that the question is not automatically whether federal legislation should be passed to define marriage, for example. Instead, the first question is whether defining marriage falls under any of the enumerated powers. If it does not, then the argument is over. If it does, then we may debate how a law should be crafted so it is in accordance with the general means, and thus such a law will subsequently attain the ultimate end of general happiness. For a person who understands the power of passion and emotion, the elimination of senatorial election by state legislatures (or in other words, the substantial mitigation of the use of reason) opens the door to establishing a precedent for legislation in any area, regardless of constitutionally enumerated powers.

As Aristotle noted, appetite and desire are the cause of all action. Also, desire results in impelling people toward immediate satisfaction. It is only reason that allows men and women to consider the future, as reason constitutes a determination of what means are suitable to achieve the end. By utilizing reason, we may determine what consequences the future may hold based on actions to satisfy a particular desire in the present. When reason is lost, the concern moves from the future to the present. "Now desires arise which are contrary to one another, and this occurs whenever reason and the appetites are opposed, that is, in those animals which have a perception of time. For intelligence bids us resist because of the future, while appetite has regard only to the immediate present; for the pleasure of the moment appears absolutely pleasurable and absolutely good because we do not see the future."[377] Making the means of election in the Senate the same as in the House increased the likelihood of sinister combinations.

Let us now move on to the second topic of this Article: the

---

377   ARISTOTLE, DE ANIMA 76 (R. D. Hicks trans., Barnes & Noble Publishing, Inc. 2006) (c. 330 B.C.E.).

1913: From General To Specific Welfare

mitigation of reason and the increased influence of passions due to the 17th Amendment. The previous quotation from Madison was his first of four inconveniences that would result without a Senate whose members were elected by the states. The next two inconveniences concern the heightened influence of passion. Madison's second inconvenience is the following:

> *Second.* The necessity of a senate is not less indicated by the propensity of all single and numerous assemblies, to yield to the impulse of sudden and violent passions, and to be seduced by factious leaders into intemperate and pernicious resolutions. Examples on this subject might be cited without number; and from proceedings within the United States, as well as from the history of other nations. But a position that will not be contradicted, need not be proved. All that need be remarked is, that a body which is to correct this infirmity, ought itself to be free from it, and consequently ought to be less numerous. It ought moreover to possess great firmness, and consequently ought to hold its authority by a tenure of considerable duration.[378]

In short, the influence of passions has already been examined fairly extensively. The framers of the Constitution noted that one purpose of the Senate was to prevent endless appeals to passion, which at the time was to be secured by state legislatures electing senators. With ratification of the 17th Amendment, not only was this security compromised, the influence of passions became more pronounced.

---

378   THE FEDERALIST NO. 62, at 344 (James Madison) (George Stade ed., Barnes & Noble, Inc. 2006).

Moving on to the third inconvenience, Madison noted:

Third. Another defect to be supplied by a senate, lies in a want of due acquaintance with the objects and principles of legislation. It is not possible that an assembly of men, called, for the most part, from pursuits of a private nature, continued in appointment for a short time, and led by no permanent motive to devote the intervals of public occupation to a study of the laws, the affairs, and the comprehensive interests of their country, should, if left wholly to themselves, escape a variety of important errors in the exercise of their legislative trust. It may be affirmed, on the best grounds, that no small share of the present embarrassments of America is to be charged on the blunders of our governments; and that these have proceeded from the heads, rather than the hearts of most of the authors of them. What indeed are all the repealing, explaining, and amending laws, which fill and disgrace our voluminous codes, but so many monuments of deficient wisdom; so many impeachments exhibited by each succeeding, against each preceding, session; so many admonitions to the people, of the value of those aids which may be expected from a well constituted senate?

A good government implies two things: first, fidelity to the object of government, which is the happiness of the people [general welfare expressed as the end of the Constitution]; secondly, a knowledge of the means by which that object can be best attained. Some governments are deficient in both these qualities: most governments are deficient in the

1913: From General To Specific Welfare

first. I scruple not to assert, that, in the American governments, too little attention has been paid to the last. The federal constitution avoids this error: and what merits particular notice, it provides for the last in a mode which increases the security of the first.[379]

Once again, if concerned with re-election, a senator must pursue the interests of those who elect him. In theory, although by no means a certainty in practice, election by a state legislature entails distinctly different interests than the interests of the people. The interests of the people were secured in the House while those of the states were originally secured in the Senate. With senators concerned with election and re-election by the people, passion becomes superior to reason.

Perhaps the effects of the 17th Amendment are subtler than the 16th Amendment or the Federal Reserve Act of 1913. Despite the potential subtlety, the result of the 17th Amendment is nonetheless just as significant as the other two. From the perspective of using ambition to counter ambition, or maintaining a balance of power, and supplying a source of reason to help choose those means which will be necessary and proper to attain the general happiness of all, the election of the Senate by the state legislature was critical. The states, with their own taxing powers that would act as a source of power to balance that of the federal power, were thought to be sufficient checks on the ambition of the central government. A body of legislators—generally well educated in cause and effect, jurisprudence, and logic—chose two members to represent the interests of the state. These two senators in theory then supplied the faculty of reason that was intended

---

379   *Id.* at 344-45.

to counter the ambition and passions of the people represented in the House.

However, state legislatures electing senators would not prevent all corruption within the Senate. In fact, to expect no corruption in such case would be to deny the very nature of people.[380] Nonetheless, election of senators by state legislatures is a necessary means to supply reason. Without any means to supply reason into debates surrounding legislative acts, it would be surprising if the intended end were ever achieved.

We can see how pivotal the 17th Amendment actually is, regardless of how subtle its effects may be. There were, and still are, very substantive reasons for electing the senators via the state legislatures. The change to elect senators directly by the people upset the balance of power between the central government and the states, and it placed an undue proportion of weight upon passion and emotion versus reason. The results of the 17th Amendment may not have been readily apparent in 1913. However, with an understanding of its importance, we quite readily see the effects when viewed through one hundred years of hindsight.

ARTICLE IV: SYNTHESIS

Now that we've examined the conditions surrounding our tax system, the Senate's electoral process, and our monetary system as they existed both prior to and after 1913, it is now time to bring into focus our premise: that the three events of 1913 (16th Amendment, 17th Amendment, and the Federal Reserve Act) transformed our system of governance from one whose end was general welfare to one of specific welfare.

---

380   In the sense used here, corruption is really nothing more than a group of men and/or women in a position of trust who have demonstrated that the trust was misplaced.

We began with the natural law of a fundamental, self-evident truth: that all people act to maximize their satisfaction. This law manifests itself through people acting for the benefit of others, or through people acting to seek personal benefits. All may act on emotion, or they may act on reason. Why people act in a certain way is not our prime concern. Rather, our overriding concern is that people act in order to maximize their satisfactions, and we recognized that this principle is at the heart of the reason for instituting any system of government, which has the potential to maximize the satisfactions of the people, or the general welfare.

This potential depends on the stated end of government and the means afforded to attain that end. In the case of the United States and the Preamble to the Constitution, the end of the government is a noble one: the general welfare. The means are to protect rights, where rights are the liberty to act or not act, and liberty is freedom from arbitrary authority. The challenge is to construct a government with enough power to secure the rights and liberty of the citizens from external threats, while at the same time restraining the natural tendencies of individuals in governmental positions in order to prevent the misuse of governmental power, which would enslave the people from within.

History and the law of human nature have demonstrated such a task as nearly impossible, due to the application of general principles that may sway an individual's beliefs, needs, desires, and subsequent values.

While we may hear that knowledge is power, the truth is that knowledge without action achieves nothing. It is applied knowledge that affects future results in a desired manner that counts: that is in fact power. If a person has special knowledge that few others have and such knowledge is applied in a manner that results in the desired future effects, then that knowledge becomes a tool for immense power, leading either to the betterment or the dissolution of government.

Next we looked at reason, a faculty employed to help an individual determine whether his actions will be appropriate to attain a given end. However, an appeal to emotion often overpowers a person's ability to reason. For individuals who understand this aspect of human nature, they may make a successful appeal to another's emotions to get him to act in the manner desired. Reason may prevent one from being duped while another may use it to dupe others.

Tying these concepts together, we see that we all act to maximize our satisfactions. A government that protects its citizens' rights and liberties has the potential to promote the general welfare. However, in order for all members of a society to enjoy their rights and liberties, each individual has an obligation to respect the rights and liberties of others. Ironically, when the majority respects the rights and liberty of others, that situation creates opportunities for those willing to "cheat." Based on the writings from the time of our republic's creation, the Founders understood these concepts. Their solution was to create a government where the method to prevent such cheating was to pit an individual's natural inclination to maximize his satisfactions against those of others, or to pit ambition against ambition. Three pillars to that strategy are found in our system of taxation, election of the Senate, and the monetary system.

These three pillars interact with each other, and their interaction strengthens each such that the result is an effect more powerful than any of the three on their own.[381]

From our review of taxation we saw that it was directly tied to representation. That system was designed in such a manner that the people were taxed through their representatives. This was accomplished by having two categories of taxation: direct and indirect taxes. Direct taxes were those that effectively could not be avoided while indirect taxes were those that could be avoided. The former included terms such as capitations and poll taxes, and they were taxes on the people or their property. Short of death, direct taxes could not be avoided.

On the other hand, indirect taxes could be avoided since they were realized as an excise, duty, or perhaps a use-tax. Granted, it may be impractical to forgo using a particular item or service simply because you wanted to avoid the tax.

There were two key restrictions placed on each category: direct taxes had to be apportioned according to representation while indirect (duties, imposts, and excises) had to be uniform throughout the United States.[382] Additionally, bills of revenue, or tax legislation, had to originate in the House. Because of the crucial link between taxes and representation, that was one of the key reasons for making the election of the representatives occur every two years. Therefore, if a tax was unavoidable, then the sum would be collected from the citizens of a state in proportion

---

[381] Similar to how the emotions of individuals feed off of each other to the point where together they are more powerful than any one's particular emotion on its own, *see* CHARLES MACKAY, EXTRAORDINARY POPULAR DELUSIONS & THE MADNESS OF CROWDS, at xviii (Three Rivers Press reprt. 1980) (1841) ("Men, it has been well said, think in herds; it will be seen that they go mad in herds, while they only recover their senses slowly, and one by one.")

[382] U.S. CONST. art. I, § 2, cl. 3; U.S. CONST. art. I, § 8, cl. 1, respectively.

to the number of representatives that a particular group of the people had in the House. It would be up to the state to determine how it would tax each person, but the theory was that people would understand who was responsible for the additional tax. It would be straightforward compared to an arcane indirect tax such as debasement of the currency, or any other tactic that would confuse the issue. In the case of direct taxes, the intent was that another person's representative would not be able to levy a tax against someone from another state.

Indirect taxes needed to be uniform, and in this case a representative could legislate a tax that we would pay only if choosing to purchase a good or service. This was a fundamental balance of power between the people and their representatives. A direct tax tapped a vast source of wealth, but the method of collection was intended to be painful and obvious with regards to who was the source of the taxation.

Turning to the Constitutional monetary system prior to 1913, it fit hand in glove with the taxation system. The central government was granted the authority to coin money, regulate its value, and borrow money on the credit of the United States.[383]

---

[383] The manner in which gold and silver eventually were regulated is quite interesting. Based in no small part on the efforts of Alexander Hamilton (see 1 EDWIN VIERA, Jr., PIECES OF EIGHT: THE MONETARY POWERS AND DISABILITIES OF THE UNITED STATES CONSTITUTION 183-90 (RR Donnelly & Sons, Inc. 2d rev. spec. ed. 2011) (explaining Hamilton's efforts as the Secretary of the Treasury in drafting the Coinage Acts of the 1790s), Congress implemented the monetary power of regulating the value through effectively intervention in the monetary markets. Instead of establishing the dollar as a fixed weight and fineness of silver, as the dollar was known at the time of ratification, and letting other metals fluctuate around the dollar based on the market, Congress implemented a monetary system based on price fixing via a fixed ratio between gold and silver. That initial fixing of price, at the heart of the monetary system, was arguably incompatible with the very concept of securing rights and liberty. What it did was set the stage for Congress to tax directly (by

However, the central government was not granted the power to declare legal tender or emit bills of credit. Additionally, people could bring their bullion to the mint to have it coined, and the expense of the mint was to be paid by the revenue from taxes. The only two methods the government had to obtain access to the money of the people, short of whatever bullion happened to be on federal territories or selling government property, was to tax or borrow.

On the other hand, the states' monetary powers were restricted such that no state shall ". . . make any Thing but gold and silver Coin a Tender in Payment of Debts. . . ."[384] Therefore, in order to borrow—as allowed by the Constitution—a state was required to pay its debts in either gold or silver coins. The coins could be minted either by the United States or by some other foreign government (as the states of the Union were prohibited from minting coins). The coins tendered to repay a state obligation had to be gold or silver that was either minted by the United States or declared "current Coin" by the United States.[385] In order for a state to borrow, the United States had to either mint gold or silver coins or declare as current some gold or silver coin minted by a foreign government. If the United States failed to do those tasks, then the federal government effectively cut off the ability of the state governments to borrow and still be in compliance

---

changing the ratio so as to increase the value of either gold or silver depending on the metal of which the government held more) without apportionment. What this power effectively did was to grant the United States a power to intervene in the monetary market of that period and effectively grant itself a power to generate purchasing power (or revenue) by setting the price between gold and silver. The ability to fix the price of money, as we have examined, is perhaps the most significant power that could be granted to any one person or group.

384   U.S. Const. art. I, § 10, cl. 1.
385   U.S. Const. art. I, § 8, cl. 4, 5.

with the Constitution, which specifies "Coin," not just gold or silver.

The Constitutional monetary system, which in fact has not ever been amended but instead has been implemented by numerous statutes, made the central government, state governments, and the people all dependent upon each other. If we were forced to pick which entity held the most influence, it would have to be the entity that provided the source of funding, whether that was from taxes or from borrowing. That entity is the people, which is what you would expect in a constitutional federal republic.

Moving to the Senate, at the time of our nation's founding that body consisted of members chosen by the state legislatures. As they were not chosen directly by the people, the expectation—or at least the intent—was that the Senate would instill reason in the legislative process of the U.S. Congress. The House, elected directly by the people, was understood to be more susceptible to passion and emotion. A state's legislature would be expected to understand cause and effect, and we would also expect the legislature to choose a representative with the wisdom to know how legislative acts would affect the general welfare. That was the theory as expressed by numerous Founders and other contemporary political writers.[386]

Then we considered the three significant enactments that

---

386   Interestingly, if one compares the writings found in *The Federalist* and those in *The Complete Anti-Federalist*, one will find that the Anti-Federalists often expressed fears of what would occur if the Constitution were to be ratified while the Federalists tended to soften those fears roused. In hindsight, however, the fears and predictions raised in *The Complete Anti-Federalist* have in large part come to pass while the safeguards espoused in *The Federalist* have been shown to be inadequate. Based on the law of nature expressed in this exposition, the fears expressed in *The Complete Anti-Federalist* are exactly what one would expect, regardless of what safeguards are erected.

occurred in 1913: the Federal Reserve Act, the 16th Amendment, and the 17th Amendment. These enactments dismantled significant pieces of the Constitutional structure that provided for a balance of power. As the federal government has the power to make law throughout its jurisdiction, which is a coercive power that compels individuals to obey or suffer a penalty, it is reasonable to expect that those so inclined will seek methods to use this power for their own satisfactions. Some of the tactics that may be used are as old as humanity, and have been described as far back as Aristotle in *The Art of Rhetoric*.[387] The foundation of the tactics is special knowledge exploited by an individual or a group. From this special knowledge spring various other tactics such as: appeals to emotion and opinion while avoiding any use of reason; the importance of relations to emotions; and the abuse of words. These tactics manifest themselves in various ways, such as an emphasis on being *for* something versus *against*, or emphasizing a vague notion of progress. Once again, with an understanding of human nature, the fact that an instrument inevitably turns into an institution should come as no surprise.

Returning to the enactments of 1913, the Federal Reserve Act alone did not transform the monetary system into what it is today. To avoid the tediousness of tracking each statute that altered the initial Act, we assumed that the Act was a necessary event that allowed the monetary system to reach our current state. As of today, the Act provides for what was traditionally considered bills of credit (FRNs of one of the Federal reserve banks, which is guaranteed by the United States Treasury) to pass as money. The FRNs are created by a bureau of the Treasury and provided

---

[387] *See generally* ARISTOTLE, THE ART OF RHETORIC 140-71 (H.C. Lawson-Tancred trans., Penguin Books reprt. 2004) (c. 350 B.C.E.) (describing the use of emotion as just one tactic to persuade).

to the Board of Governors, which then provides the notes to the Federal reserve agent representing their particular Federal reserve bank.

Only the government produces the money used by the people, and the money is redeemable in either more of the same paper, or in coins that are overvalued.[388] Because the coins that may be obtained through redemption are overvalued, there is no monetary reason to exchange FRNs for coins. On the other hand, gold or silver coins may only be purchased with FRNs, and the price is substantially more than what the market would bear for the raw bullion. Moreover, because they are stamped such that the nominal value makes them significantly undervalued for the purposes of paying any tax or buying any good or service, there is no practical reason for gold or silver coins to circulate. The legal structure surrounding Federal reserve notes essentially allows the government to issue an unlimited amount of them to the Federal Reserve System, which the FRS can and does use to purchase the government's debt securities.

More importantly, the legal structure of FRNs creates what amounts to a self-funded government. Instead of a requirement for the government to tax or borrow from the people it represents, the people must exchange their labor, land, or capital for FRNs in order to pay a non-apportioned income tax to the government. Before turning to the 16th Amendment, some examples are necessary to explain the results when the source of money becomes inverted from the original system.

---

388 The coins have been in general overvalued. Recently, due to the substantial creation of more FRNs, some of the coins - such as nickels - have become undervalued. This will ultimately result in what one would normally expect when something is artificially undervalued – scarcity. Based on the nature of the monetary system's fractional reserve lending, eventually all of the current coins will become undervalued (assuming the content is not changed).

As one example, imagine how a family's hierarchy would be undermined if one of its children was the source of money versus one or both of the parents. Given enough time, would we expect the parents to continue to make the rules, or would it be the child? Remember, the person who pays the piper calls the tune. It is not too far-fetched for the child to determine how and when the money was spent. Granted, due to the special-knowledge advantage about finances that a parent has over a child, it would also be plausible that in a short time the parent would control all of the money.

As another example, imagine a business selling a good to consumers. In order to compete in a market economy where others are free to sell the same good, the business must either produce a better good or sell it at a cheaper price. If the business fails to do one or the other, there is a high probability (short of a law mandating that a consumer must purchase the good regardless) that the business will eventually shut down.

Now imagine if that business finds a way to generate its own FRNs. A self-funding business no longer has any monetary incentive to produce a better-quality good or sell it at a cheaper price, and it has no monetary interest in pleasing its customers. This pertains to a government that is self-funding as well. Such a government no longer has an incentive to be responsive to the needs of the people.

Both of these examples prove the following point: An entity created to fulfill a particular need will quickly turn into an institution, as described by Quigley, once it becomes self-funding. The entity will remain an instrument fulfilling a need as long as it requires funding from those it aims to serve. As shown in the example of the family, the entity with the money makes the rules. Those who seek the money serve those with the money.

It is unreasonable to expect that a government that is self-funded would have any chance of achieving its end of general welfare by securing the liberty of all. People's natural inclination to maximize their own satisfactions will undoubtedly result in individuals or groups seeking ways to secure special favors from the source of the money for themselves. The perpetuation of this result is only compounded when combined with the 16th and 17th Amendments.

Turning to the 16th Amendment, it resulted in the direct taxation of income that no longer required apportionment in accordance with the number of representatives each state had in the House. With this change to the fundamental structure linking direct taxation with representation, the results today are exactly what we would expect. Once again, a couple of examples demonstrate our point.

Imagine a large group of parents spread over a fairly large county. The parents decide they would like to build a school for their children. The parents realize that building and managing a school will require funding. The parents use the representative structure of the Constitution as a basis for establishing their school. Then, they divide their area into districts, and they create a school board to manage the system. Next, they decide how many members each district may place on the board, which is based on how many children they expect each district to send to the school. Each district will be charged a fee in proportion to how many members their district places on the board. They create a charter that grants certain powers to the board, defining how the money generated by the fees will be spent. The school is built, children enrolled, and parents inevitably debate how the money should be spent. Some want more arts while others want more sports. As the powers are inevitably expanded and money is spent, those people with more board members pay their apportioned share. If the burden of these fees becomes too burdensome, we would expect board members to be replaced with members who are more mindful of the fees' effect on their constituents.

Now imagine if there was a change to the method for collecting revenue. Instead of fees being apportioned, the current board had the power to alter the charter such that fees were charged to each parent equally, let alone based on their income levels. The districts still retained the same proportional number of members on the board, but the link between representatives and fees charged was severed. There would be a pool of resources secured from the revenue generated by the fees with no link to apportioned representation. If there were a group of parents from one district who banded together to secure additional money for sports activities, they could be successful in attaining their desires. Remembering the tactics people employ to achieve their end, such as using special knowledge and appeals to passion, it should become even more obvious that eventually such a group will be successful.

Of course, once the precedent is set, other groups will form to receive their share of the pool of resources. Over time, the original charter loses meaning. Fees must be increased as more and more groups organize to secure their share of the pool. Even though some parents may have moral reservations about such actions, their reluctance to act may cost them dearly in fees. We would also expect that with increased revenue, the board and the entire system would transform from the instrument intended to educate their children to an institution with members of the board seeking their own interests. The general result would be each parent or group of parents versus the other. Moreover, imagine the further ramifications if the board became self-funding, and the board required the fees to be paid in their type of currency.

Addressing now the 17th Amendment, we see that it altered how the Senate was elected. As noted by Justice Story, the two branches of the legislature prior to the 17th Amendment served as a balance due to the mechanism for choosing the members of each branch. "The legislative power being that which is predominant in all governments ought to be, above all, of this character [proportional and equal representation]; because there can be no security for the general government or the State governments, without an adequate representation, and an adequate check of each in the functions of legislation. Whatever basis, therefore, is assumed for one branch of the legislature, the antagonist basis should be assumed for the other."[389] In other words, if one branch is based on representation of the people, then the opposite basis would see the other branch representing the States. Because Justice Story so eloquently summarized the effects of the eventual 17th Amendment (despite the fact he wrote these words in 1833, well prior to the 17th Amendment in 1913), his thoughts are included at length:

> Another and most important advantage arising from this ingredient [a proportional House and a Senate fixed upon an absolute equality as the representative of State sovereignty] is the great difference which it creates in the

---

[389] 1 JOSEPH STORY, COMMENTARIES ON THE CONSTITUTION OF THE UNITED STATES 502 (Thomas M. Cooley ed., The Lawbook Exchange, LTD. 4th ed. 2008) (1873).

elements of the two branches of the legislature, which constitutes a great desideratum in every practical division of the legislative power. In fact, this division (as has been already intimated) is of little or no intrinsic value, unless it is so organized that each can operate as a real check upon undue and rash legislation. If each branch is substantially framed upon the same plan, the advantages of the division are shadowy and imaginative; the visions and speculations of the brain, and not the waking thoughts of statesmen or patriots. It may be safely asserted that, for all the purposes of liberty, and security, of stable laws and of solid institutions, of personal rights, and of the protection of property, a single branch is quite as good as two, if their composition is the same and their spirits and impulses the same. Each will act as the other does; and each will be led by the same common influence of ambition or intrigue or passion to the same disregard of the public interests, and the same indifference to, and prostration of, private rights. It will only be a duplication of the evils of oppression and rashness, with a duplication of obstructions to effective redress. In this view, the organization of the Senate becomes of inestimable value. It represents the voice, not of a district, but of a State; not of one State, but of all; not of the interest of one State, but of all; not of the chosen pursuits of a predominant population in one State, but of all the pursuits in all the States."[390]

After the 17th Amendment, the Constitutional structure no longer caused the Senate to act as a balancing power to the

---

390 *Id.* at 502-03 (citation omitted).

potentially clamorous and passionate House. As Justice Story noted, the United States Congress effectively became unicameral. Most, if not all, of the advantages of the Senate had been negated, leaving only disadvantages. The effects previously described from the 16th Amendment and the Federal Reserve Act had no restraining force of reason from the Senate. Instead, the 17th Amendment served to do just the opposite. It actually amplified the results. The influence of money, controlled by the government and the banks, greatly increased. Additionally, those who received first access to the money rose in influence and importance.[391]

These factions not only sought to secure access to the new money, but they had a powerful tool to hamper their competition or to simply use as a bludgeon against their enemies: the power of taxation. Granted, the United States always had nearly plenary powers to tax within its jurisdiction. However, the 16th Amendment deleted the requirement to apportion any income tax. As previously examined, when this power is abused, it can be used as a means to punish. It may be used in more than a monetary sense, as the power to tax is also the power to destroy. The tax code may be used by any particular faction to achieve moral ends by taxing any group whose beliefs are in disfavor with those in power. With the 17th Amendment, instead of the Senate tempering such abuse of taxes (when compared to what was said in the Preamble and the stipulation that taxes be used to pay debts and provide for the common defense and general welfare), the present structure of the Senate is adding to the abuse.

---

[391] Given enough time as more and more of the populace understands the system, it is inevitable that the trend will be towards a state of nature where it is each human versus each human armed with the force of government coercion.

This occurs because Senators are all susceptible to the same influences as the House.

In light of our examination, it is wholly expected that we would have the symptoms we presently experience: onerous laws created to grant specific welfare by transgressing citizens' rights and liberty instead of securing rights and liberties to promote the general welfare. The Federal Reserve Act, combined with the 16th and 17th Amendments, transformed the government in a way that removed the fundamental balance that checked ambition with ambition. The FRA gave the government power to create the Federal Reserve System and what we today call money; a tax system that allowed factions to inevitably spring up around the government and the banks to either grant tax exemptions to themselves or assess taxes upon those not part of their group. This arrangement is not conducive to the general welfare, nor does it promote the rights and liberty of all. Without laws used to secure rights and liberty, there can be no justice. Without justice, there will be no domestic tranquility. Without domestic tranquility, there will be no environment to produce wealth, and without the generation of wealth, there can be no means for the common defense. When all of these factors are absent, there will be no government except in name only.

We've seen how the law of nature determines that each individual acts to maximize his own satisfactions. It is this same law that is the impetus for the formation of government, and is also responsible for turning the government's end from one of general welfare to one of special or specific welfare.

PART VI:
CONCLUSION

Fortunately or unfortunately, there is no limit to the ingenuity of men and women. Sometimes this ingenuity is used to promote the general welfare, and other times it is used to subvert that process in the pursuit of securing special welfare. However, there is a seemingly glaring contradiction in a general population that attempts to achieve general welfare by establishing a government: the knowledge that must be obtained by the few in order to successfully establish a government may be used by them or others to subvert the end. As Ben Franklin astutely observed, in order for a republic to achieve the end of general welfare, it will require a well-educated citizenry, legislative body, and governors. When it comes to the special knowledge and ingenuity of the few, Mr. Bryce provides this perceptive illustration:

> In 1866, when Congress was in fierce antagonism to President Johnson, and desired to prevent him from appointing any judges, it reduced the number, which was then ten, by a statute providing that no vacancy should be filled up till the number was reduced to seven. In 1869, when Johnson had been succeeded by Grant, the number

was raised to nine, and the legal tender decision given just before was presently reversed by the altered court [some issues are seemingly forever in contention]. This method is plainly susceptible of further and possibly dangerous application. Suppose a Congress and President bent on doing something which the Supreme court deems contrary to the Constitution. They pass a statute. A case arises under it. The court on the hearing of the case unanimously declares the statute to be null, as being beyond the power of Congress. Congress forthwith passes and the President signs another statute more than doubling the number of the justices. The President appoints to the new justiceships men who are pledged to hold the former statute constitutional. The Senate confirms his appointments. Another case raising the validity of the disputed statute is brought up to the court. The new justices outvote the old ones: the statute is held valid: the security provided for the protection of the Constitution is gone like a morning mist.[392]

This might be too much, to expect the public, engaged and immersed in their own affairs, to exert the effort needed to keep tabs on their representatives. Although it may be too much to ask, such action is necessary if the people expect to have their liberty honored and their general welfare protected.

In light of our examination, the events of 1913 have certainly resulted in special welfare, particularly for those engaged in the practice of creating new money and credit. With a basis from *The Federalist* and *The Complete Anti-Federalist*, there is a very low

---

[392] 1 JAMES BRYCE, THE AMERICAN COMMONWEALTH 269 (Neil H. Alford et al. eds., Leslie B. Adams, Jr. The Legal Classics Library spec. ed. reprt. 1987) (1888).

1913: From General To Specific Welfare

likelihood, if any at all, that the conventions of the 1780s would have ratified the Constitution if it provided for the creation of paper currency by the government, or a bank the government created; non-apportioned taxation of income; and a Senate that was elected by the people of each state. It is just as unlikely that the people of that era would have ever contemplated such a revision to the Constitution, let alone agreed to such radical change within the same year. But in hindsight and with an understanding of human nature, we shouldn't be surprised that it both happened and manifested these results.

We discussed how pleasure and pain are powerful motivators, and relieving the pain of another is often even more powerful than pleasure alone. We must note here that fear caused by uncertainty is also a cause of mental pain. And it is the fear of external threats that compelled people to band together to provide a common defense. As Hobbes noted, "[f]eare of oppression, disposeth a man to anticipate, or to seek ayd by society: for there is no other way by which a man can secure his life and liberty."[393]

Fear may manifest itself in any number of ways: from an external menace caused by other people; from disease; natural catastrophes; and, of course, economic disasters such as monetary panics, runs on banks, and ruinously high interest rates. And there are those who exploit the people's susceptibility to fear and will wait for the opportune time to use their special knowledge to exploit others.

During times of crises and fear, such circumstances may induce people to relax the Constitutional constraints in the promise for security or safety. However, in a government whose aim is general welfare, relaxing the Constitutional constraints in

---

[393] THOMAS HOBBES, LEVIATHAN 61 (Barnes & Noble, Inc. 2004) (1651).

Conclusion

a search for safety would hardly serve the end of general welfare. Appeals to emotion may certainly persuade enough of the populace that the only way to assuage their fears is to exchange liberty for safety, but such legislation would be contrary to the Preamble's end of general welfare by securing rights and liberty. As Ben Franklin once wisely said, "[t]hose who would give up essential liberty to purchase a little temporary safety deserve neither liberty nor safety."[394] This is a maxim for the ages. For those who place specific welfare over general welfare, however, the opportunities to secure specific welfare during conditions of fear and panic are plentiful. In truth, the only safeguard is in the wisdom of the people.

When all is said and done, the people of the United States must continuously make choices, and those choices have long-lasting consequences. Decisions will be made based on either emotion or reason, or a combination of the two as explained by Aristotle. The decisions made to address our needs and desires, as well as our methods chosen to fulfill them, are influenced by our knowledge, experience, and wisdom.

But governance is a paradox. The best method to secure general welfare is to secure the rights and liberty for all, but the power necessary to achieve this end may be used instead to promote special welfare for a select few.

Imbalances of power—especially those concerning our monetary system—have seemingly made reform a remote possibility. That is not to say that reform could not be attempted, and it may yet work. Even still, securing rights and liberty through abolishing the 16th and 17th Amendments along with the FRA would

---

[394] THE QUOTABLE FOUNDING FATHERS 204 (Buckner F. Melton, Jr. ed., Fall River Press 2008) (citing Franklin's speech to the Pennsylvania Assembly November 11, 1755).

likely create such upheaval, panic, and fear that it would create the opportunity for some to secure even more special privileges at the expense of the general welfare.

Instead, it may be more appropriate to let the current system run its course and concern ourselves with being in a position to secure the rights and liberties of all when the root cause of our misery—the 16th and 17th Amendments and the FRA—has been identified by the majority and compelled them to act accordingly. Perhaps then, we could once again attempt to form a more perfect Union whose end is to promote the general welfare by securing the rights and liberty of all.

This would by no means be an easy task. Those who successfully achieved their ends in 1913 had the concrete rewards of special favors and privileges. Those rare individuals who run for office or attempt to persuade others with no goal other than securing rights, liberty, and general welfare are seemingly tilting at windmills. These are abstract concepts to promote with no monetary gain whatsoever.

Luckily, history has demonstrated that when the time is right, there have always been enough like-minded men and women who will make the necessary sacrifices to obtain their liberty. In our case, our Founders accomplished that task when they drafted and established our Constitution. Even then, the process of preserving the general welfare against those scheming for special welfare soon continued again. The only question is when will liberty be secured before human nature exerts its force and allows tyranny to once again prevail.

When I first began drafting this book, my goal was to obviously maximize my satisfaction by taking steps to secure my own rights and liberty. I was also well aware that this cannot be done by me alone. Furthermore, I realize that to secure my rights and liberty, they must be secure for all, which will require the actions of the many compared to those of the few.

If by placing my thoughts on paper I have helped even one person understand how the three events of 1913 transformed our government from one of general welfare to one of specific welfare, and if my work helped to shed light on how we may yet return to a system that secures everyone's rights, liberty, and general welfare, then I have reached . . .

My End.

BIBLIOGRAPHY

Saul Alinsky, Rules for Radicals: A Practical Primer for Realistic Radicals (Vintage Books reprt. 1989) (1971).

St. Thomas Aquinas, On Law and Justice: Excerpts from Summa Theologica (Neil H. Alford et al. eds., Leslie B. Adams, Jr. spec. ed. reprt. 1988) (1485).

Aristotle, De Anima (R. D. Hicks trans., Barnes & Noble Publishing, Inc. 2006) (c. 330 B.C.E.).

Aristotle, The Art of Rhetoric (H.C. Lawson-Tancred trans., Penguin Books reprt. 2004) (c. 350 B.C.E.).

Aristotle, Nicomachean Ethics (F.H. Peters, M.A. trans., Barnes & Noble, Inc. 2004) (350 B.C.E).

Marcus Aurelius, Meditations (Martin Hammond, trans., Penguin Books 2006) (150 A.D.).

Bernard Bailyn, The Ideological Origins of the American Revolution (The Belknap Press of Harvard University Press 1967).

M. Frederic Bastiat, Essays on Political Economy (G. P. Putnams & Sons 3rd ed. reprt. 1874).

Frederic Bastiat, The Law (Dean Russell trans., Foundation for Economic Freedom 2d ed. 1998) (1850).

Christopher M. Bruner, *The Changing Face of Money*, 30 Rev. Banking & Fin. L. (2010).

JAMES BRYCE, THE AMERICAN COMMONWEALTH (Neil H. Alford et al. eds., Leslie B. Adams, Jr. The Legal Classics Library spec. ed. reprt. 1987) (1888).

DALE CARNEGIE, HOW TO WIN FRIENDS & INFLUENCE PEOPLE (Dorothy Carnegie & Arthur R. Pell, Ph.D. eds., Simon & Schuster 2009).

THE COMPLETE ANTI-FEDERALIST (Herbert J. Storing, ed., The University of Chicago Press 1981).

THE DECLARATION OF INDEPENDENCE (U.S. 1776).

JESÚS HUERTA DE SOTO, MONEY, BANK CREDIT, AND ECONOMIC CYCLES 285 (Melinda A. Stroup trans., Ludwig von Mises Institute 2006).

ALEXIS DE TOCQUEVILLE, DEMOCRACY IN AMERICA (Harvey C. Mansfield & Delba Winthrop eds. & trans., The University of Chicago Press, LTD. 2002) (1835).

EMER DE VATTEL, THE LAW OF NATIONS (Béla Kapossy & Richard Whatmore eds., Liberty Fund, Inc. 2008) (1758).

JOHN DEWEY, HOW WE THINK (Barnes & Noble Publishing, Inc. 2005) (1910).

THE FEDERALIST (George Stade ed., Barnes & Noble Inc. 2006).

FEDERAL RESERVE BANK OF CHICAGO, MODERN MONEY MECHANICS: A WORKBOOK ON BANK RESERVES AND DEPOSIT EXPANSION (reprt. 1994) (c. 1992).

SIGMUND FREUD, CIVILIZATION & ITS DISCONTENTS (Joan Riviere trans., Martino Publishing 2010) (1930).

MILTON FRIEDMAN & ANNA JACOBSON SCHWARTZ, A MONETARY HISTORY OF THE UNITED STATES, 1867-1960 (Princeton University Press 9th prtg. 1993) (1963).

MILTON FRIEDMAN, CAPITALISM AND FREEDOM (The University of Chicago Press 40th Anniversary ed. 2002).

Thomas Gordon & John Trenchard, Cato's Letters (Ronald Hamowy ed., Liberty Fund, Inc. 1995) (c. 1720).

Hugo Grotius, On the Law of War and Peace (Kessinger Publishing reprt. (1625).

Sir Matthew Hale, The History of the Common Law of England, and an Analysis of the Civil Part of the Law (6th ed. reprt. 1820) (1713).

Thomas Hobbes, Leviathan (Barnes & Noble, Inc. 2004) (1651).

David Hume, An Enquiry Concerning Human Understanding (Prometheus Books, 1988) (1748).

David Hume, Essays Moral, Political and Literary (Henry Frowde reprt. 1904) (1741-42).

David Hume, Of Political Society, *in* Hume's Political Discourses (The Walter Scott Publishing Co., LTD n.d.) (1752).

Hylton v. United States, 3 Dall. 171 (1796).

William Stanley Jevons, The Principles Of Science: A Treatise on Logic and Scientific Method (Adamant Media Corporation 3rd ed. reprt. 2008) (1879).

Lord Henry Home Kames, Sketches of the History of Man (A. Strahan & T. Cadell reprt. 1783).

John Maynard Keynes, The Economic Consequences of the Peace (Skyhorse Publishing reprt. 2007) (1919).

John M. Keynes, The General Theory of Employment, Interest, and Money (Classic House Books reprt. 2008).

John Maynard Keynes, A Tract on Monetary Reform (BN Publishing reprt. 2008).

Gary Lawson & Guy I. Seidman, *Necessity, Propriety, and Reasonableness, in* The Origins of the Necessary and Proper Clause (Cambridge University Press 2010).

JOHN LOCKE, *An Essay on Toleration, in* POLITICAL ESSAYS (Mark Goldie ed., Cambridge University Press 1997) (1660).

JOHN LOCKE, *Essays on the Law of Nature V, in* POLITICAL ESSAYS (Mark Goldie ed., Cambridge University Press 1997) (1660).

JOHN LOCKE, AN ESSAY CONCERNING HUMAN UNDERSTANDING BOOK I-II (Adamant Media Corporation reprt. 2006) (c. 1690).

JOHN LOCKE, *First Tract on Government, in* POLITICAL ESSAYS (Mark Goldie ed., Cambridge University Press 1997) (1660).

JOHN LOCKE, *Morality, in* POLITICAL ESSAYS (Mark Goldie ed., Cambridge University Press 1997) (c. 1677-1678).

JOHN LOCKE, OF THE ABUSE OF WORDS (Penguin Books 2009) (c. 1689).

JOHN LOCKE, *Second Tract on Government, in* POLITICAL ESSAYS (Mark Goldie ed., Cambridge University Press 1997) (1660).

JOHN LOCKE, THE SECOND TREATISE ON CIVIL GOVERNMENT (Prometheus Books 1986) (1690).

NICCOLÒ MACHIAVELLI, THE PRINCE (David Wootton ed. & trans., Hackett Publishing Company, Inc. 1995) (1532).

CHARLES MACKAY, EXTRAORDINARY POPULAR DELUSIONS & THE MADNESS OF CROWDS (Three Rivers Press reprt. 1980) (1841).

JACKSON TURNER MAIN, THE ANTI-FEDERALISTS CRITICS OF THE CONSTITUTION 1781-1788 (W. W. Norton & Company, Inc. 1974).

KARL MARX & FREDERICK ENGELS, *Communist Manifesto, in* ECONOMIC AND PHILOSOPHIC MANUSCRIPTS OF 1844 AND THE COMMUNIST MANIFESTO (Martin Milligan trans., Prometheus Books 1988) (1847).

Joshua Matz & Laurence Tribe, Uncertain Justice 257 (Henry Holt and Company, LLC 2014).

Carl Menger, Principles of Economics (James Dingwall & Bert F. Hoselitz trans., Ludwig von Mises Institute reprt. 2007) (1871).

John Stuart Mill, Dissertations and Discussion: Political, Philosophical, and Historical (William V. Spencer reprt. 1864).

Montesquieu, The Spirit of the Laws (Anne M. Cohler, Basia Carolyn Miller, & Harold Samuel Stone eds. & trans., Cambridge University Press 14th prtg. 2009) (1748).

Albert Jay Nock, Jefferson (The Ludwig von Mises Institute 2007) (1926).

Thomas Paine, The Crisis (Prometheus Books 2008) (1776).

Ron Paul, The Revolution (Grand Central Publishing 2008).

Plato, Gorgias (Walter Hamilton & Chris Emlyn-Jones trans., Penguin Books rev ed. 2004) (c. 380 B.C.E.).

Plato, The Republic (Betty Radice ed., Desmond Lee trans., Penguin Books 2d rev. ed. reprt. 1987) (c. 380 B.C.E.).

The Political Writings of Thomas Jefferson (Edward Dumbauld ed., The Bobbs-Merrill Company, Inc. 1955).

Pollock v. Farmers' Loan Trust Co., 157 U.S. 429 (1895).

Carroll Quigley, The Evolution of Civilizations (Liberty Fund, Inc. reprt. 1979).

The Quotable Founding Fathers (Buckner F. Melton, Jr. ed., Fall River Press 2008).

Murray Rothbard, Man, Economy, and the State: A Treatise on Economic Principles with Power and Market (Ludwig von Mises Institute 2nd ed. 2009)

Jean-Jacques Rousseau, The Social Contract (G.D. H. Cole trans., BN Publishing 2007) (1762).

Bibliography

Joseph A. Schumpeter, Capitalism, Socialism, and Democracy (Harper Perennial Modern Thought 2008) (1942).

Algernon Sidney, Discourses Concerning Government (Thomas G. West ed., Liberty Classics 1990) (1698).

Adam Smith, The Theory of Moral Sentiments (Classic House Books 2009) (1759).

Adam Smith, The Wealth of Nations (Edwin Cannan ed., Bantam Books 2003) (1776).

John Lord Somers, The Security of Engli[s]hmen's Lives: Or the Trust, Power and Duty of Grand Juries of England 78 (Kessinger Publishing reprt. n.d.) (1681).

Joseph Story, Commentaries on the Constitution of the United States (Thomas M. Cooley ed., The Lawbook Exchange, LTD. 4th ed. 2008) (1873).

Sun Tzu, The Art of War (Dallas Galvin ed., Lionel Giles trans., Barnes & Noble Classics 2003) (c. 512 B.C.E.).

Abel Parker Upshur, A Brief Inquiry into the True Nature and Character of Our Federal Government: Being a Review of Judge Story's Commentaries On the Constitution of the United States (Kessinger Publishing) (1868).

Edwin Vieira, Jr., *The Forgotten Role of the Constitution in Monetary Law*, 2 Tex. Rev. L. & Pol. (1997).

Edwin Viera, Jr., Pieces of Eight: The Monetary Powers and Disabilities of the United States Constitution (RR Donnelly & Sons, Inc. 2d rev. spec. ed. 2011).